The Connected Parent

Mike and Sarah,

Blessings on this journey!

Love,
Kristin O...

The Connected Parent

—m—

Uncovering Your Peace

Kristen Oliver, MOT, OTR/L

Cover design by Sallie Aceto of Design & Media Group,
www.DesignandMediaGroup.com
Author photograph by Susanna Marie,
www.susanna-marie.com
Interior graphics by David Lewis,
www.DavinoMariDesign.com

The author of this book does not provide medical advice or suggest the use of any technique as a form of treatment for any physical, psychological, or emotional condition.

The intent of the author is to offer information of a general nature to aid readers in their journey as a parent. In the event that you use any of the information provided in this book for yourself or your child, the author and publisher assume no responsibility for your actions or the outcomes.

Published in the United States

First Printing, 2016

ISBN-13: 9780997197808
ISBN-10: 0997197803
Library of Congress Control Number: 2016916924
CreateSpace Independent Publishing Platform
North Charleston, South Carolina

For Infinite Love and Your Reflection in My Life

Contents

Acknowledgements

My Deepest Gratitude to:

My beloved children, Andrew and Tessa,
for it is through You that I more deeply know Me.

Mike,
for who you are in my life—my healing partner.
LOVE.

Maureen Ryan Griffin,
for your countless hours of editing, your insight, encouragement and dedication to this book, and for believing in me throughout this process.

Annie Maier,
for your attention to detail and your diligence and commitment in helping me refine my message.

Renate Schubert,
for your friendship, guidance and love. No words can express my gratitude for your presence in this experience.

Sheila Kilbane, MD,
for your unending support of my work and your unwavering commitment to the health of all children and families. You are a blessing in my life.

Mom and Dad,
for your love and assistance through all of my life stages.

Meredith Oliver,
for breaking all mother-in-law stereotypes and being just amazing.

Dr. Joe Dispenza,
for your advice on this book and your continuous inspiration for humanity.

All my friends and family,
for your compassion, love and emotional nourishment as I live my life's purpose.

Thursday night GC members,
your sisterhood means the world to me.

My clients and every parent I know,
you inspire me every day.

Kiddos everywhere,
for your endless forgiveness, understanding and knowing that, as parents, we are all doing our best.

And to all others who offered their time and expertise in support of the creation of this book: Cindy Calderwood; Connie Merk; Adele Schiessle; Nancy Tilton and the ALC Mosaic community; Arthur Brock, Agile Learning Centers; Nadia Miller; Nancy Gordon, PhD; Nick Maglosky; David Lewis; Richard Griffin; Lori Ives-Godwin; Sallie Aceto; and Miguel Carvalho.

Thank you!

Introduction

ARE YOU STRUGGLING to help your child with sensory, social, emotional, learning or behavioral challenges? Are you feeling frustrated and overwhelmed, like you have tried everything—and it is just not enough? Worse yet, do you fear that your child's anxiety, tantrums, homework battles, sibling rivalries or other difficulties are your fault? If you desire heart-based connection, effective, compassionate communication and family harmony, look no further. *The Connected Parent: Uncovering Your Peace* is the solution you have been searching for.

Like many of my clients, you may have difficulty imagining peace is possible for you and your family. When you're steeped in chaos, feeling hopeless and exhausted, it can seem light years away. I would like to assure you—through my personal journey and through the work I have done with many stressed-out parents and children, I know that peace and ease *are* possible and that they do not have to take years to materialize. In fact, I created the process behind *The Connected Parent* to give other parents quick access to the concepts and tools that made such a difference in my life.

My story starts over thirteen years ago, when I found myself in a personal health crisis. I sought assistance from various medical professionals, receiving only limited results. Then, a friend shared an inspired way of thinking that allowed me the insight to experience a life-changing shift: There was no way I could create health and wellness from the same thoughts and beliefs that had created illness. I saw that I was not meant to be sick and that different, more loving ways to think and feel were available for me to discover.

After taking the time to soak this possibility in, I sent a message out to the Universe. Envisioning all of my limiting thoughts and beliefs as grains of sand in a bucket, I turned the bucket over and dumped them out. As I flipped the bucket upright again, I calmly and clearly asked to be guided to a new way of being.

Through a steady flow of abundance, I met friends who shared encouraging stories, discovered a wealth of inspiring authors and speakers, and began to meditate. Along the way, I was introduced to a multitude of spiritual theories and techniques, which I later found were all backed by the latest scientific developments. Throughout this journey, my heart opened. My body healed.

An even more monumental shift came after my husband and I started our family. Many of the subconscious anxieties and beliefs that I thought I had previously cleared resurfaced with a vengeance. The results of my fear-based thinking were no longer housed only in my body. Now my children were reflecting them back to me, through a variety of challenging behaviors, sleep disturbances and sensory sensitivities. Despite all I had learned, I did not handle these in a very enlightened way!

A Little Window into My Past

In the years that chaos erupted between my preschool-aged kids, sometimes the only thing I could do was walk (or run!) away from the room, lock my bedroom door, and then go into the bathroom, where I knew I would have roughly 2½ minutes to myself before the kids made their way in. Maybe some small part of me believed we would be visited by a saving angel who would wave her sparkly wand, bless the kids, and have them apologize and promise never to argue again.

In reality, by the time the kids found a penny and unlocked both doors, I was usually ready to face the situation. More than once, I held the bathroom door shut until they gave up. Powerful parenting, right? The handful of occasions when I did this stand out much more than all of the times I stayed with them, triggered by their choices and actions, trying to work things out.

The fact of the matter is, neither of these approaches brought the peace I was looking for.

I knew there was another way—many other ways. Hadn't I read all about them? But every time I attempted to integrate a new theory into my thoughts and actions, I just ended up berating myself over perceived mistakes. I was truly my own worst enemy. Guilt, blame and shame, based on patterns from the past, held me in place, denying me the peace I most desired.

In spite of this, through grace and diligence, I began to awaken into my True Self. I may have struggled as I implemented each new concept but at least I was taking action. Bit by bit, I peeled away the layers of patterning that had taken years to create. What I did not realize is that, in this journey to discover my True Self, I had unearthed much of the underlying support I needed to modify my conscious and subconscious behaviors. I knew I did not need to move through life constantly triggered, in a state of perpetual fear or waiting for the next tumultuous event to befall us. Everything I had studied provided the awareness and understanding that it was possible to live differently. And I was determined to do just that.

As I did my inner work, returning to the techniques I had learned during my health crisis, happiness and health returned to me and to my family. Before long, it became clear that my life's purpose was to incorporate these concepts and tools into my work as a pediatric occupational therapist. ***The Connected Parent*** is the result of these personal and professional experiences.

The step-by-step process offered in these pages will assist you in addressing root causes rather than bandaging surface symptoms. Unless the necessary inner work is done, common, practical tactics intended to help children with attention issues, anxiety, tantrums and poor self-esteem are futile. Why? Because our brains are strongly wired by our old beliefs, and until we re-wire we live on autopilot, experiencing different versions of the same problems over and over and over. The accompanying thoughts and underlying patterns so strongly influence our experience and surroundings we typically find a way to perpetuate our symptoms, however unpleasant. The resulting challenges appear not only in ourselves but in those around us, including our children. And all the while, we may be completely unaware of this process.

As you embark on this journey, know that you are not alone; if at any time, you would like more information or support working with the following concepts, please visit my website at www.kristenoliver. com.

Kristen
October, 2016

How to Use This Book

My INTENTION IN writing this book is to offer you what I needed most when I was in the depths of parenting despair. My thirteen years of experience in personal growth, eighteen years as a pediatric occupational therapist (OT), and eleven years as a parent are all rolled into the following fifteen chapters. Whether your challenges are great or you are simply experiencing everyday difficulties, the concepts and strategies in this book will be of value; over and over, clients tell me that everyone in their family is happier after practicing the tools you will learn here.

The Connected Parent: Uncovering Your Peace provides a framework for you to reveal and transform the underlying negative patterns and limiting beliefs that produce and reinforce the situations you're trying so hard to avoid. Clarity, connection and peace are all possible if you are willing to do the work described in this unique approach.

The primary obstacle many of us face in our quest for harmony is believing that a shift is possible in the first place. If I had not regularly seen transformations both large and small in my family and in the lives of my clients, I would not have believed it either. I know this shift can happen because in my role as a parent I, too, felt overwhelmed and desperate at times.

Life is not free of challenges. *The Connected Parent: Uncovering Your Peace* will lead you to discover peace in these challenges by seeing them as opportunities to love and forgive yourself, your children and everyone/everything in your life. The hidden peace that you are searching for is revealed—it's within and has been there all along.

The Connected Parent is organized into three main "Peaces."

The First Peace—*Getting Clear* will:

- Support you in identifying the underlying negative patterns and limiting beliefs that helped you create your "story"—the current dynamics of your family.
- Describe common triggers—events, people or situations that elicit anger, frustration, upset, etc.
- Explain how we develop our ego, and forget our True Self in the process.
- Share the concept of the "Backpack" —the invisible, expanding storage place for heavy emotions we have not yet addressed.

The Second Peace—*The Power Tools* will:

- Explain what it means to do our inner work.
- Detail how to do this work in the moment of being triggered or shortly thereafter.
- Provide exercises to peel away the layers and get to the root causes of your upsets and frustrations.
- Introduce specific tools for change, what I call "The Four C's," along with options for implementing them in your life. Briefly, the Four C's are:
  - Consciously Observe—*Step Out to Look In*
  - Connect—*Join with Infinite Love*
  - Choose—*Select a Way to Let Go*
  - Create—*Powerfully Intend a New Path*

The Third Peace—*Moving Forward* will:

- Guide you to a place of self-love, forgiveness and harmony.
- Clarify the difference between judgment and discernment.
- Encourage you to take responsibility for your part in any situation and commit to do the work, for yourself and your family.
- Empower you to explore the role of intention and intuition in creating what you most deeply desire.

- Inspire a strong connection between you and your child(ren).
- Offer a children's story specifically crafted as a fun and age-appropriate way for you to share the Power Tools with your kiddos.
- Support you in creating a Family Connection Plan that ensures time for bonding, sharing and fun.

In addition to the concepts described above, each chapter contains personal stories and Client Triumphs to provide support, guidance and encouragement. When we witness how major shifts occur for others, it helps us see that change and growth are possible for us, too.

At the end of each chapter, you will find several Action Peaces—exercises meant to enable you to practice and solidify the concepts covered in that chapter. Taking advantage of these opportunities for growth will support you in your journey.

There are a few additional points I would like to add:

- The concepts in this book are a process, not a quick fix. Each of us has our own story, time line and path to transformation. Give yourself the gift of discovery.
- The personal stories shared in this book are true and permission has been kindly granted for their publication. To protect the identities of my clients and their families, I have changed all names and identifying details.
- For the purposes of this book, I use the words "feelings" and "emotions" interchangeably.
- I share a good deal about our automatic programming (subconscious/unconscious mind). In an effort to keep things simple, I use subconscious mind when referring to this concept.
- The information in this book is intended for everyone, regardless of religious, spiritual or philosophical beliefs. I use the words Infinite Love when referring to the highest love—the most powerful forces of light and truth in existence. Some may call this force God, Creator, the Universe, Spirit, Oneness, Life Energy and the Field of Possibility.

To me, these all mean unconditional LOVE! Feel free to replace Infinite Love with the term or entity that represents the highest power for you.

If you are ready to experience a life-changing shift for yourself and your family, read on!

The First Peace

Getting Clear

THIS IS THE beginning of a new opportunity for you and your family. If you picked up this book, there is a reason. Maybe your child has specific challenges—a learning difference, disruptive behavior, or other special needs. These challenges can bring up frustration, sadness, anger, resentment, and a variety of other emotions that can lead you to feel out of control or stuck in a rut. You want to help, but don't know how. Or, maybe your child is typical—whatever that means!—and you just want to better navigate your family's dynamics. Either way, I am offering to meet you where you are and travel with you on a journey toward experiencing abundance within yourself and your family.

I don't share any quick fixes or offer a bandage-the-surface-symptom approach. I've found, in my own life, that these only provide temporary relief. **The First Peace—*Getting Clear*** is about taking first steps: Identifying the root cause of our discontent, bringing awareness to that root cause and shifting it from the inside out.

Part of this process requires that we do some digging. We dig into the situation, our feelings and maybe even the past. We do our best to understand the hows and whys of what we are experiencing with our kids. And then we prepare to do the necessary work to shift from a state of chaos to one of peace, clarity and lasting change.

Imagine that you splurge on a beautiful, newly sodded lawn for your yard. On the surface the grass is green and there are few weeds. Then, before you know it, the grass starts to brown and the weeds peek through. You discover that the soil underneath is sub-par. Without realizing it, you placed your fresh sod on dry, malnourished earth. In this moment, you have a choice.

You can replace the sod, hoping you will get better results this time. (Though it is often said that insanity is doing the same thing over and over while expecting different results!) Or, you can take on the belief that all challenges are opportunities and decide something must be done to improve the earth beneath the sod. It took me quite a while to discover that our challenges are often our biggest gifts. I used to resist them and, like crabgrass, they lingered and hid for a while only to resurface with a vengeance.

Once you decide to do this work, you start to dig. The once thick and meticulously groomed grass is torn up, embedded in piles of dirt. As you sift through that dirt, you remove toxins and impurities you didn't even know were there. You get into this process, seeing that it's messy but not as bad as you expected. You clean and clear the earth and start to feel good about what you will put in the soil. Carefully, you till and fertilize and start to plan what you will do with this space.

Suddenly, you're inspired… a garden! You want to plant a garden here. No longer set on the perfect-looking lawn that ended up dying anyway, you decide to try something entirely new. Something that feeds your creativity and is an extension of your true essence.

It isn't an easy process but in the end you have a fabulous garden. You know you're not done, because all gardens need maintenance, but you feel strong and secure knowing you have the wisdom and tools to nourish the soil, prune whatever isn't thriving and make additional changes as needed. You feel supported, relieved and fulfilled in each moment you spend in your garden. It's a unique creation, like none other in the world!

The next six chapters will guide you through the process of digging and clearing your family garden and help you gain the understanding necessary to create this lush new environment. You get to choose your plants and accents. This may look like knowing how to set loving boundaries for yourself and your kids, communicating effectively or enjoying a harmonious family vacation. It *is* possible to go from a weed-filled lawn of a family life to a beautiful garden.

Let's get started. Opportunities abound!

CHAPTER 1

Awareness
Identify Your "Story"

"I don't know. It's just what I've always done,
what I'm used to."

~ ANDREW, AGE 5½

THE QUOTE ABOVE is from my son, in response to being asked why he was so
upset following a tantrum that seemed to come from nowhere. As parents,
mothers in particular, we are often overloaded, overwhelmed and over tired.
And, like Andrew, we all have habitual responses to the stressors in our lives.
Having one or more children in this day and age is the equivalent of a full-
time job, with significant overtime requirements. The amount of attention,
orchestration and time required to navigate a basic daily routine is enormous.
Any learning, behavior or sensory challenges your children may have will
provide additional factors that need to be taken into consideration, adding to
the intensity of the parenting experience.

Days of stress can lead to months, which can then lead to years of difficulty. By the time a child is only two or three, we most likely have an elaborate
story to tell about sleepless nights, tantrums, or whatever struggles we face as
a parent. And the story keeps growing as your child grows.

It's important to remember that there is a difference between information
and your story. Information includes things like the hospital where your child
was born, the city you visited on vacation last summer and the name of your
child's second grade teacher. I use the word "story" to represent our perception of life events, circumstances and relationships, as well as the feelings and
emotions that accompany them.

Your story can be likened to an intricate production in which you are both the writer and the star. Everyone involved in your life is either an actor or engaged in behind the scenes activities. Throughout this detailed production, you wear various costumes that fit your role in any given moment—the wardrobe department is massive and constantly expanding. There is tragedy. There is victory. There is anything and everything in between.

We parents often get extremely attached to the story of how our children act and what our family life is like. How could we not? It is our life. We can feel driven to share this story with friends, family and coworkers. The more we tell it, the more we believe it and the more we continue to "write" the same material. We may unintentionally use the story to receive sympathy or validation. It can dominate our every thought on a conscious and subconscious level, allowing the tragedy and drama to overshadow finding solutions and creating new experiences of peace, love and joy with our children.

The story you have to tell about your child(ren) or your family life can be a sensitive topic. It might even be the reason you are seeking guidance. After all, if everything were effortless and going just the way you always dreamed it would, chances are you would be doing something else besides reading this book right now.

Before delving into the specifics of your story, let's look at a simple example of a mother who, when dealing with a challenge, deliberately chose one possible scenario over another.

Client Triumph—What Story Do You Believe?

One fall day, Karen noticed a strange mark on her two-year-old son's right shoulder. At first she thought it was a bug bite. After watching it for a couple of days, she noticed it was growing in size and becoming bright red in color. When Colin noticed the bump and started to worry, Karen told him, "Lots of people get bumps on their skin and they just go away."

While participating in a pilot program with me, another professional, and an integrative pediatrician, Karen shared a photo of the growth. After asking a few questions, the pediatrician offered her thoughts (she believed it wasn't anything to worry about) and ended by saying, "It may just go away on its own."

Karen continued to check the bump daily. She and Colin often discussed it, very matter-of-factly, without fear, as Karen knew in her heart it was not an issue. Each day, she told him that, though the mark was still there, she knew it would go away soon.

During a routine visit, Colin's doctor noticed the bump. The size concerned her enough that she called a busy dermatologist and got Colin in the next day.

Although the dermatologist concurred with Karen and the pediatrician that the bump wasn't anything serious, he recommended surgical removal as soon as possible so it wouldn't continue to grow. The very next day, Colin was seen by a surgeon, who agreed with this recommendation. The procedure was scheduled for the end of December.

Surgery for this little guy was not something Karen wanted. Rather than focus on this possibility and the accompanying trepidation it created, she stuck with her original story that all would be fine. She believed with complete clarity that the growth was simply going to fall off and her son would not need surgery.

Karen's parents, who are highly involved in Colin's life, asked questions like "Aren't you worried about how the surgery will go?" and "What if Colin has a negative reaction to anesthesia?" Karen held strong, knowing in her heart that all was well, and refused to join in the story others were telling.

Six days prior to the surgery, Karen was changing Colin out of his pajamas when she noticed that the mark on his shoulder was gone. She told him the growth had fallen off, just as they had discussed. Without an ounce of surprise, she called the surgeon's office to inform him. Both the nurse and doctor were startled to hear this news and said something along the lines of "This never happens." As Karen so steadfastly believed, the surgery was cancelled.

Who knows what would have transpired had Karen chosen a fear-based story. Would Colin have ended up needing surgery? We will never have that answer. But we do know that the time between her seeing the mark and having it fall off was peaceful and calm, not filled with anxiety.

And, there was a secondary benefit as well. Karen felt, firsthand, the power of standing firmly in her "all is well" story, versus the fear-based story perpetuated by well-meaning family and friends. She wasn't irresponsible or naive. She took the necessary steps, keeping appointments and scheduling the surgery. She simply trusted her gut and never believed her son would actually need to have the growth removed.

During our individual sessions, I often referenced this occurrence with Karen, commending her commitment to seeing things positively. Although Colin occasionally worried about various things in his environment, he never went into a state of panic about the growth because his mother, the one who represents safety and security to him, was so strong in her knowledge that all was well.

Karen's story helps us see that unlimited choices of perception are possible. This may be an oversimplification, but I want to emphasize that consciously selecting which ones we give our attention to is no small matter.

Are We Rewriting the Same Story?

Are we unknowingly addicted to the same scenarios and their repercussions? Being entrenched in a story allows it to define us, with no idea there is a way out. Comfort is available in that which is familiar, so we cling to the "blankie" of our narrative.

When our story is filled with anxiety, worry, guilt and fear, our bodies become accustomed to those sensations. Though we don't necessarily want to feel this way, it's what we know. It's what is familiar. Anything else—peace, ease, joy, relaxation—feels unfamiliar and, therefore, foreign.

Over time, such responses to life events become automatic, unintentionally creating an internal, cellular environment that is also filled with anxiety, worry, guilt and fear.

In his book *Breaking the Habit of Being Yourself*, Dr. Joe Dispenza states it this way:

> Every time you think a guilty thought, you've signaled your body to produce the specific chemicals that make up the feeling of guilt.

You've done this so often that your cells are swimming in a sea of guilt chemicals.

He goes on to say:

The receptor sites on your cells adapt so that they can better take in and process this particular chemical expression, that of guilt. The enormous amount of guilt bathing the cells begins to feel normal to them, and eventually what the body perceives as normal starts to be interpreted as pleasurable. It's like living for years near an airport. You get so used to the noise that you no longer hear it consciously, unless one jet flies lower than usual and the roar of its engines is so much louder that it gets your attention. The same thing happens to your cells. As a result, they literally become desensitized to the chemical feeling of guilt; they will require a stronger, more powerful emotion from you—a higher threshold of stimuli—to turn on the next time. And when that stronger "hit" of guilt chemicals gets the body's attention, your cells "perk up" at that stimulation, much like that first cup of java feels to a coffee drinker.

And when each cell divides at the end of its life and makes a daughter cell, the receptor sites on the outside of the new cell will require a higher threshold of guilt to turn them on. Now the body demands a stronger emotional rush of feeling bad in order to feel *alive*. You become addicted to the guilt by your own doing.

As we move into understanding our story and bring awareness to how we perceive our experiences, we notice patterns that tend to replay in our lives. What do I mean by "bring awareness"? Pay attention to your thoughts during and after an upsetting or frustrating incident. Listen to what you say to yourself. Be mindful of your feelings. And be compassionate—the thoughts, feelings, beliefs and patterns that create our stories are on auto-pilot until we begin to take notice and choose something different.

You may be deeply familiar with these topics and concepts, somewhat new to them or somewhere in between. We'll further explore each throughout the book. For now, give yourself the gift of being open to seeing your life from a fresh perspective.

Speaking about awareness reminds me of a vision I once received during meditation.

A Personal Peace—An Unnecessary Struggle

I was in on a mission in some sort of battle zone, yet I felt safe. Dressed in camouflage from head to toe, including a heavy helmet, I was combat-crawling through a low, narrow tunnel. There was light ahead—the end of the tunnel—which I was persistently moving toward at a snail's pace. I was willing to do anything for the relief that light represented.

At one point, I was overcome with an awareness to look up. As I did so, I saw that I was not in a tunnel at all. There was, in fact, nothing overhead but blue sky. I'd been wearing my helmet so low, I hadn't noticed I was in a narrow but open passageway, rather than a covered tunnel.

At that moment, I simply stood up. Walking upright wasn't easy because the space was tight, but I was able to complete the journey without any further struggle.

Coming out of the meditation, I saw immediately what this meant in my life. I had gotten stuck in my story around a particular conflict. I even valued the battle to a degree, giving myself a pat on the back for the level of upset, and even suffering, I could endure.

I share this because I believe many of us are combat-crawling through our lives, unaware that we have an opportunity to look up and that there might be an easier way to mitigate our struggle.

Moving Past Feeling "Stuck"

Of course, when we are in the trenches, it can be difficult to seek another way out. Know that I have been in that place multiple times. I have felt the anger of being hit by my kids, the exhaustion of being repeatedly awoken long past the age when my child was *supposed* to sleep through the night, and the stress of feeling judged by family and friends for my style of parenting. And these examples just scratch the surface.

In such moments, I was deeply entrenched in my story, feeling desperate and convinced I was serving a life sentence of ever increasing difficulty. I often went on what ended up being another fruitless search for what was "wrong" with my child, believing *I* should be able to fix it. I looked for external solutions, seeking the advice of popular parenting books, medical professionals and, occasionally, my peers. Many well-intentioned resources provided varying degrees of temporary relief for my family; we tried different diets, new discipline strategies, and kind suggestions from friends with children very different from my own. I am not saying that these things were not helpful—in some cases they were. But what I really discovered in this process was that, until I was ready to release my story, new challenges would always find their way into my experience.

In the meantime, as I undertook this external search for solutions, I became a master at covering up my emotions and the truth of what I was experiencing. To this day, I am sure many people had no clue what I was actually thinking and feeling during those difficult times, partly because I didn't want to spread my story but also because I was filled with guilt, blame and shame. Just to be clear, I can be totally open about my true feelings and experiences now because I no longer suffer that guilt and shame, and because I know this kind of sharing contributes to others being empowered to let go of their own guilt, blame and shame.

You may wonder how you could possibly experience living guilt-free. That will become clear as you move through this journey. For now, I will say I know it is possible because of where I came from and where I am now—happier and healthier than ever before.

Bring Awareness to Your Story

Whether you are steeped in an elaborate story or hiding what you really feel, I am here to tell you there is a way out of the trauma and drama. As I mentioned earlier, there is power in awareness—in bringing the details of the story you are telling or experiencing to the forefront of your mind, identifying your feelings and recognizing that this story has, to some degree, been defining who you think you are for a very long time. Now is your opportunity to choose awareness.

To begin with, your story identifies the who, what, when, where, why and how of your life, as well as all of the thoughts and feelings that go with these details. It consists of multiple key players and supporting roles, along with a collection of elaborate plots and intricate details. Your personal history includes past occurrences, reactions and behaviors, and is made up of a lifetime of similar stories that ultimately influence how you perceive yourself, others and life in general. This includes your children. As parents, much of our story centers around those we love—how you react to a child who resists doing their homework, for instance, or the feelings that arise when you find out about a big social studies project the night before it's due.

Any given experience offers an infinite number of stories that can be written and believed. Fortunately, we always have a choice, a fact that will become clearer and clearer as you put the ideas and practices in this book to work in your life.

Our Story Can Also Include Areas That Are Going Well

Although tragedy or trauma scenarios are typically the more dominant and pressing pieces of any story, I invite you to note that not every component of our story is an issue. Even when we are stressed about the challenges we are facing, we likely have a number of areas in life that are not in turmoil. If, for example, our family life is a strain, maybe our job, finances or relationships with close friends are going well. If your schedule is stressful, maybe your tennis game is fabulous. (Who has time to play tennis? Oops, that's part of my story—no time to do things for myself. I told you I would share openly!)

Why Do We Stay in Our Story?

I try not to speak in absolutes, so I will say *most* of us are steeped in our story and don't know it. We share our story with anyone who will listen in the hopes of receiving sympathy or support. Why? Because it feels good. There is comfort in connecting with others and feeling seen and heard when they really listen. When we don't see a way out of a situation, we naturally seek the only thing that might help, and so we share the story, sometimes over and over. When we feel trapped and believe life is filled with constant trauma and drama, at least we know there is the possibility of receiving some empathy—unless, of course, feeling alone and unsupported is part of the story.

But how much does empathy alone help us? Does it lead us to take the steps necessary to release and change the story? Or do we find ourselves stuck in that story, ensuring that we get more and more of the same?

I will never argue that genuine empathy is not powerful. It is so important to feel heard, and heartfelt listening is a significant component of my work with clients. *And,* I also believe that being listened to and empathized with can, without our awareness, keep us in our story.

Before you close this book, hear me out. Empathy can be highly beneficial. I just don't feel it is enough to free us from the trap of our stories.

For example, there were many things that kept me in my story. So many, I could write another book on them. But that wouldn't help you, other than to let you know that you are not alone. Here are some thoughts, beliefs, behaviors and payoffs I allowed to feed my story:

- Self-punishment—I deserved a difficult life.
- Self-blame—Things weren't that bad. Others have so much more on their plates. I should be able to deal with my challenges.
- Martyrdom—I received some sort of invisible reward in being able to handle difficulties and still keep smiling. Of course, I was crying behind closed doors, but others didn't know that.
- Tough gal—I told myself this was my life and complaining wouldn't solve anything. It was best to just suck it up and deal.
- Disillusionment—I tried to make the best of things, yet again, and then gave up, reminding myself that positive thinking had failed in the past.
- Distraction—I held onto the knowledge that the next season of *So You Think You Can Dance* would start soon. Not a joke. I really loved this reality show and used it to get me through some tough times.

- Hopelessness—I knew things didn't have to be this way, but told myself I was too tired to do anything about it.
- Self-pity—I repeatedly told myself "This situation sucks."
- Playing the victim role—I asked, "What did I do to deserve this? Why is this happening to me?"
- Blame and self-deprecation—I kept repeating, "I'm an idiot. If only I would do this or that, everything would be okay."
- Fear—It was easier to stay in my story and live a mediocre life, doing what I had always done, than to do the work required to change.
- Ignorance—Even when I knew that what I was doing didn't work, I didn't know how to change or what else to do.
- Validation—I believed challenges, and how I handled them, proved that I was working hard and being a really good mom.
- Addiction to empathy and camaraderie—I reassured myself that I was not alone. Other moms felt exhausted, had sensitive kids and other, endless challenges. I could commiserate with them and it felt good to be seen and heard.
- Guilt and Shame—I told myself I knew better than to get stuck in negative patterns and, yet, I did so anyway. Repeatedly.
- Resignation—I had just had it.

I could go on. No, really, I could go on and on. I was in my story.

Does any of this sound or feel familiar? You may be telling yourself some of the same things, or you may have different components of your story, such as:

- Feeling hopeless—"You don't understand. My child's condition is neurological. There is nothing we can do about it."
- Withdrawal and rejection—"I have no support. My family is not in town. My husband travels. I am in this all alone."

As challenging as all of these thoughts, beliefs and behaviors can be, there's good news—recognition is a powerful first step in shifting from chaos to harmony, for yourself and your family.

In later chapters, we will uncover how your story started and how/why it may be serving you. For now, let's work on bringing awareness to your particular story.

Action Peace—Being "In Awareness"

By bringing focus and awareness to your story and recognizing when you are stuck, you can heighten conscious understanding and self-reflection. This is empowering, as we cannot shift what we are not aware of.

In the space below, list five to seven areas where you will heighten the attention you place on your story and its accompanying thoughts and feelings. Choose situations where you tend to feel frustrated or upset, or where you experience a lack of power or peace. Some examples may be at breakfast, after school, while your children are playing or doing homework, or when you are interacting with your spouse.

1.

2.

3.

4.

5.

6.

7.

Action Peace—What Is Your Story?

As you fill in responses to the following prompts, practice being in awareness rather than judging yourself or others. Write the first thoughts that come to mind. Notice the feelings that arise.

1. The story (about myself) I unintentionally received from my parents (or other adults):

    Feelings that come up:

2. My story about my childhood:

    Feelings that come up:

3. My story of a past trauma:

    Feelings that come up:

4. My story of myself as a parent:

    Feelings that come up:

5. My story of myself in relationship with _____:

    Feelings that come up:

Action Peace—Harmony Rating Scale

This scale will serve as a baseline for how you feel your child performs in various areas. This will help you become aware of how you see your child right now. You may find that both "story" and "information" show up.

Later, we'll come back to this Action Peace, and you will be able to see and track your growing awareness as you apply the principles and tools of *The Connected Parent.* You'll also see your child's progress and the increase in your family's level of harmony.

Using a scale of 1 – 5 for each area of concern below, reflect on and rate the level of harmony you've perceived in your child over the last three to six months. Another way to think of this is, "What areas are the most challenging for our family?" Note that the more challenging an area is, the less harmony will be present for you, your child and the family in general.

Included at the end of the chart are areas specifically focused on you as the parent. Rate your level of harmony from 1 – 5, just as you did for your child.

As you rate your current experience of your child and yourself in these areas, add a few notes in the "Current Observations" column for those of the greatest concern. You'll have a chance to work with these areas, using the Power Tools in **The Second Peace**.

Today's Date: _____

Scale:

1 = Almost No Harmony
2 = Very Little Harmony
3 = Some Harmony
4 = Frequent Harmony
5 = Almost Total Harmony

AREA OF CONCERN	RATE 1-5	CURRENT OBSERVATIONS
Your Child's Areas of Concern		
Academic Performance		
Attention to Tasks		
Following Instructions		
Problem Solving		
Ability to Plan/Organize		
Impulsivity		
Ability to Complete Familiar Routing		
Motivation		
Behaviors at Home		

AREA OF CONCERN	RATE 1-5	CURRENT OBSERVATIONS
Your Child's Areas of Concern		
Behaviors at School		
Frustration/Tolerance		
Tantrums/Meltdowns (+Duration/Frequency)		
Handling Transitions		
Adapting to Change		
Anxiety		
Self-esteem		
Mood		
Social Skills		
Interactions with Parent(s)		
Interactions with Sibling(s)		
Interactions with Peers		
Appropriate Play		
Sensory Challenges		
Self-care		
Physical Strength		
Motor Skills		
Coordination		

AREA OF CONCERN	RATE 1-5	CURRENT OBSERVATIONS
Your Areas of Concern		
Anxiety		
Stress		
Family Dynamics in General		
Relationship with Spouse		
Relationship with Child(ren)		
Self-care		
Other (Note Area)		
Other (Note Area)		

CHAPTER 2

Patterns and Beliefs
Reveal Conscious and Subconscious Forces

"Do you know what I want to grow up to be?
I want to grow up to be myself! Then, I can do
anything I want.
If I want to do something else, I can just change my mind."

~ Tessa, age 4½

THE MATERIAL WE draw from when developing our stories are our life's patterns, our underlying beliefs and our memories from the past. These start in childhood and are a result of our environment as well as accumulated years of acting, saying and doing things a certain way.

Our patterns are driven by our thoughts, feelings, actions and beliefs, which in turn spring from our conscious and subconscious mind. Because of the disproportionate influence of the subconscious—research shows 95% of our thoughts, actions and beliefs are a result of our subconscious—it takes a bit more digging to reveal the underlying themes that reside there. (See Figure 2.1.) However, it is by delving into the powerful themes of the subconscious that we receive clarity and understanding as to how and why we do the things we do. One way the subconscious serves us, for instance, is through the storage of basic routines. We don't have to relearn how to tie our shoes or drive a car each day. That said, the subconscious also holds the memories and past stories that create the patterns and beliefs that so strongly influence our experience today.

Guilt, blame, shame, lack of self-worth, victimhood and martyrdom are just a few of the big issues that often get exposed within the subconscious. Bringing the resulting patterns and beliefs to the forefront of our awareness

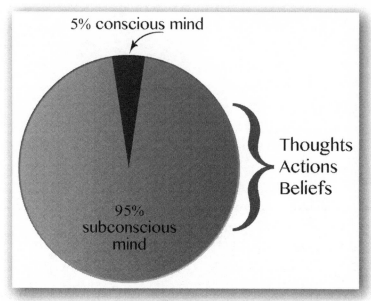

Figure 2.1

reduces the fear that surrounds these feelings and the power they have in our lives. Revealing them can also lead to healing.

As my daughter notes in the quote that begins this chapter, if we want to do something different in our lives, we can simply change our minds. It can be that simple. We don't need decades to reprogram, although shifting beliefs does take some work. We only need to remain in awareness of our stories so that we can begin to uncover the patterns and beliefs that influence our perceived reality.

The following story concerns a student I worked with years ago. The transformation he and his mom underwent in a handful of months remains an inspiration to this day.

Client Triumph—Observing with Trust

As I was getting to know Matthew, a fifth grader, it became clear that we would have to build a strong rapport before we could address the yearly goals his school assistance team had set for him. Matthew had mild autism and ADHD and had been on and off meds for years. Despite an above average intelligence, he performed poorly with regard to academics. Still, whenever I brought up schoolwork, he insisted everything was fine.

Matthew was also "clumsy"—falling and getting hurt regularly. On each of our first three meetings, he was wielding an ice pack or had a visible bandage on his body. In addition, less than ideal social skills had resulted in his having few friends and being bullied on the bus… by a first grade girl.

Because we shared a mutual interest in science, I introduced him to the double-slit experiment, a well-known trial in quantum physics that demonstrates how the presence of an observer can alter the way matter behaves. Like me, Matthew found this idea mind-boggling.

Together, we watched a segment from *What the Bleep Do We Know: Down the Rabbit Hole* in which Dr. Quantum, a white-haired cartoon superhero, explains an experiment meant to determine whether matter is a particle or a wave. In this experiment, scientists discovered that the mere act of adding an "observer" or any type of measuring device changed the results! As Dr. Quantum demonstrates, everything (energy) lies in a state of possibility until it is observed, at which point what was once a "wave of infinite possibilities" is forced to take a path. Therefore, by changing how you see, or observe, yourself, you can change the outcome of a given situation or experience.

After the video, I gave Matthew a personal example related to my performance on the high school tennis team. Back then, I had no idea that my thoughts influenced my skills and abilities. I was always nervous during matches and tended to focus on what I feared or didn't want (hitting the ball out), rather than on winning or even being able to return a good serve. As a result, I was often right. If I worried about double-faulting, I often did so. If I felt evenly matched with my opponent but found myself thinking I was going to lose, I did so. I observed myself from a place of lack and my observations were confirmed in my performance.

As I explained to Matthew, this did not go unnoticed by others. My fear and negative self-talk were so extreme and so powerful, my teammates and coach often commented on the difference between how I played in games as opposed to practice.

Matthew and I then talked about how he is, like everyone, always his own observer. As the double-slit experiment demonstrates, many, perhaps infinite, possibilities exist until an observer lands on one particular option. Often, it is our subconscious mind that makes the selection.

Matthew agreed that, as his own observer, it would benefit him to rethink some of the views he had about himself. He chose to begin by shifting his belief about getting hurt. Rather than focusing on statements like "I don't want to get hurt anymore," I coached him toward choosing the positive approach: "I move through my day safely." Matthew went with it. He turned his own life into an experiment. By shifting this one belief about himself, he was able to directly affect the outcome, as he went from observing himself as clumsy to observing himself moving confidently through his day. In this way, he *landed on* a different outcome, one that was outside anything he had experienced in the past.

After a couple of weeks without injury, Matthew was ready to move on to how he was observing the bully on the bus. He decided to see her with indifference rather than with the dislike, even hatred, he had previously chosen. In no longer viewing this child with animosity, Matthew was able to release both the frequency and the effect of her behavior. In other words, once he no longer cared, she no longer cared, a fact he shared with me via a "thumbs up" communication system we came up with so he could let me know how it was going when we passed in the school hallway.

Only then was Matthew ready to address his academic performance. Once again, by shifting how he observed himself, his teacher and his assignments, Matthew was able to see school from a completely different place. He released old patterns and beliefs and consciously chose new ones. Needless to say, Matthew's grades quickly improved. He even set a goal to get the highest possible scores on his end of grade tests, and did so!

Equally important to note is the lengthy support conversation I had with Matthew's mom. I listened to her fears and concerns and lent a compassionate ear. I explained my approach and told her I believed the whole family would benefit if she could take a break from worrying. Then I asked if she was willing to trust that her son had what it took to be successful in school, both socially and academically.

Our time together was transformative. After moving through some intense emotions and many tears, Matthew's mom decided to observe her son differently. She committed to the notion that he already possessed everything he needed and that she could trust him and our process. By doing so, she helped to create a new environment for Matthew—one of infinite possibilities!

She told me later that everything in her life changed in that moment.

A few years later, in preparation for a speaking event in which I planned to share his story, I reconnected with Matthew's mom. I was beyond thrilled to hear how his middle school years were going. With occasional encouragement, he had maintained his high academic performance and was now captain of the golf team. In fact, his coach had gone out of his way to attend Matthew's annual education meeting to tell everyone how grateful he was to have such a confident leader and positive influence on his team.

Matthew just "got it." Having discovered his inner observer, he now knows that he is the master of his reality. As a result, he is able to spread positive energy throughout his home and school.

More Science on the Matter

How is it that Matthew's whole life shifted over the span of a few months? And is this possible for you and your children? Yes, it is. Let's discuss how and why.

We tend to get stuck in repeated cycles of thinking and events that play over and over. In fact, according to Dr. Joe Dispenza, 90% of the thoughts we will have today are the same as the thoughts we had yesterday. Scary, right?

You might be thinking, "Sure, it's nice to think we can shift our life to a more joyous and successful experience, but where is the science to back up this idea?"

First of all, it's important to understand that our conscious mind—the analytical part of us that is aware of our surroundings, knows when soccer practice is and remembers we have a dentist appointment tomorrow—is not writing our stories. I will restate what I mentioned earlier: 95% of our thoughts, actions and beliefs are determined by the subconscious mind, the part of our being that is a result of automatic programming.

This high percentage is why we have such difficulty breaking habits. For example, if we want to break a longstanding habit of hitting snooze three times before getting up, we can typically use will power, our conscious mind, to succeed for two or three days. More often than not, our subconscious patterning then kicks in and we fall back into our old ways, which leads us to beat ourselves up for being incapable of change.

The seeming inability to change leaves us feeling as if we are victims of our subconscious, stuck in a life sentence of our own patterning. But not only is it possible to change this patterning, according to stem cell biologist Dr. Bruce Lipton, it is also possible to escape the repercussions of our genetic coding. Yes, you read that correctly. In his book, *The Biology of Belief*, Lipton explains how studies in the field of epigenetics show that our genetic coding is only minimally responsible for our health and wellness or the way we experience our world.

So, if not DNA, what does determine our characteristics, tendencies or physical and emotional health? Dr. Lipton (along with others in the forefront of epigenetic research) believes it is our environment. On a microcosmic level, the environment of a cell—hydration, nourishment, chemical and neurological input—greatly determines the health of that cell. Experiments have proven that if the environment of a cell in a petri dish is one of malnourishment, the cell will not thrive.

On a larger scale, let's consider the entire body. If we feel tension and pressure as a result of the outer environment, our inner environment responds by releasing cortisol, a stress hormone that places us in a state of fight or flight. In small bursts, cortisol is helpful when we are in danger. For example, it helps channel blood to our extremities to help us run faster if we encounter a vicious dog. This is an appropriate response, one that may save our lives. The problem today is that many of us live in a constant state of fight or flight, and our cells respond accordingly. When we are out of balance in this way, we inadvertently create a stressful cellular environment that compromises the integrity and function of our whole system.

On a macrocosmic level, we can see how this same effect occurs in our home environment. If a child is predisposed to ADHD due to family genetics *and* experiences high levels of stress in the home, he or she is more likely to exhibit symptoms consistent with that diagnosis. On the other hand, a person genetically prone to a condition has a healthy inner and outer environment, with nourished cells, a nourished mind and a calm, supportive family life, he or she may experience little or no symptoms.

Dr. Lipton cites a variety of fascinating stories that support such findings in his book, *The Biology of Belief.* My favorite is one in which he relates how a woman with multiple personality disorder experienced a potentially fatal allergy to pet dander in one personality but not in others. In a similar case, a patient's eye color changed from one personality to another. This means that each person's genetic coding shifted according to who they thought they were in the moment!

These and the many other examples in this fascinating book exemplify why Matthew was able to change his entire experience of reality. He modified his inner environment to one of positivity, focusing on what he wanted rather than on being a victim of his circumstances. As Dr. Joe Dispenza would put it, Matthew created a new mind (his thoughts) and a new body (his feelings), thereby accessing his genetic blueprint in a new, supportive way.

The point is, our DNA or past history is not a life sentence of illness, distress and doom for us or our children. By shifting beliefs, we shift outcomes. By creating and inhabiting a loving inner and outer environment, we are able to access the highest genetic expressions of ourselves.

Changing Our Thoughts to Change Our Neurochemistry

Dr. Joe Dispenza is another scientist conducting compelling research in neuroscience, biology, psychology, hypnosis, behavioral conditioning and quantum physics. In his book *You are the Placebo: Making Your Mind Matter*, he presents "before and after" brain scans of patients healed from chronic diseases simply through changing the perceptions and beliefs that were limiting them.

On the flip side, Dr. Dispenza also references the stories of people who were misdiagnosed with a fatal illness and died, even though they did not have the illness, because they believed so strongly in the prognosis that accompanied that misdiagnosis.

If we apply these findings to Matthew's story, it's clear that what he did was reprogram the underlying negative patterns and limiting beliefs lingering in his subconscious. Additionally, his mother actively created a fresh home environment as she began to fully trust he had what it took to attain social and academic success. Together, these changes shifted Matthew's neurochemistry and allowed him to create new neural pathways—made of the replacement beliefs from which he chose to live his life. He went from being clumsy, getting teased and performing poorly in school to feeling safe and physically coordinated, forming meaningful relationships, and thriving academically.

When Do Negative Patterns and Limiting Beliefs Begin and Why?

Throughout our lives, we gather information and experiences that cause us to create (subconsciously, of course) our own patterns and beliefs. Such experiences can run the gamut from joyous to tragic, from loving and supportive to emotionally or physically abusive, and they all serve to influence our patterns and beliefs.

As you may acknowledge, we do not experience all patterns adversely. Maybe you learned the benefit of putting an item away when you were done with it at an early age, resulting in a pattern of keeping a neat and tidy living space that serves you well as an adult.

I would like to take this opportunity to state that I only advocate digging up patterns and beliefs if doing so is helpful. Some of my clients find this process highly beneficial because it offers a piece to their puzzle and aids in healing. Others skim right past such introspection. I am not a proponent of judging our parents or childhood experiences or engaging in a "blame-fest" that can keep us from our real intention—revealing patterns in order to move past their limitations.

Instead, I find it helpful to come from the stance that the patterns and beliefs we dig up are not good or bad, they just are. If you experienced an abusive childhood, please know that my saying this does not mean that what happened is okay, or that we should allow abuse to continue if we find ourselves in another abusive relationship. It just means that what happened in the past happened, and we have the power to choose what we do in the present and in the future. And, what we find in unearthing our patterns and beliefs can help us understand why we respond to our children the way we do and what we can do to shift those (re)actions.

For instance, upon doing reflective work as an adult, I traced one of my familiar patterns to an early childhood experience.

A Personal Peace—Reflecting on the Effects of Childhood Injury

One day, when I was about seven years old, I was playing on my swing set with my best friend. After a pretty hard fall and a trip to the ER, it was determined I had broken my right arm. Back in the early 1980s, we didn't have the colorful, streamlined casts of today. Instead, I was given a massive, white plaster cast that extended from my wrist to my upper arm. None of my shirts fit over the cast, which ended up being pretty cool, as I got to wear my dad's white undershirts while I recovered on the couch at home. Plus, I got all of the benefits of being sick without the sore throat, tummy ache, or diarrhea! For several days, I got to stay home from school, watch tons of TV, eat special treats and, best of all, receive lots of extra loving from my parents. Despite the occasional throb and the discomfort of the itchy cast, I was living the life!

If I thought home pampering was great, I had no idea what I was in for at school. As I entered the classroom, everyone asked me what had happened and fought to sign my cast. I even made a new friend, one I remained close with through high school.

It was not until I looked back at this event with a critical eye that I saw it as the start of a pattern—playing the role of victim. The secondary gain I'd received from this mini-trauma was a ton of attention. And oh, did it feel good. On a biological and neurological level, the neural pathway of

physical trauma = attention

was seeded in my subconscious. The only drawback was that my mind didn't know the difference between an incident that would bring positive attention and one that would bring negative attention. Over time, this pattern was sealed through a number of incidents, from falling on the playground and tearing a hole in my new white jeans to majorly embarrassing party fouls.

Looking at life events with an objective eye and seeing why and how a pattern started helps us be compassionate with ourselves. As we step out of guilt, blame and shame, we can gain helpful insights from this type of reflection.

We Always Have a Choice

When it comes to our lives and our children, learning to identify our patterns and beliefs is a highly useful tool. Imagine your reaction to the below scenarios, as presented by a teacher or therapist:

"Testing reveals your child has a learning disability.
She will need special help."

versus

"Your child learns differently from the method she is being taught. Let's work together to find a more effective strategy."

How might you react to each of these statements, which represent two very different ways to communicate the very same diagnostic results? The first implies a lifelong struggle with no way out. Hearing this, many of us would go immediately to a doom and gloom reaction, based on the underlying fear that there is a problem with our child. The second offers a proactive viewpoint, one that leads to a pattern of hopefulness and possibility.

I am not advocating denial for anyone who receives similar news about their child. Rather, I am pointing out how different patterns and beliefs come into play according to how information is presented and perceived.

Sometimes we can choose how and when we receive information. For example, during my first pregnancy, I noticed that I experienced an increase in negative symptoms every time I read the "What to Expect This Month" handout presented at each checkup. Eventually, I skipped reading the handout, giving it straight to my husband instead. I told him that if anything arose that was of concern, I would tell him and he could look it up to see if it was typical. From that day forward, I experienced significantly fewer "expected" symptoms.

And, even when we don't have control over how information is presented, we always have the opportunity to reframe our perceptions.

Back to Matthew's Mom—Allowing the Shift

Many times, new clients want me to start working with their child immediately, as they are perceived as "the one with the problems." These include unproductive behaviors at school or home, issues with anxiety, learning challenges, trouble paying attention or following instructions—the list goes on. The reason I no longer bypass parents to work with their kiddos is that I've learned—I can help only so much if a child returns to the same home and school environments and to the same parents and teachers with the same engrained patterns.

As we discussed above, our environment is key in terms of influencing outcomes, health, wellness, peace and harmony. In Matthew's case, his mother played a huge role in supporting his shift. She was open, ready and willing to own her piece in Matthew's environment, and to do the necessary work in moving through her story.

When I got in touch with her several years after working with Matthew, she told me that our discussion about trusting Matthew had been monumental in her life and imperative to Matthew's transformation. Previously, she'd seen him as "incapable" of many things. She wondered how this child, who had always been accident-prone, socially awkward and seemingly unable to apply his brilliant intelligence, could possibly meet the demands of school. And, she also felt she was holding him back, stuck as she was in her own thoughts and patterns. She knew her perception of her son as lacking stemmed from her past experiences and her beliefs that he just did not have the skill to be successful. She was even aware that she had "released" her older son from such fears and limitations and that he thrived as a result. Why, then, had she been unable to free Matthew?

As we worked together, Matthew's mom realized that she did not trust that he could be successful. After some diligent digging, she clearly saw that this was because she didn't trust herself, as a parent or as a person. On an emotional level, she released a good deal during our discussions. As she owned what was hers—the fear and limiting beliefs—and let it go, she came to trust Matthew and, more importantly, to trust herself. This shift created space for her son to make similar changes. In addition, she empowered herself as well, returning to school to complete her degree.

What Patterns and Beliefs Influence Our Story?

In **The Second Peace**, you will learn specific techniques, tools and strategies that lead to real life solutions. But before we jump into such transformational work, it can be helpful to understand what is behind your story.

Over and over, as parents, the temptation is to focus on our children—what they are doing or not doing, their choices, tendencies, flaws and fears, as well as how their behavior manifests in present day challenges. Once we recognize that our patterns and beliefs form the root of our influence on our children and their environment, however, we can choose to move toward shifting them. This, in turn, creates a space that frees our children from perpetuating their version of our patterns.

Action Peace—How Open Are You?

The extent to which you *believe* you can experience something different in any aspect of your life will determine the extent of your ability to make a shift.

Believing there is only a small possibility that our thoughts affect the world around us will permit an equally small change. Being wide open to potential will allow us to receive an immense shift in perception—even a miraculous one.

On the lines below, mark where you fall in each area:

1. I believe it is possible to live a more joyous life.

_____

Not at all   Absolutely

2. I am willing to do what it takes to change my thoughts and feelings in order to change my story.

_____

Not at all   Absolutely

3. I know that my child and entire family will benefit from me doing this work.

_____

Not at all   Absolutely

This Action Peace will help prepare you for the following chapters. Remember, the more open you are, the greater your opportunity to experience a shift. No matter your responses, you are always free to reassess or make different choices.

Action Peace—Reveal Your Beliefs

List three to five thoughts you have about yourself and your life. If you need help, try these prompts:

1. I feel happy until _____.
2. I am usually pretty stressed unless _____.
3. I try really hard to _____ but _____ always gets in the way.

4. I know I am doing my best as a parent but _____.
5. I used to love (choose an activity you enjoyed prior to having kids) _____, but I don't anymore because _____.

Now, identify the root belief behind each thought and when you think it came into your life. Typically, this will not be something that arose last week. You will most likely see a lifelong pattern or theme to support your findings.

For example, if, for number 5, you wrote, "I used to love to travel, but I don't anymore because I have so many commitments with the kids," the underlying belief might be "Parenting and sacrifice go hand in hand. I can't possible take time for my own hobbies or interests and still be a good parent."

Underlying belief and when it originated:

1.

2.

3.

4.

5.

Action Peace—Uncover Old Patterns

If you find it difficult to get to your core belief(s), take time for the following exercise.

Sit quietly and allow events from your younger years to flow through your mind. Be alert to anything that may have influenced the opinions your formed about yourself. If it helps, keep a pen and paper handy to record your thoughts.

Now, dig in a bit to uncover an underlying idea or consistent theme. Were you required to take care of a sibling, leading you to feel overwhelmed with responsibility? Were your needs met, or did you often feel overlooked or even abandoned? Did love seem conditional, bestowed only when you did certain things?

The practice of sitting quietly and reflecting may not be automatic for you. If you have trouble focusing and start to think of items on your "to do" list, that's okay. Just observe and let them go. If you can't get past the distractions, write them down. Once you know that you will, say, remember to pick up kidney beans for chili tonight, it will be easier to bring your focus back to the task of uncovering core beliefs.

The intent of this exercise is to experience being your own observer. As you move through your days, commit to taking the opportunity to observe your thoughts and reactions. As recollections come to mind, be aware of what you may be bringing to the table.

CHAPTER 3

Triggers
Acknowledge Your Part

"I can't believe I am going to tell you this. When I
am mad at you,
I try to say as much as I can that will get you mad…
on purpose."
(long pause)
"I feel so much better."

~ ANDREW, AGE 8

WHEN AN EVENT, situation or encounter with a person results in our feeling angry, upset, frustrated, etc., we call that a "trigger." Triggers do not make us feel good and they can be difficult to face. It's easy to emphasize someone else's role in what has happened, but our reaction and the resulting emotions belong to us, even if they are the result of our subconscious choice(s).

As my son so freely communicated, he and I play off one another. When he is angry, his intention is to share that feeling, hoping to take me to the same place. I'm sure that, on some level (conscious or subconscious), when I'm upset, I want to share that with him, or with others in my life. So, where do you think he learned that pattern? I'm not blaming myself here, just pointing out a possibility. If I'm not living from a conscious place, it is likely that I will unknowingly pass this pattern to him.

This is clearly not the way to bring forth the happiness and harmony that we all want. But awakening to the pattern that is presenting itself for a shift can be.

Each and every triggering event in our life can be seen as an opportunity. We can learn just as much from the littlest, most inconsequential incidents as we can from the granddaddy, seemingly life-shattering ones. I'd like you to try on the idea that all of life's occurrences provide a possibility for growth.

And here's a radical idea that can completely alter your experience of being triggered: All obstacles are Divinely orchestrated to offer the exact lesson we need at a particular time. If we choose not to take the lesson, there is no judgment, just the recognition that the lesson will be offered again, sooner or later and possibly in a different way.

Further on in the book, we will talk about how we can shift from learning our lessons through strain, struggle or even tragedy, to learning them with grace and ease.

For now, simply being aware of how our children's choices, attitudes and behaviors affect us can provide a window into healing. By doing our work, we gain an ability to identify the events that trigger us, as well as their corresponding thoughts and feelings and the beliefs that underlie them. We can then move from understanding to action.

Let's examine what doing our work can look like.

Client Triumph—Seeing Through a New Lens

Janie's son Alex experienced high levels of anxiety. Whenever there was an unexpected event at school or a change in his schedule, he developed a severe stomachache and was sent home. This drove Janie crazy because she knew it was not a digestive issue or the flu but anxiety that caused the stomachaches. She felt helpless and frustrated, not knowing how to assist her son. She also felt annoyed, at times, and worried that allowing him to come home sent a message that he didn't have the tools to handle such challenges himself. Needless to say, Alex's stomachaches were a big trigger for Janie.

For Alex, change was unbearable, so he found a way to meet his need to feel protected and secure in a predictable environment. If he got a tummy ache, he knew he could go home to "safety," and thus avoid the event or situation that had triggered him. Janie and Alex's teacher made tremendous efforts to inform him well ahead of time of any changes in the daily schedule. This strategy was certainly helpful, but Janie knew it did not allow him the opportunity to move through the root issue—a fear of change and an underlying insecurity that kept him from feeling safe.

As Janie and I worked together, and she started recognizing her own story and underlying beliefs, she allowed a shift in how she was seeing her son.

One morning, Janie was at Alex's school for a meeting and she unexpectedly ran into him in the hallway. There was a new girl in his class and Alex explained to his mom that he was nervous and had an intense tummy ache. Rather than taking her old approach, one of frustration and concern, Janie held strong in a fresh view of her son—she *knew* he had everything he needed to comfort and calm himself within.

Though she empathized with Alex, she didn't allow herself to feel triggered. She simply held in her mind this positive new image. After sharing his concerns, rather than begging to come home, Alex seemed open to her suggestion that he introduce himself to the new girl. She agreed to walk him back to class and facilitate their meeting. Her son did wonderfully, with no sign of a tummy ache and no additional requests to go home.

Janie confirmed that doing her work on how she viewed her son did, in fact, help him through the challenge. Because she did not feel triggered, she was able to observe his anxiety, while remaining calm and peaceful. Without attachment to the outcome, Janie made a suggestion, supported her son, and observed as he successfully returned to his classroom for the remainder of the day.

Alex is starting to learn a new pattern as well. He felt safe to express his feelings to his mom and is learning the necessary tools to handle his triggers. Through continued support, Alex will learn that he has what it takes and move past the trigger on his own.

If Only...

Janie only felt a shift in her son after doing work on the part she played in such situations. We have all heard the adage that we can't change others, only ourselves. Why then do we continuously attempt to "fix" our children, our spouses and external situations?

Often, it seems that if others just did not do what bothers us, then we would not need to be upset. This is untrue. Triggers continue to resurface over and over, through various scenarios, until we get the intended message and do the corresponding work. This is why I believe the dominant paradigms of discipline in our culture are ineffective. (But that's another book.)

Our children offer myriad opportunities for us to feel triggered and then choose to work through our stuff. When we can tell the story below, filling in the blank with our version of life, we know there is an opportunity for us to grow:

"If my child would only _____, everything would be okay."

The feelings that arise during or after a triggering event are a result of our own patterns, beliefs and perceived, unmet needs. When we see that we have a story to fill in the blank above, we also see that we are unknowingly expecting our children to meet our needs. Is it possible for a five-year-old or even a 15-year-old to meet *our* need for peace, order, ease and harmony? No. Not only are our children incapable of meeting our needs, it is unfair to expect them to do so.

Nor is it fair to expect anyone else (spouses, parents, friends) to meet our needs. For that, we must learn a different approach, which will happen as we move through the tools and methods that open us to possibility and awaken us to our True Self (discussed in the next chapter).

As we acknowledge our part in triggering events, we gift ourselves with a new perspective. Becoming aware of our automatic responses will help us break down old patterns based in limiting beliefs.

Commit to being aware as you watch yourself move through your life. Making conscious decisions as to how to react to a challenge shifts the energy behind our triggers. Sometimes it's as simple as doing something different from what is typical for you.

For example, say I am triggered by my daughter's reaction to a seemingly small difficulty. When I am in awareness of my thoughts and feelings, I consciously stop myself from saying what comes automatically to mind. Sometimes, when I don't know what to say or do in a tough situation, I simply tell her, "I don't know what to say right now." It's so freeing. I can then explain how I am feeling and even empathize with her about how she feels.

If in the past I've tried a particular approach and it didn't work, why would I keep trying the same thing? Instead, I accept the opportunity to "Just do it differently." The act of doing or saying something out of the ordinary builds new neural pathways for us *and* for our children.

Pulling Together the Whole Story

As mentioned above, a trigger is a person, place or situation that brings up unpleasant feelings. Typically, the stories we build are initiated by such a trigger.

1. The trigger elicits certain thoughts. (The *mind* component)
2. Our brain releases neuropeptides and hormones, which leads us to experience certain sensations or feelings. (The *body* component)
3. Each thought follows its own neural pathway. And, as Dr. Joe Dispenza says, "Neurons that fire together, wire together." This is a fancy way of saying that, as these thoughts wear a groove into the tissue of our brain, the groundwork is laid for a recurring story.
4. As this cycle occurs over and over, we solidify strong neuropathic loops. With every loop of repeated triggers, thoughts and feelings, we develop certain beliefs and perceptions, based on the past, that appear and feel like the "truth."
5. With a repetition of beliefs, we form a pattern or habit—an unconscious set of thoughts, behaviors and emotions. These often encompass themes like victimhood, martyrdom, self-sabotage and more.

We can observe the entire story loop in Figure 3.1, below.

Figure 3.1

Over time, the emotions associated with any given story create a baseline feeling that becomes the norm. In other words, we become so accustomed to the feelings of stress, say, that we now associate them with our normal resting state. They're certainly not comfortable but they are familiar. As I said in Chapter 1, it's "what we know, the result being that we no longer require the trigger to elicit that same state of stress—our body is automatically and already there. As high levels of the stress hormone cortisol course through our bodies, we require more of the same, which keeps that feeling alive. One could almost say that we become addicted to this feeling. In time, we require more trauma and irritation to elicit the same levels of pressure or to feel "normal."

Many of my clients confirm this, saying that as they wake in the morning their bodies are already prepared for the challenges the day will hold. Maybe this is a form of post traumatic stress disorder (PTSD). When the last six months have been filled with difficulty, we are programmed to expect more.

Due to the power of our subconscious patterning (as discussed in Chapter 2), we typically cannot elicit any type of change without intentional reprogramming. Remember, 95% of our thoughts, actions and beliefs are influenced by our subconscious mind, and 90% of our thoughts today will be the same as yesterday.

Now, the feelings—the body component of the story loop—and the resulting experiences are predictable. With the same thoughts (same mind) and the same feelings (same body), we end up with the same story, or different versions of the same story, as depicted in Figure 3.2. After all, how can we forge a new story while operating on auto-pilot when none of the components have changed?

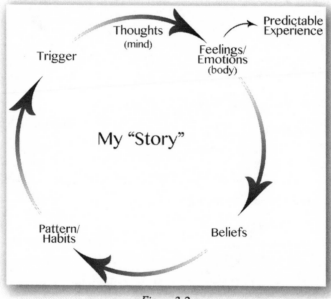

Figure 3.2

What This May Look Like—Who's Triggered Here?

Dana could not stand it when her kids "plugged in" and played video games for hours. She did her best to set limits, but her eight-year-old son was often triggered when told his screen time was up. He threw tantrums or tried to manipulate his mother to see if he could get more time. Dana felt as though she were constantly negotiating with him about this, and that no activity was clear of this technological component. Her son's peers even brought their devices to swim meets so they could play during down time. This was allowed and even encouraged by adult staff, as it kept the kids "manageable" while others were competing.

And, of course, Dana's son wasn't the only one feeling challenged. The quantity of screen time and her son's reaction to it were also triggers for Dana. She expressed feeling frustrated and concerned about her child's dependency on using technology as a distraction. She wanted more for him—to see him socializing and interacting with peers in constructive play was one of her strongest desires. Instead, she saw a group of kids who sat next to one another while gaming, without even communicating.

As Dana and I delved further into our work together, she shared her own difficulty managing time. She was late to almost everything and felt like she rarely ever chipped away at her to-do list. The house was a mess, her schedule was crazy and she was a nervous wreck.

Once she realized that she had created a plethora of distractions in her own life, Dana was able to recognize why her son's seeming dependency on technology was such a trigger. She did the same thing—unconsciously engaging in meaningless activities in order to avoid what she really wanted to be doing.

From there, we dove deeper. Dana dug into her story about why she avoided certain tasks, and why she was not mindful of time with regard to appointments and commitments. Dana shared that her mom had died when she was a young child. She and her brother were under the care of an aunt and uncle who did not have children of their own. Without going into details, it's safe to say that Dana didn't receive the support she needed as a child, and the concept of having "enough time" had become a big issue. She felt constantly criticized at home, and was always rushed through self-care tasks like getting dressed and ready for school. Dana compensated by daydreaming. If she took a couple of hours to clean the bathroom, that meant less time to interact with unsupportive and abusive family members.

These patterns lingered in her subconscious. Although she has little to no contact with her aunt and uncle today, the habit of taking a long time to complete chores and the underlying fear of not having time for herself presented a major opportunity.

In learning to identify her triggers and the feelings that accompanied them, Dana was able to take responsibility for what was "hers" in each situation.

Mapping the cycle illustrated in Figure 3.2, here's what the "My Story" components looked like for Dana, as reflected in the initial challenge with her son:

1. **Trigger**: Son's excessive screen time and tantrums when allotted time was up
2. **Thoughts**: Why can't he play with his friends? What's wrong with him? What's wrong with me?
3. **Feelings:** Distress, frustration, worry, fear
4. **Beliefs**: My son is dependent on technology to be comfortable and is unable to socialize appropriately. He'll never be successful in life.
5. **Pattern/Habit:** Needing a distraction, difficulty identifying priorities, self-sabotage

After releasing her deepest fears and limiting beliefs, Dana was able to make significant changes in her life (prioritizing tasks, time management, etc.), which led to being better equipped to support her son in transitioning away from his distractions and moving toward activities that involved creativity, socialization and movement.

Having the honor of working with Dana and her son, I was in awe of both. His brilliance, self-awareness and unbridled creativity reflected the fact that he was being raised with such love, words can't even begin to describe. Although she carried some big traumas from her own childhood, this love is the prevailing influence in their family.

How Did That "Make" You Feel?

What is the best way to support a child, and ourselves, when we feel triggered? How can we best take advantage of the opportunity triggers provide, while understanding we have a choice in how we respond to challenging events or people in our lives? And, how can we help our children see this as well?

So often, when mediating between our children, and even spouses and other adults, we say things like: "When Sam hit you, how did that *make* you feel?" Or, "You *made* me sad when you didn't put your clothes away."

Yikes! When this seems the appropriate response, we really need to take a step back and assess what we are teaching our children and what we ourselves believe. If Jane is triggered and feeling upset because her brother hit her, when we say, "How did that make you feel?" we plant a couple of pretty big seeds. For one, we teach Jane that other people have control over her feelings. This can lead to a sense of powerlessness and low self-worth. Secondly, Jane learns that she gets extra attention when someone does something *to* her, enforcing the ever so common victim/villain pattern. She may find it serves her to play out the victim role in order to get extra attention from parents, teachers or even peers.

When describing this cause and effect scenario to parents, I often think of those who inspire me—Gandhi, Dr. Martin Luther King, Jr. and Mother Theresa, to name a few.

Imagine this hypothetical, yet realistic, scenario: A government official visits a health clinic in which Mother Theresa cares for people with infectious diseases. This official observes Mother Theresa, without a mask or gloves, working closely with patients who have contagious and deadly diseases. Triggered by her apparent disregard of rules and his own unrealized fears, he blurts, "You are a raving mad lunatic! How can you work with these people without any protection?"

Would Mother Theresa have broken down in tears and said, "When you say that, you make me feel bad"? Personally, I can't imagine such a thing. I believe she would have kindly and quietly blessed the official and then returned to her work with the sick and dying.

I realize that it's a big leap from Jane to Mother Theresa, but can you see how the ability to take responsibility for our own thoughts, actions and responses can free and empower us?

To reiterate a few key points:

- Others cannot make us feel any certain way unless we allow them that power. Our reactions to adverse situations or to what others say and do are always a choice.
- When we are empowered and connected with who we really are, we do not allow others to have control over our feelings or reactions.
- Mother Theresa was able to work with the sickest of the sick because she had complete trust and faith that she was safe and protected. She was not often triggered by what others said or by the prognosis of her patients. She stood solid in knowing her Divine mission.

As easy as it is to place blame on others, we hand over our power when we think someone else has control over us. In reacting to something our child says or does, we tend to think they are the ones with the problem or the ones who need to change. Our kiddos would likely benefit from some loving guidance, but that can't occur until we first take care of the part of us that is feeling triggered!

Do we have a need for peace and ease? Do we want to feel like we are good parents, unconditionally loved and respected? Once again, we cannot expect our children to meet our needs. The most useful thing we can do to start with is identify what is triggering us and accept the accompanying feelings.

To put it another way, the best way to support our children and ourselves, and the best way to take advantage of the opportunities triggers provide, is to do the work on our own story loop. Like the proverbial oxygen mask on an airplane, we can only help our children choose their responses to challenging events and/or people in their lives *after* we help ourselves.

A Personal Peace—From Trigger to Gratitude
Many of us can relate to feeling triggered around the holidays. I was no exception. I always found it odd that Thanksgiving—a holiday

that actually has the word "thanks" in it—seemed to be more about stress and excess busyness than being grateful.

Now, the "giving" part, I definitely witnessed. In my family, Thanksgiving was all about one or two women giving up their day to feed a room full of people who virtually did nothing to help. I could not imagine what the women in this situation could possibly find to be thankful for, other than the whole thing being over. To be clear, I am aware that some women truly enjoy being in the kitchen and feeding droves of people, but that is not me.

As a child and young adult, I was in the receiving group—the group that should have been giving thanks. With the exception of a few last minute tasks, I did nothing. Maybe, on a good year, I would set the table. (Sorry for being a slug, Mom. And thank you!)

So, when it came time to host my first Thanksgiving dinner, I was a bit apprehensive, to say the least. Once I had put the offer out there, I experienced a myriad of emotions—from excitement and nervousness to dread.

As the day approached, my anxiety built. Looking back at what typically arose for me during family gatherings, I saw a tendency to turn simple, meaningless comments or questions by others into personal attacks. If someone suggested I use a different pot for the mashed potatoes, for example, I heard "You don't know what you're doing." If someone said, "Can I help you with that?" I heard "You are incapable and unworthy." Ill intended or not, these comments were triggers. Due to underlying fears of not being good enough, I felt angry, worthless and fearful, and my reactions reflected these feelings of inadequacy and defensiveness.

Once I became aware of this pattern, I saw I had several choices: I could continue what I perceived as a generational pattern of struggling to make the entire meal myself; I could ask for help and be triggered by a multitude of comments I would take the wrong way, which would then lead to the "You made me feel this way" mentality; or, I could create an entirely new experience.

Excited to see this holiday from a new place, I chose to create something new for myself and my family. I knew that, in addition to countless siblings, nieces and nephews, both sets of grandparents would be attending and I asked my mom and my mother-in-law for help. I knew I needed to be highly intentional in order to create anew, and, just prior to the big day, I made a list of everyone attending, with five things I was grateful for written next to each.

Sprinkled through the lists were things like:

- "I'm grateful that my dad likes to show his love by helping out with projects around the house."
- "I'm grateful my mother-in-law and my mom get along."
- "I'm grateful that my father-in-law is fun-loving and enjoys playing games with the kids."

My list for Mom looked like this:

- I'm grateful Mom has tons of experience making Thanksgiving dinner.
- I'm grateful Mom is always willing to help in the kitchen.
- I'm grateful Mom loves to laugh.
- I'm grateful Mom is supportive.
- I'm grateful Mom loves being together with our family.

The day's events were amazing. At one point, my mom turned to me and said, "Let's laugh! Tell me a funny story." I was overjoyed to retell one of her favorite stories and to hear her giggle with happiness as we peeled the sweet potatoes.

In addition to the preparations listed above, I arranged an activity and requested participation from each guest, from kiddos to grandparents. I gave everyone three strips of paper and asked that they write one thing they were grateful for on each. Then, we linked the strips to make a paper chain. Once that was complete, we strung the chain around the window in our dining room. It felt so good to consciously bring gratitude into the holiday.

I enjoyed seeing a genuine connection across the generations as my kids and their grandfathers played Monopoly. I enjoyed even more hearing my son ask, "Why are all of the boys playing games and all of the girls making food?" I was astounded by his observation.

After dinner, my father-in-law asked how he could help. Rather than giving the typical, "Oh, don't worry about it" response, I asked him to clear the table. Watching my dad and my father-in-law do the dishes, I was filled with real thankfulness.

What about you? What family patterns have you become entrenched in? What would you like to create anew for yourself and your family? Think about your triggers, and ways to release them.

Whose Trigger Is This, Anyway?

As we move further into awareness, we have the opportunity to gain increasing clarity regarding what is our work and what belongs to another. In any situation, if anger, guilt, shame or any other emotions arise and we feel triggered, we have the choice to do our work and discover why.

If, on the other hand, others feel triggered by something we've said or done, it is important to remember that their reactions and feelings belong to them. You are never responsible for making anyone feel any particular way. This does not give us free reign to purposefully instigate arguments with our children, partners, exes, coworkers or friends. In fact, becoming more conscious of our word choices and being aware that what we say and how we act can promote peace and harmony are beautiful side effects of this work.

Once you become adept at identifying your story, thoughts, feelings, beliefs and patterns, and then releasing them, you may begin to notice that situations that once triggered you no longer have such power. This is a phenomenal thing. It's as if you have renewed vision, and can now support your loved ones from a place of abundance.

Let's move forward by discovering what triggers exist for you. Then, we'll take a look at the whole story.

Action Peace—You're Driving Me Crazy!

Write a few triggers and the feelings that accompany them for each category in the table below. Keep in mind that feelings may include frustration, fear, dismay, anger or sadness. "I just want them to stop doing that" is not a feeling.

AREA	TRIGGER	FEELINGS
Children		
Spouse/Partner/Ex		
Extended Family		
Career		
Personal/Body/Health		
Living Situation		
Other		

Now, take another few minutes to look over each trigger, seeing it as an opportunity for growth. Can you imagine what it would be like if you still felt peace whenever that trigger occurred?

Action Peace—Observe Your Story

The following exercise is a wonderful opportunity to bring together everything we have discussed in the first three chapters.

Fill in the diagram below in order to observe your story in its entirety. As you do so, don't worry about getting anything perfect. The opportunity here is to enhance your understanding of your story.

Remember:

- Your **story** represents your perceptions of life events, circumstances and relationships, as well as their accompanying feelings and emotions.
- A **trigger** is a person, place, or situation that brings up unpleasant feelings for you.
- Your **feelings** are described with words like frustration, anger, sadness, guilt, regret, etc.
- A **belief** is a perception based on the past that appears and feels like the truth.
- A **pattern or habit** is an unconscious set of thoughts, behaviors and emotions that often include themes of victimhood, martyrdom, self-sabotage, etc.

Story Loop

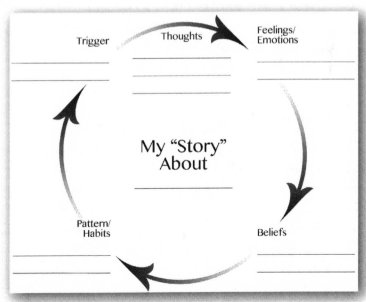

CHAPTER 4

True Self versus Ego

Understand Who You Are

"Mommy, I just realized Love can be different colors.
When I look with my third eye, I can see all the colors."

~ Tessa, age 6

Throughout our lives, many people feel the need to tell us who we are. Via everyday, seemingly benign conversations, we hear that someone finds us funny or critical, smart, kind, or mean-spirited. Or, we are called lazy, bright, successful. On top of the labels we receive from others, we have our own perceptions about ourselves. So, who's right? Which perception is the correct one? The one we should believe?

We create an **ego** as we expand on all of these perceptions—the physical, emotional and mental traits that we *think* describe us. Often, they come to form the basis for how we define ourselves. Some of these descriptors change from day to day or year to year, and can include marital status, title (if we have one), number of children, accomplishments, failures and on and on.

In contrast to the ego, our **True Self** is a Divine being of pure love. This is who we *really* are, and it never changes, regardless of status or circumstances.

What possibilities reveal themselves when we become attuned to our True Self? For one, we see all of life differently. By viewing others from a place of connection, self-love, empowerment, peace and joy, we open to a whole new way of being. Witnessing who our children really are from this perspective is just as powerful. We see past their behaviors, upsets and fears about themselves into the eyes of their divinity.

As my daughter Tessa states at the beginning of this chapter, when we open our perception, we receive new insights about things we thought we already completely understood.

Client Triumph—Coming Home "On Pink"

Erin and her new husband came to see me because her seven-year-old son was experiencing behavior challenges at school. Wesley had been through a lot in his short life. Among other difficulties, he was often teased at school, had motor skill delays and, due to his parents' divorce, split his time between two very different home environments.

Erin's description of her son matched that of many kids I've worked with in the past. He was impulsive, always on the move and had poor eye contact skills. Despite awkward social tendencies, it was important to him to form positive peer relationships, and he tried hard to get his needs met—to make himself feel seen and heard—which often resulted in being disruptive during class. As a result, he received special treatment from teachers and was assigned his own area of the classroom to sit.

Wesley's school used an elaborate color system to monitor classroom behavior for each child. Rather than the common green (good), yellow (warnings) and red (problems), his school used seven colors. Wesley often came home with one of the colors that corresponded to the various problems he exhibited at school.

Erin wanted to have outside testing done for Wesley, but she held off on pursuing the entire battery. Instead, she came to me. After a few individual sessions, she understood that she had a choice as to the lens through which she saw her son.

Erin chose the route of empowerment, helping Wesley see who he really was. She spent extra time with him in the evenings, and coached him to alter how he viewed himself. One evening, while guiding him in relaxation exercises for the central nervous system, Erin asked Wesley what color he wanted to receive at school the next day. They went through a visualization where he demonstrated appropriate behaviors, like raising his hand, waiting his turn and, consequently, coming home with a positive report.

Wesley responded beautifully and soon started shifting his experience at school. More and more, he came home "On Pink," the most desirable color of this particular system. As a result, his self-esteem improved and he began forming more meaningful relationships with adults and peers.

Shortly after I wrote this section, Erin contacted me by email. Wesley's growth had been remarkable, and she no longer felt his current school setting was meeting all of his needs. She took the steps she was guided to take and enrolled her son in a charter school with a very child-centered, loving approach. Wesley was, she reported, shining like never before!

If Erin's first step had been to find a new school, their family may have missed the opportunity to work through their triggers, feelings and patterns (their old stories). When we jump immediately to changing our outer circumstances, problems often resurface fairly quickly. Erin took charge of her feelings first and was able to coach her son toward a new perspective. Only then did she move to find the setting that would support him in his new story—and in seeing himself as he really is.

A Deeper Understanding of Who We Really Are

What or who is our True Self? Is it the best version of who we think we are? No, our True Self goes beyond our personality, to our innermost being—the truth of who we are at our core.

The heart in Figure 4.1 represents the Divine Source of Love. As I shared earlier, my belief is that God is all-loving and encompasses infinite peace and love. For purposes of simplicity, I use the words Infinite Love to indicate this concept. Feel free to use whatever word(s) you find most meaningful. For some, that will be Life-Energy or the Universe. I've listed a number of synonyms. Regardless of what is right for you, our shared understanding will be that this force is at the center of all life.

Figure 4.1 Infinite Love

Synonyms for Infinite Love:
Perfect Love
Field of Potential
Unconditional Love
Oneness
Wisdom
Creator
Spirit
Truth
Mind

We are each a unique expression of Infinite Love. In Figure 4.2 below, the small heart above Infinite Love represents our True Self. This is the truth of who we are, that which never changes, regardless of age, marital status, parental roles, social roles, skills and abilities, perceived mistakes and lifetime accomplishments. Our True Self is one with Infinite Love and with everyone and everything around us. As described in Neale Donald Walsch's children's book *The Little Soul and the Sun,* it is as if Infinite Love is the sun and each one of us is a candle on the sun. When even one candle cannot shine, the light is just not the same.

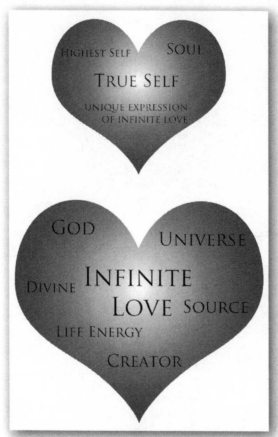

Figure 4.2 Infinite Love and True Self

For some of us, this concept may make perfect sense, and, for others, this can take time. Am I implying that we are, at our core, perfect and Divine beings? I am. Stay with me here. Have you ever witnessed the awe and wonderment of a sleeping, newborn baby? How in the world could anyone say that newborn is anything but a perfect creation? Well, what about kids who are rushed to the Neonatal ICU with breathing difficulties, heart issues or other complications? Are they perfect? Absolutely! At our core we are all unique, Divine expressions of Love.

So, when is it that we come to believe otherwise? Certainly an infant crying from hunger is simply communicating a need for nourishment. But what if that crying goes on for hours and hours? Are we still able to see that child as a perfect expression of Infinite Love? Maybe, because he or she is still young. And maybe not, if we are a parent who is exhausted and overwhelmed. My point is this:

The True Self remains pure and perfect Love through
Illness or disease
Perceived disability in any area
Ability/performance in any area (academic, athletic, creative)
Perceived mistakes
Conformity to socially accepted definitions of beauty
Perceived accomplishments
Financial status
Marital/divorce status
Career status
Hobbies/interests
Criminal record
Volunteer record
Addictions
Sexual orientation

Our Ego—Who We Think We Are

When young, we don't really see or feel ourselves as separate from our parents. For the most part, we live in the here and now, feeling connected to everyone and everything. We cry if we are upset and laugh if we are happy. At any given moment, we experience what arises without judgment or analysis. We don't wonder how we can be upset about not getting a cookie one moment and then be happy and laughing the next. Can you imagine a three-year-old saying, "Mom, isn't it crazy that ten minutes ago I was screaming about that cookie and now I am happy and playing? Strange, huh?" This would never happen because young children live purely in the moment, not in a state of judgment about the past or fear of the future.

Around the age of seven, we start to develop an idea of who we *think* we are. The first thing that influences this process is the environment in which we spend most of our time. This environment is created by the conscious and subconscious thoughts, actions, feelings and beliefs of our parents or caregivers. Unintentionally, they pass their beliefs, and sometimes their whole story, to us. Over time, we hear and feel their opinions and start to believe these things to be true. Along with ideas about ourselves, we are also given ideas about society, culture, etc. This provides a reference point from which we begin to judge ourselves and others. In other words, we unknowingly adopt the beliefs of parents, siblings, teachers, etc. to be true and then expand on those beliefs to develop our personality.

Here are a few examples of parental beliefs (and possible interpretations) that can be passed to a child:

- You're too sensitive. (Don't feel your emotions. Cover them up.)
- You should eat your broccoli like your sister. (You are not as good as your sister. You are not healthy enough.)
- Don't talk to strangers. (Be fearful of anyone you don't know.)
- Stay away from people who live in that area. (Judge others according to certain standards—socioeconomic status, physical appearance, etc.)
- Little girls/boys don't do that. (Follow all spoken and unspoken rules of socially acceptable gender roles.)
- Work hard so you can be successful. (Your value is based on your accomplishments.)

Once we take on these beliefs, they become the basis of our identity—our ego self. In this way, we learn to see and experience ourselves as separate from our parents, siblings and friends, and, ultimately, our True Self and Infinite Love. This feeling of separation brings about fear and promotes judgment, and we begin to evaluate ourselves and others accordingly.

An extreme but powerful simplification is that our True Self and Infinite Love operate from a *love*-based perspective, while our egos operate from a *fear*-based perspective.

As you can see in Figure 4.3, our ego (personality and identity) is seemingly separate from our True Self. Along with our ego, we receive the metaphorical equivalent of a durable, expandable, invisible **backpack**. Until recognized for what it is, this backpack becomes a storage place for all of the heavy emotions we have not addressed—anger, frustration, upsets, negative self-image, judgments, traumas, tragedy and much, much more. It isn't something we consciously choose and wear only on occasion; it just comes with our ego.

In addition to the "free gift" of a backpack, we also receive an imaginary scorecard. This is where we evaluate and judge ourselves and others. Subconsciously, we give ourselves points for being or doing "good," and we take away points for being or doing "bad." The most important concept to remember about this scorecard is that it is based upon lessons learned from our teachers, parents, society, religion, etc., and it is the method our ego uses to analyze our words, actions and abilities. Steeped in judgment and fear, the scorecard reinforces our separation from everyone and everything around us.

Figure 4.3 My Ego, My True Self and Infinite Love

Synonyms for Ego:
Personality
Identity
Fear-based perception of myself
Who I *think* I am

Adding Others to the Picture

In our ego state, each of us is a "me," and each "me" is constantly interacting with one or more "you." Place yourself in Figure 4.4 below. The small heart at the top center represents your True Self: The truth of who you really are—pure and perfect Love. The person with the backpack and scorecard at the left of this heart represents your ego self. This is your personality: Who you *think* you are, as you learned to define yourself beginning in early childhood. As stated above, the ego self is constructed from what is presented in our environment, which is comprised of the conscious and subconscious thoughts, feelings, beliefs and patterns of those with whom we spend our younger years.

The small heart at the bottom center represents the True Self of each person you interact with—like you, pure and perfect Love. The person with the backpack and scorecard on the bottom right represents the ego self of each person you interact with. As with your own ego self, this ego was consciously and subconsciously created over time in response to that person's environment. In the center of this figure is Infinite Love.

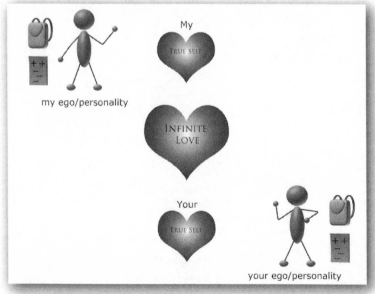

Figure 4.4 My Ego and True Self, Infinite Love, Your Ego and True Self

Our ego beliefs, what we carry in our backpack and how we score ourselves and others create our perception of the world—the lens through which we see everything. This happens to everyone, so we all perceive the world through a unique lens. We converge on similar beliefs or perceptions at times, of course, but, ultimately, we can never really experience the world through another's eyes.

How We Perceive Each Other

It gets more complicated! Additional images have been added to Figure 4.5, representing the way we experience one another. To use myself as an example, if I am seeing the world through my ego—the one carrying the backpack of stories and the scorecard of judgments—then, when I meet you, I create an idea of who I *think* you are.

In other words, I take in how you look, act and sound, and subconsciously use my ego understandings to create an idea, or ego image, of you. This may or may not be similar to how you perceive yourself or how others see you. It is certainly vastly different from who you really are—a Divine being, a unique expression of Infinite Love.

The ego image I create for you is the person I communicate with when we speak. I talk *from* who I think I am and *to* who I think you are. You do the same when you meet me, using all of your personal and worldly knowledge to assess my physical appearance, how I speak and act, and what you may already know about me to create an idea, or ego image, of who you think I am. And, you talk *from* who you think you are, *to* who you think I am. As these ego images communicate and interact with each other, we keep adding details. Before we know it, we have a full picture of one another locked into our conscious and subconscious minds.

As this model illustrates, not even our egos interact with one another. We each communicate and interact with an *idea* of who the other is via our own, subconsciously created perceptions. And, again, these images have little or nothing to do with who either of us really is.

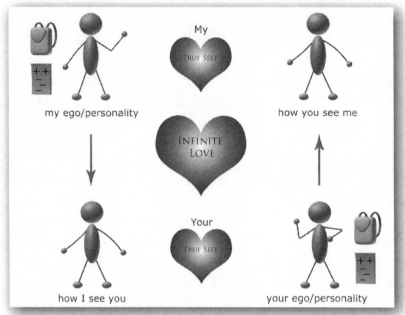

Figure 4.5 Our Egos and Ego Images of One Another,
Our True Selves and Infinite Love

What This May Look Like—An Ego in the Making

If the idea of our ego versus our True Self is new to you, the following example may help bring it all together.

When my parents found out they were expecting a second child soon after their first, they most likely started forming conscious and subconscious ideas of who I would "be." For instance, they would have had underlying beliefs of what life would be like with two little ones under the age of two, and how that would change if I were a boy or a girl. If you had asked them, they may not have been aware of these beliefs on a conscious level, but they were there.

After I was born and started to develop, I was exposed to myriad influences in my home environment, based on beliefs about who I was, cultural expectations, judgments, fears and much, much more. Like all children, I was told, "This is good," "Don't do that," etc. Some of these things are necessary for safety and survival, and some are not.

As I started to walk, talk and pass through various stages of development, I was exposed to more and more beliefs, ideas and experiences. And then I reached my school years.

My mom often tells me, "You were such a happy child until first grade." Hearing this after I learned about how we form identities, I realized school marked the stage when I started to "buy into" the influences from my environment. I no longer felt free just to *be*. I started noticing what others wore and how they presented themselves. I felt embarrassed about certain articles of my clothing, and wanted particular shoes and jeans so I could be like the popular girls in my class. This was the beginning of comparing and evaluating myself on an unrealistic scale on which I could never measure up. No matter what I did, I always came up short. I was developing an ego.

You can see this when looking at my "personality." I was an emotional child. Within the safety of my home environment, my first reaction to many upsets was to burst into tears. At school, I was much better at hiding my sadness and frustration, bottling them in for later. When I did have an occasional explosion, I was told to stop crying. I heard, "It's okay, stop crying" and "You're too sensitive" what seemed like hundreds of times. And like so many children, I interpreted this to mean it was not safe to express my feelings. I continued to cry when I felt sad or angry for a little while, but over time I became a master at covering up my emotions.

The sense of freedom and happiness that once ruled my life dissolved, replaced by the ideas and beliefs of who others thought I was—and who I thought others thought I was. Soon enough, I began owning those thoughts and beliefs, and, as I grew, I kept adding to them, creating an elaborate, complicated ego.

The Gift of True Perspective

I want to add that my parents are, and have always been, wonderful and amazing people. They are both loving and supportive, and I hold no judgment for any of the above. Though the development of my ego was influenced by my environment, I was the one who accepted, as human beings unknowingly do, the information and ideas that were presented as truth. We all operate from an ego perspective until we know otherwise. Now, living what I share in this book and knowing I always have a choice as to how I respond, I am empowered. I released any blame I ever felt toward my parents because I recognized that it only served to weigh down my backpack.

And clearly, my memories are filtered through my own ego perceptions. Who knows what really happened? Each of us has our own viewpoint of even shared experiences. This was confirmed for me when talking with my brother, whose take on much of our childhood is totally different from my own. Of course it is. He has his own backpack, scorecard and unique personality, and has created a lens through which he witnesses and observes life.

When I tune in to the perspective of my True Self and of Infinite Love, I see and feel only the love that my parents' True Selves had and have for me. And it is abundant!

Also, I would like to add that we don't always pick up negative patterns in childhood. Every once in a while, I meet a client who reports having felt totally supported and unconditionally loved as a child. (I tip my glass to those parents.) For these folks, a trauma or difficult situation during young adulthood was the trigger that brought out fear-based ego thoughts. Regardless of when and how we create our ego, it isn't a life sentence. It doesn't take thirty years to undo the effects, even if we have been in a cloud of ego beliefs for that amount of time.

What's available to us in awakening to our True Self goes beyond the limitations of our language. My wish for you, and my main intention in this book, is that you release your baggage and experience who you really are! From the viewpoint of your True Self, you will awaken to a world of infinite possibility. Your family will benefit in turn, as they experience the new environment you create from a place of love and possibility.

More on the Ego (or "Moron, the Ego," ha ha)

When I use the word "ego," I am not referring to the work of analysts like Freud. As stated previously, I use it to represent our personality—who we think we are. The original purpose of the ego was to perceive danger and keep the physical body from harm, thus allowing our spirit—our True Self—to have a human experience. Without an ego, early humans would not have known to run from sabre tooth tigers or learned to use fire for cooking and warmth.

Over the centuries, the role of our ego expanded to the point that it is now out of control. (Our egos really are rather moronic.) Humans moved into a space of perceiving high levels of fear on a daily, moment-to-moment basis. This manifests as depression, anxiety, tension and dis-ease. This is not, say, due to fire-breathing dragons lurking in the produce aisle but to the multitude of stressors we experience in ordinary life. Our overscheduled, emotionally intense lives cause our brains to release high levels of cortisol, a stress hormone. Pulsing through our bodies in response to this pervasive stress, cortisol leaves us feeling like we are in "fight or flight" mode much of the time.

Whether consciously and/or subconsciously, this affects everyone around us. As parents, we are key players in creating the tone of our home environment. When we are in a state of increased tension, those feelings becomes available for our kids to absorb. This is true whether caused by the loss or illness of a loved one, deadlines at work, poor grades or the discovery that our daughter has her first boyfriend.

In order to ensure we do not pass our negative patterns and limiting beliefs to our children, we must first understand how our baggage and our stress affects how we view them. In other words, the anxiety, anger, grief and whatever else we are holding onto influences our perception of all we encounter—especially our kiddos.

How You See Your Child

What is influencing your perceptions? Let's apply the concepts in this chapter to your family dynamics.

Place your child in Figure 4.6 below, along with Infinite Love and your ego and True Self. Your child's True Self is at the bottom center, representing that they are a unique expression of Infinite Love. Their ego is at the bottom right.

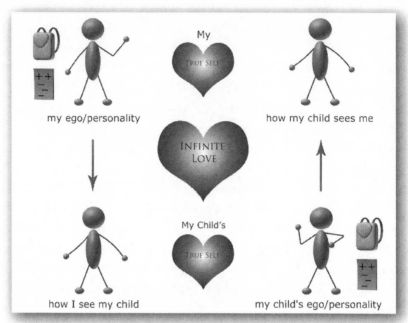

Figure 4.6 How You Perceive Your Child

If we view our child through ego eyes, we create an idea of who that child is through the lens of our story. As we've discovered, this perspective is often fear-based, which causes us to view him or her as having a range of limiting tendencies and characteristics.

For instance, let's say a child has received a diagnosis, or displays symptoms of one. As with any "label, we form preconceived ideas of what that diagnosis means. Whether we intend to or not, our perception will necessarily be affected by our personal experience of that diagnosis, including the influence it has on both our child and the family as a whole. Medical information and societal beliefs also come into play.

Only on rare occasions have I worked with families who feel empowered in such a situation. One mom, a client, said to her daughter, "We found out there is nothing wrong. You have ADHD and that just means that certain doors are closed. We will do whatever we can to help you open those doors." Far more often, we go to the internet and read everything there is about a diagnosis, only to end up feeling like our child, and therefore our family, has been handed a life sentence of struggle.

All of this is to say—there are a multitude of influences that help create our perception of our children. Fortunately, there are also a multitude of possibilities available, once we know we have a choice.

The Influence of Observers and the Environment

So far, we've examined Your Story, Patterns and Beliefs, Triggers and True Self versus Ego. This information will help expand your ability to create a new dynamic for yourself and your family. Let's look at how this process can unfold.

When you feel triggered by something your child does, you can choose to bring awareness to the stream of thoughts and emotions that arise. You can then notice that it is as if the trigger activated the traumas and difficulties stored in your backpack—your old stories that continue to course through their strongly rooted, neural pathways.

After multiple triggers, you see that your stories' accompanying thoughts and feelings led to beliefs and patterns that continue to replay. In fact, you may be observing your child through the eyes of the one wearing the backpack filled with fear, guilt, anger, sadness and more. When you see with these eyes, it's not surprising that your child appears disrespectful, incapable, selfish, disorganized, etc.

Let's look at this another way. Have you ever wondered how that same child manages to "keep it together" at school? Or why your friends say he or she is always so well behaved and respectful? The difference is the observer, each wearing their individual backpack and seeing with their singular eyes. Our children know this at a core level.

It's also the case that our children feel safe within their family environment—at home, in the car, etc. They hold things in throughout the day, then lash out at us. I once asked my son why he didn't "act like this" around his friends. He said he knows I will love him no matter what. I was grateful for his honesty, and I realized I had some more work to do—first to address my triggers and emotions and then to release them in order to get to a place where I could support my son. That doesn't mean I encourage him to direct his anger toward me. I just know

now that when I am centered and clear, feeling free of my baggage, I can create the space he needs to release his frustrations in a healthy way.

There are rare times that a child exhibits difficult behavior at school or in other settings and not so much at home. There can be a number of reasons for this. And, I still feel it is important for parents to do the work in identifying their story, revealing their underlying fears and limiting beliefs, acknowledging their part, and understanding who they—and their children—really are. Releasing our subconscious patterns and intentionally reprogramming allows us to remember our connection with Infinite Love and create a new story—one that includes a more loving way to interact with and experience our children.

A Unique Way to Release

I recall a time when my son was experiencing some intense emotions about a disagreement he'd had with a friend. The story and his negative feelings reignited when I told him this friend was coming to visit. The intensity of his anger surprised me, as the incident he was upset about had occurred months earlier. Though I was not completely aware of what had happened, it was clear to me that he was holding onto quite a bit, if not all, of the accompanying emotions. There was anger, sadness, upset and even rage.

Despite knowing that the friend would arrive in just a couple of hours, I wasn't triggered by the strength of his emotions. Listening and empathizing with my son, I allowed and even encouraged him to experience all that had arisen. I did not judge him, nor did I have an agenda that he *work through* his emotions in a certain time frame.

As the feelings heightened, so did his apparent need for a physical expression of his anger. In a moment of inspiration, I grabbed an old t-shirt and suggested he tear it to pieces. He looked at me as if to say, "Really, I can do this?" I assured him it was okay and that the shirt was a rag we no longer needed.

For twenty minutes, he tore at the t-shirt, shredding it into strips. As the last bit of physical exertion exited his body, I suddenly had my son back. It was as if nothing had happened. Via the physical act of demolishing a rag, he was able to release the emotions he'd carried for months over this situation.

The wildest part is, when his friend showed up at the door, my son gave him a big hug and went off to play as if nothing at all had happened!

An Important Note about the Ego

Before going any further, I want to discuss how I used to feel about my ego. My intention in sharing this is to spare you from time spent resisting this part of yourself.

As I began to understand the concept of the ego, I entered a rabbit hole of guilt, blame and shame. Any time I felt angry or upset or frustrated, I told myself things like, "You know better!" or "This is all because of your ego. You let it get out of control and brought this on yourself."

This type of thinking was a distraction from what was really going on and, ironically, led to even more ego thoughts of blame and shame. I ignored the feelings and stuffed them, unresolved, into my backpack. Fortunately, I came to realize that the hate I was directing at my ego only added fuel to the fire. I also understood that the time I had spent in the rabbit hole had gotten me no further along in healing. I had emerged right where I'd entered—in need of a drastic shift.

I now view my ego for what it is—the part of me that acts as a magnet to draw the exact right challenges into my life in order to reveal my next lesson. I am grateful, as I am able to choose to see life's trials as opportunities rather than difficulties. This simple shift in perception relieved me of the heavy weight of guilt and shame. Now, when a trigger arises, I take note, acknowledge and feel my thoughts and emotions and do the work needed to release the old pattern and create a new one. (Don't worry, we will go into detail about this process in **The Second Peace**.)

Delving Deeper into Our True Self

Ego beliefs can shift and change from day to day and even minute to minute. So, where does the heart, or True Self, fit in? Let's revisit Figure 4.5 as we consider an answer to this pivotal question.

In Figure 4.5, our True Self appears separate from the ego and the body. For one reason or another, many of us have completely forgotten that our True Self even exists. Or maybe we have never been exposed to the idea that we have a True Self. The reality is, our True Self is right here, in our body, along with our thoughts, feelings and beliefs. It may have hibernated for a number of years but, by taking particular steps to bring awareness to our thoughts and feelings, we can awaken to the Infinite Love and possibility within and start living more and more from a place of clarity, peace, love and grace.

When we become attuned to our True Self, have all our needs met from this place and stay committed to the love within that never changes, we begin to see ourselves and others from a new, more enlightened perspective. We are filled with love and forgiveness, peace and harmony. We shift how we perceive and even create our environment. Often, lasting changes result in both our inner and outer world.

By viewing others from this place of connection, self-love, empowerment, compassion and joy, we also experience them differently. It's as if we are able to *feel* their truest essence.

One of the challenges of introducing the concept of our True Self is that it is difficult to describe, and understand, intellectually. It is more an experience, or a *knowing*, that occurs when we are clear of the limiting beliefs and negative patterns of our ego.

So, how in the world do we release years of ego beliefs in order to connect in to our True Self? In Chapter 9 we will go through a variety of methods to let go of the thoughts, ideas, feelings and beliefs that shape how we view ourselves and others. In the meantime, let me share a personal story.

A Personal Peace—The Last Night Terror
As a young child, my son experienced night terrors. More accurately, my *family* experienced night terrors. If you or your child has ever been there, you need no explanation. If not, consider yourself fortunate.

A night terror often occurs in the middle of the night but can happen during naptime as well. It's very different from a nightmare. Rather than waking up from a scary dream, those experiencing night terrors look awake—their eyes are open—but they are still asleep. It is almost like sleepwalking in the middle of a nightmare.

I imagine such experiences can be different for different people. For my son, a night terror consisted of screaming, kicking and inconsolably crying, non-stop, for 30-45 minutes, three or four times a month. I have heard that we were among the lucky ones—some kiddos experience terrors like this three or four times a week. Regardless, I went to bed each night in a state of fear. Would this be a night terror night? How long would it last? Wasn't there anything I could do to help?

Without being too dramatic, I would say it was torturous to witness my son's night terrors. There was nothing I could do to console him. He didn't want to be touched, he couldn't be soothed and nothing my husband or I could do decreased either the intensity or duration.

Witnessing my son as he came out of a night terror was just as strange as the experience itself. After screaming and flailing about for up to an hour, he would wake up, yawn a few times and look around, bewildered.

My husband or I would gently guide him back to bed, with a tiny bit of relief, hopeful we would have a few days until the next night terror.

When I mentioned my concern to our pediatrician, he told me there was no known cause and that my son would eventually grow out of them. Like many parents, I started doing my own research, exploring new and integrative medical approaches. Were the night terrors linked to a food sensitivity? What other factors might come into play? I wasn't about to wait this one out to see when he would "grow out of it." I had to attack the problem now and find a solution. I was 100% dedicated and determined to help my child.

Then came the miracle.

One night, as my husband and I were watching a movie, we heard Andrew start to cry. We knew the sound and what we were in for. My husband went in and carried him to the family room so he wouldn't wake our daughter.

As Andrew stood before me, sobbing now, something came over me. It is very difficult to describe in words but I will do my best. I suddenly had an awareness that I was considering the situation from an inaccurate viewpoint. I was angry and felt a great deal of resentment toward Western medicine and, because my ego was in full force, I was seeing my son from a place of distress.

My ego eyes saw a helpless child in pain, in terror. My ego thoughts directed me to *attack* the problem. If Western medicine wasn't the answer, there had to be another approach. Focused on this belief, I felt as if *I* was the one who needed to find the answer.

Then it happened. As if my thoughts were removed from my head and replaced with a new, enlightened viewpoint, I saw the error in these fear-based, ego thoughts. I knew that the solution was not in any approach I might take, but in how I was seeing the problem and from what viewpoint I was observing my son. And, like that, I saw the following possibilities:

What if this night terror is not even real?

What would happen if I didn't believe night terrors had any power over my son or my family?

What if this is not even a problem?

Ultimately, this lead to:

The truth of my son is that he is pure and perfect love and light. Not that he is a "child with night terrors."

In that moment, I saw Andrew in a new light, with new eyes. I knew from a deeper place that he was a child of Infinite Love and infinite possibility, and I no longer believed in night terrors as something that defined his or our experience.

Though only about five minutes into the experience, Andrew stopped crying. He walked to where I sat and curled up in my lap. Everything seemed to be happening in slow motion. As he nestled in, I held him, knowing with every cell of my being he would NEVER have another night terror.

And, he never did.

What happened during this miracle moment was that I *truly* saw my son, *truly* saw myself, and knew that the night terrors had nothing to do with Andrew's True Self. They weren't even *real*. They were simply the result of a misperception I had first blamed on various external factors and then blamed on myself. Only when I was totally willing to take responsibility for this perception did the situation shift. I had the utter privilege of choosing to realize that nothing, in fact, was "wrong" with my child. He was and is perfect. And, on some deep level, he sensed this knowledge as well.

Ultimately, I became a different neurological being. If anyone had taken a brain scan prior to this revelation and another after, I can almost guarantee that my brain would have looked different. That's how big the shift felt. In that moment, my thoughts (my mind) changed, my feelings (my body) changed, and the part of my backpack that was filled with night terror stories was emptied.

I saw my son from the perspective of my True Self and what I saw was his True Self, whole and complete and expressing his unique manifestation of Infinite Love.

Figure 4.7 Two True Selves Really *Seeing* One Another

I'll never know what happened during that last night terror from Andrew's perspective. I will say that the concepts based in quantum physics that I discussed earlier appear to come into play. I, as the observer, saw my son through a fresh lens. Sharing a heart, mind and spirit connection allowed him, in the quantum field of possibility, to tune into this vision and to release the night terrors. Like Matthew's mom in Chapter 2, I let go of my limited views and beliefs and my son joined me.

After I told this story in a recent class, one attendee shared that her daughter also had night terrors. When her mother-in-law babysat the children overnight, she would meditate outside of Angela's daughter's bedroom door. She focused on her granddaughter's well-being and imagined her sleeping soundly through the night—and she always did. On the other hand, when Angela's mother stayed with the kids overnight, she was petrified of the night terrors. On those evenings, the daughter always had one. Angela, seeing the correlation between how her daughter "responded" to the state of mind of the person caring for her, started to meditate and release her fears and beliefs about the night terrors. Not surprisingly, they decreased dramatically.

Miraculous Mirror Neurons

Another concept that comes into play in close relationships concerns mirror neurons. A mirror neuron is a brain cell that fires when someone completes an action, as well as when they observe someone else complete that same action. In what is also known as "imitation learning," the neurons of the observer *mirror* the behavior of the other person, just as though he or she were performing the action. Pretty wild, huh? This explains why, when we see someone fall or drop something, we gasp or reach to catch the object, even when we are not involved. As I made the change in how I perceived Andrew, it is quite possible that his mirror neurons fired as well, allowing him to share this perception.

I want to be clear that I believe I have experienced an abundance of miracles in my life. Some, like the night terror experience, occur in an instant. In fact, one of the biggest gifts that resulted from that night was that I learned it is possible to witness a massive shift in a very short period of time. Other miracles take place over the course of days, weeks or months. And, though I'd love to have all life shifts happen in a matter of minutes, I do see the value in those that take longer. Often, I experience a sort of awakening that is more powerful because of the way, and time frame, in which the situation unfolds.

I have a handful of these stories from my own life and even more from my clients. The key to real transformation is believing that a shift is even possible in the first place. If we can't imagine how a situation can change, it will be virtually impossible to experience a new story. Revisit the Action Peace—How Open Are You? in Chapter 3. Has anything shifted for you?

Action Peace—Who's Doing the Thinking and Reacting? My Ego or My True Self?

Ego thoughts are typically automatic and based in fear. Our ego, or personality, feels separate from loved ones and separate from Infinite Love, thus learning to judge and evaluate ourselves and others from a place of lack.

Our True Self, on the other hand, remains in conscious awareness. Thoughts from our True Self are more of a *knowing*—an ability to watch what goes on around us while remaining in a state of peace, grace and ease.

In the space provided below, list three ego thoughts you've had. For example, "My child will never be successful" or "I've done this all wrong. My child's difficulties are my fault."

1.

2.

3.

List the feelings that accompany each thought:

1.

2.

3.

What pattern, belief or fear might be blocking you from moving through these areas?

1.

2.

3.

Consider some possible ways that your True Self might rethink these situations. For example, "I know anything is possible, and that my child is constantly growing and changing" or, "I free myself from my old beliefs and trust that Infinite Love will take care of this situation."

1.

2.

3.

Action Peace—Identifying Ego Perceptions and Judgments

Keeping score strengthens the ego and often leads to feelings of guilt, blame and shame when we don't live up to the standards we set for ourselves or those we feel are imposed by others.

In the space below, brainstorm some of the beliefs on your scorecard. Then, try writing them on a sheet of paper, tearing it up and throwing it away!

My Ego Scorecard

Three things I think I'm good at:

1.

2.

3.

Three things I think I'm not good at:

1.

2.

3.

In addition, we often subconsciously use our scorecard to evaluate our children. Whether we say it out loud, in our minds or on a subconscious level, they feel and respond to that judgment.

Three ways I evaluate my child:

1.

2.

3.

Now that you have a better idea of how this works, bring awareness to your scorecard. Consider how these perceptions may be coloring your view of yourself and others. What would life be like if we did not judge ourselves so often and severely?

Action Peace—Reflecting on Your Child
(Adapted from Janita Venema's book, *Present Child*)
Complete the written portions of this exercise prior to reading ahead. Answer the following questions.

1. What is going on with your child?

2. What seems to make the situation worse?

3. What makes the situation better?

4. What do you wish for your child?

Now, go back and re-read your answers, this time imagining that your child (or your inner child) is saying these things about *you*. Wherever you've written your child's name, replace it with "I."

Do you see any similarities? Are you experiencing some version of what your child is exemplifying? Are you experiencing the exact opposite? (That can happen, too.)

Look for metaphors or deeper parallels. For example, if you wrote something like "Bobby needs to stop playing with John because John is a disrespectful bully," this offers an opportunity to look at your life. Is there a "bully" in your midst? This may be a family member, friend or a co-worker. The same dynamic could be found in a situation as well as a person. Is there a situation where you feel like a victim?

This process can take practice and may not reveal exactly what you are experiencing. However, there are typically some pretty powerful gems to be discovered, if you are ready to do a bit of self-reflection.

CHAPTER 5

The Backpack You Carry
Uncover the Weight of Upsetting Emotions

"Mom, when you were a kid did you ever feel like
when Mimi (my mother) asked you to do something,
you just wanted to do the exact opposite?"

~ ANDREW, ALMOST 7

As YOU LEARNED in the last chapter, I use the metaphor of a backpack to illustrate how we cover up stressful emotions, causing them to adversely affect our health and well-being. Imagine that each of us stashes all of our unaddressed angers, frustrations, upsets, negative self-talk, judgments, unfavorable images of others, etc. in this durable, expandable and invisible backpack. These contents—our story, our old patterns, thoughts, feelings and beliefs—are solidly set in the neural pathways of our mind.

The contents of our backpack, produced in response to difficulties and challenges from our past, are held in our subconscious mind and strongly influence our present day experiences. As it grows, the backpack gets heavier and heavier, and harder to carry. When it gets too full, unaddressed feelings can overflow into the body, cover our Light and even form a physical ailment or dis-ease.

In the quote that opens this chapter, Andrew divulges, though somewhat indirectly, that there are times when he wants to do the opposite of what I ask, right? Of course he does! This may be because he wants to exercise some autonomy—or he may be holding onto something in his backpack, retaliating because it hasn't yet been released or addressed. I recall exactly when he said this because I laughed inside, reflecting on my own contrary tendencies as a young adult.

Client Triumph—Immediate Results from Emptying the Backpack
Haley and Tim were referred to me to deal with the stress and anxiety
they were experiencing regarding the health and wellness of their two-
year-old son, Caleb.

Caleb exhibited sensory challenges as well as speech and motor
delays. He attended therapy four days a week and had an extensive
home therapy program that included exercises his parents were told
must be performed every two to three hours.

Caleb was also under watch for seizures, though there was no proof
he'd ever had one. At the time, his neurologist had ordered a battery
of tests, one of which was an MRI that would require Caleb to be put
under general anesthesia. The MRI was scheduled four days after my
second visit with this couple. During our session, both parents vented
their concerns about the procedure and the potential repercussions of
using general anesthesia on such a young child. Through a conversation with the nurse, they knew the insurance company played a big
part in determining their son's protocol of care. This didn't sit well
with Tim or Haley, who felt the decision should be made by the whole
team, not only on what the insurance company deemed appropriate.

On an intuitive level, I felt this was not the time for this procedure. As I am not licensed to give out advice on these topics, I kept
my feelings to myself. Instead, I cleared the triggers the conversation
stirred in me and proceeded with our session.

We had discussed the backpack metaphor in our first session, and,
as we dug into their apprehensions, Tim shared that he had some past
family trauma he just couldn't get beyond. When he was ten years
old, his mother gave birth to a still-born baby girl after a full term
pregnancy. He detailed how difficult the ordeal had been for him and
his family. After discussing this sad experience, we talked about the
concerns the couple had about their own son's health.

In preparation for the MRI, we shared a meditation to release a
layer, or more, of the baggage they were each carrying. We created an
intention that if it was highest and best that the test be performed on

the scheduled day, it go through with grace and ease for all. If it was not, we intended that this, too, be made clear with grace and ease.

During the meditation, I experienced an overwhelming awareness of the energetic presence of Tim's sister—as if she were a guardian angel. I knew that, on some level, she was there with us. I went out on a limb and shared this with Tim and Haley. They were open to this possibility and, as tears welled in their eyes, I knew I had hit a sensitive spot. After they left the session, I was present to an awe-inspiring peace about the situation, accompanied by a certainty that whatever was meant to occur would occur.

Two days later, I received a text stating that Tim and Haley had cancelled the MRI as a result of a few serendipitous incidents. Tim had run into an anesthesiologist who had a child on the autism spectrum. This doctor recommended doing a particular blood test prior to the MRI to check if Caleb was sensitive to the anesthesia. The couple also consulted an integrative pediatrician, who not only offered her own advice on the topic, but went out of her way to touch base with a pediatric neurologist who was no longer taking new patients. They, too, recommended holding off on the procedure.

Finally, it seemed Caleb had his own opinion. As his parents talked about the procedure, they said something to the effect of "It's like the insurance company is dictating the decision-making here." Seemingly out of nowhere, Caleb said, "Yes." This was the first time he had ever said this word. He clearly wanted to have a say in the matter.

My next session with the couple was on the following Monday. During this visit, we unearthed more from their backpacks. After receiving news that Tim and Haley were cancelling Caleb's MRI, the attending nurse had been irritated, which resulted in a high-pressure conversation. For Haley, this stirred intense feelings of guilt and shame. Through another powerful technique, we cleared the couple's fear surrounding both the influence wielded by the insurance company and the potential reaction of the doctor who'd initially ordered the MRI.

Once again, wonderful results came through. The doctor really went to bat for this family. According to a message from Haley, "She even offered to talk to the doctor at the insurance company if necessary, for a peer to peer review... They definitely took some steps to help get a less invasive EEG approved, which I guess shows some support of our decision. Tim and I are in shock. Your support and your guidance helped make things happen!! Thank you!!!"

After addressing a few additional concerns, I sent the couple a gentle reminder: "Remember to ask Tim's sister to help. In spirit form, she can be of great assistance."

Moments later, I received this reply: "OMG! We were just watching a show where a man was talking about his stillborn daughter and his name was Keith. That's Tim's dad's name!!! It's like [Tim's sister] just threw that out there to make a big point!!!"

Upon following up months later, Haley said that Caleb's speech has taken off, and that he now talks in complete sentences. His motor skills are also improving, to the point that they have significantly decreased his therapy time.

Tim and Haley continue to empty their backpacks, creating a positive and intentional environment for themselves and for Caleb. Parents that are willing to do this level of inner work will be a helpful model for this little guy, and for his little sister. Tim and Haley are expecting.

Expanding the Metaphor

It's so easy to let small and large difficulties build as we move through all we need to do day after day. Without realizing it, we let these challenges and the accompanying feelings snowball. Even though we may know we are holding onto negativity, we don't have any idea what to do with it. So, we simply fling the problems into our backpacks to be addressed "later."

When we're dealing with a challenging situation, our goal is often to just get through it. The problem is, with each incident we make it through, we add more weight to our backpack. By the end of the day, it is so burdensome and we feel so tired, it's all we can do to shrug it off and leave it by the bedside.

The next morning, we put it on again, still packed with all that weight. Even if we have methods to aid us in letting go of our baggage, we often don't make such clearing a priority. Our self-care gets overlooked. After all, we can handle quite a bit, can't we? We can juggle our kids' schedules, drive them all over town, volunteer at their schools, manage a house, make meals, work in or out of the home, and on and on.

By incorporating the heavy lifting needed to get our backpack on over and over again, day after day, our bodies become accustomed to carrying that weight. Over time, or with the buildup of a particular emotion, the backpack gets too heavy and some of that weight gets transferred "within."

In her book *You Can Heal Your Life*, well-known spiritual author and publisher Louise Hay links emotions to physical ailments, saying, "I find that resentment, criticism, guilt and fear cause more problems than anything else." She goes on, explaining how certain patterns can manifest in the physical body: "Resentment... can eat away at the body and become the dis-ease we call cancer. Criticism as a permanent habit can often lead to arthritis in the body. Guilt always looks for punishment and punishment causes pain. Fear, and the tension it produces, can create things like baldness, ulcers, and even sore feet."

Utilizing these and other concepts, I often receive clarity about my own physical ailments. I recall like it was yesterday one particular example...

A Personal Peace—An "In My Face" Message from My Body

It was a Friday evening. One of my teeth and the surrounding gum was very tender and starting to throb. I used all sorts of tactics to distract myself, trying not to even think that I might have yet another cavity. (I'd gone through a phase of developing cavities in my twenties and thirties, even though I'd never had one in my childhood.)

After a few hours, I realized there was something pretty wrong. I couldn't sleep and was ready for whatever Western medicine magic I could find at the corner pharmacy. This was one time I was super glad they were open 24 hours a day. Upon my return home, I put some gel on my gums and went back to bed. That worked for about two minutes. If anything, the pain was steadily increasing.

Surfing the internet, I found all sorts of natural remedies, from chewing on garlic cloves to rinsing with hydrogen peroxide. I tried them all. The pain continued to intensify. I had taken some pretty humble pride in birthing both kiddos without any anesthesia, but this was getting out of control.

At least after the intensity of childbirth, I'd ended up with a beautiful baby!

Just like everything else in my life at the time, I felt I could handle this situation without "bothering" anyone. I chose not to wake my husband, telling myself he had to work early the next morning and I didn't want to disrupt his sleep. I suffered all night, rubbing garlic over my gums and holding peroxide in my mouth until it burned my tongue. Eventually, I was able to get the excruciating pain down to about a seven on a one to ten pain scale. I then distracted myself till morning by watching back to back episodes of *Project Runway*.

When my husband arose at 6:00 am to prepare for his weekend shift, I briefly told him I had been up all night with a toothache. I went into no detail and did not request assistance. He sympathized and was off. Soon, my kids woke up and joined me in the day. I had no clue how I was going to provide for two toddlers under three while in some of the worst pain of my life.

In that moment, I knew I needed to ask for help. The pain was not going away and I couldn't continue the garlic and peroxide routine until Monday morning. Luckily, my dentist had a pager for emergencies. I waited until a reasonable hour and paged the number. No return call. Paged again. No call. One of the two dentists in the office was the husband of a former co-worker and friend of mine. With tears of pain and desperation flowing down my face, I called their home. When he told me he would meet me at the office at noon, I felt overwhelmed with gratitude.

I forced myself to call my sister-in-law to ask for help. She came over to watch my kids and I was off. As I pulled out of the driveway, my gas light came on. Argh! There was no way I could risk running out of gas before getting to the office. I stopped at the station, filled my mouth with the peroxide and started pumping gas. As my tongue started to burn, I got in the car to spit in my spit cup, which subsequently spilled all over my console. I wiped that up and reached to remove the gas pump, only to spill gasoline on my pants and feet!!! I couldn't even cry at that point, I just needed to get to the dentist's office. I grabbed some extra flip-flops that were in my back seat (lucky on this one) and ran in to the gas station bathroom to wash my feet. Finally on my way, I realized I now smelled of garlic and gasoline and was about to go clinically insane from the pain. Once again, the tears flowed.

I arrived splotchy-faced and smelly, and my dentist got started. He took an x-ray, said that there was an infection under my tooth and detailed what the upcoming root canal would entail. I just lay there, trusting anything that he said and did, knowing that the pain would soon be gone. With that first injection of Novocain, peace came over my entire body. Sweet relief.

Throughout this ordeal, my husband had no clue. Why? Because I didn't want to disturb him. I didn't want to put him out or ask for what I really needed—for him to call off work to take care of our kids so I could put myself first. This is what playing the victim looks like. I had gotten pretty good at that one.

A couple of months later, I had a second experience that mirrored this one. Yet again, it was on a weekend evening. As soon as the waves of intolerable pain started, I knew exactly what was happening. And, I went immediately into the same feelings of panic and fear. After crying for a bit, I got it. I knew there was something big for me to learn here.

I was so used to handling things on my own, bottling up any emotions and hiding any needs I might have. This time, I stopped and asked Infinite Love to provide guidance on what would be the highest and best outcome. In response, I forced myself to do something that did not come naturally at all: I woke up my husband and asked for his support.

He held me, which was a real comfort, and together we visualized my pain subsiding to a manageable level. We focused on everything going smoothly, with ease and grace, at the dentist's the next day. It was such a beautiful moment of vulnerability, and an opportunity for me to ask for and receive help. My husband's love and support, combined with the grace of Infinite Love, reduced the pain and infused my body with a sense of peace and love that got me through the night.

I had the second root canal that Sunday morning with the same dentist, and I managed to make it to my appointment garlic and gasoline free. My husband watched the kids while I recovered from the physically and emotionally draining experience.

The healing did not stop there. I clearly had some work to do. What could possibly be underneath these two root canals? What had I previously denied that I now felt ready to face? What, in my backpack, was up for release?

Via a multitude of meditations and a couple of conversations with an intuitive friend, I came to realize the cavities represented aggravations, things that bothered me that I had chosen to tolerate rather than address. This was my "in my face" message that I needed to deal with the such aggravations as they arose, so they wouldn't continue to build.

With these experiences as motivators, I began working to identify situations and events when they were bothering me, and to let them go instead of stuffing them in the backpack as I had been doing.

This was a massive turning point for me. Until then, I had been inconsistent in doing my work, despite the fact that I always felt significantly better when I diligently cleared all triggers and upset feelings. The metaphor of the cavities—small, lingering irritations—and the root canals—large, painful irritations—stuck with me. As a result, I moved into a rhythm of practicing the techniques I share in this book on an hourly basis.

Soon after that, these practices almost became moment to moment. And, I'm jumping ahead. First let's review a crucial point.

Awareness Is Key

Just like identifying our story and the thoughts and feelings that comprise it, being in awareness of what we carry in our backpack helps us do the necessary work to release, so we can perceive ourselves, our lives and our children from a place of Infinite Love and possibility. What we are learning is simple but not easy. We are taking a different, or maybe renewed, approach to old problems and choosing to experience the people and events in our lives in new ways.

When we view life through our ego self, the one carrying the backpack, we often can't see our way out of difficult situations. Paying attention to our responses and moving more consciously through our day is a great start to experiencing major shifts in our lives.

What this May Look Like—Resurgence of a Physical Ailment

Jennifer, a client in my six-week class on parenting with peace, experienced a physical healing as the result of a tool we learned and practiced together. She had been suffering from severe abdominal pain for months. In less than ten minutes, she went from pain at a level of seven out of ten, to that of two or three.

At the following class, a few participants commented that Jennifer seemed different—her skin was brighter and she looked healthy and energized. As everyone excitedly requested an update, she shared that the pain was completely gone.

About a month later, Jennifer told the group she had experienced a big trigger in the previous week that coincided with a disagreement she had with a neighbor. She also reported that the pain in her abdomen had returned. (Luckily, she was able to use our earlier technique to release this pain.) She asked our help to identify the root cause of the issue—that is, what was in her backpack that had raised such strong feelings.

Jennifer soon uncovered that she had a fear of not being accepted. This, combined with the disagreement with her neighbor, had led her to feel embarrassed, ashamed and resentful all at once. Patterns of victimhood, martyrdom and self-sabotage came into play.

In the coming weeks, Jennifer did the subsequent work needed to clear both the patterns she had discovered and their effects on her body—abdominal discomfort brought on as a result of bottling things up and burying them in her backpack.

The Benefits of Routinely Emptying the Backpack

Earlier, I shared Louise Hay's thoughts on the connection between our emotions and physical ailments. Author and MD Lissa Rankin expands on this idea in her blog post, "10 Signs Fear Is Running Your Life (and How to Get Back on Track)":

> Fear isn't just an uncomfortable emotion that holds you back from following your dreams, connecting soul-to-soul with your true tribe, and serving out your life's purpose. It also triggers stress responses in the body that put you at risk of disease and make it hard for the body to heal itself. Fearful people are more likely to get heart attacks, cancer, diabetes, autoimmune diseases, inflammatory disorders, chronic pain, and even the common cold. They're also more likely to experience milder symptoms, such as insomnia, low energy, obesity, dizziness, headaches, backaches, decreased libido, and gastrointestinal distress.

I have seen this a number of times in myself, my clients and my kiddos. We don't always know exactly what our physical conditions are linked to, but research confirms that stress compromises bodily functions, influencing the efficiency and efficacy of all physiological systems.

Pamela Grout addresses this idea, maintaining that "Sickness is optional" in her best-selling book, *E2*:

> Instead of seeing sickness as a problem, something to correct, we accept it as a fact of life. We have all agreed to this arbitrary set of

rules that says sickness can't be escaped, illness is natural. Most of us can't even imagine perfect health.

Long ago, our minds established this false pattern of perception. Once a mind thinks it can't do some task (like unclog an artery), it informs the brain…, which in turn informs the muscles. The "virus" in our consciousness has limited our ability to utilize our bodies' great wisdom.

On many occasions, I have had the experience of feeling a physical release after clearing emotional baggage. This can also can occur in the reverse—I clear a physical ailment and the underlying emotions dissipate.

What is available to us, always, is Infinite Love. We just need to put ourselves high enough on our priority list to make the time and space to do this clearing, connecting work. It's the most loving thing we *can* do, for ourselves and our families.

Action Peace—What's in Your Backpack?
List a challenge you had as a child:

What feelings came up during this challenge, or even come up now?

Did you start to create a story about yourself in response to this difficulty? If so, what was it?

Action Peace—Your Childhood Needs
Set aside about 20 minutes for this Action Peace.

Step One
Read through the following steps a few times and then take yourself through the meditation.

1. Sit quietly and take a few, deep breaths.
2. Imagine yourself as a child—at whatever age comes to mind. See yourself in a room in your childhood home, and imagine your mom or another caregiver entering that room.
3. Reflect on the type of communication or interaction you experienced with this person.
4. What feelings came up as a result of that interaction?
5. What was the deeper feeling or fear beneath that initial reaction?
6. Without any judgment or blame, take note of any needs you had that were not met.
7. Say thank you to your mom or caregiver and let them leave the room.
8. Repeat steps 2-7 with your father or another applicable caregiver.
9. Open your eyes and jot down your observations.

Step Two
Take a little time to more fully explore your responses in this meditation.

Describe the type of communication and interaction you experienced with your mom or another caregiver:

Describe the feelings that accompanied that interaction:

Describe any underlying fears:

Describe any unmet needs:

Step Three
Describe the type of communication and interaction you experienced with your dad or another caregiver:

Describe the feelings that accompanied that interaction:

Describe any underlying fears:

Describe any unmet needs:

Step Four
Take note! Don't miss the opportunity this last step provides!
Return to the Action Peace—Reflecting on Your Child in Chapter 4. Compare what you wrote about your child and see if there are any similarities with what you revealed above. Sometimes we see similar themes, and sometimes it turns out that we manifest the exact opposite in our experiences. Typically, there is some sort of pattern that, when brought to our attention, offers clarity to our current challenges.

This process often uncovers our unmet needs. As we've discussed, we cannot expect others to fulfill those needs for us. Once identified, we can do our inner work, connect with our True Self, and experience them being met through our beautiful and intimate connection with Infinite Love.

CHAPTER 6

Power Up
Shifting Your Experience

"Mom, you can heal everything backwards and forwards."

~ ANDREW, AGE 3

ARE YOU TIRED of carrying that backpack full of heavy emotions throughout your busy days? Are you ready to transform how you view yourself as a parent? Do you want to experience true connection with yourself and your child?

In my role as an occupational therapist, I've worked with hundreds of families who came to me in the throes of difficult situations. What is important to know is that you can heal or change what you are currently going through. It might not happen in minutes but nor does it need to take five years or longer. Since committing to my health and well-being and, therefore, the health and well-being of my family, I have witnessed shifts that occurred right before my eyes. In other instances, it has taken us days, weeks or even months to alter a pattern that no longer served us. The point is, there is another way.

If we, as parents, continue to do what we have always done, in the same way we have always done it, we will continue to get the same results. The methods we adopt are often subconscious and, as we discussed in **The First Peace**, have been unintentionally passed down from generation to generation. And, at some point, we unknowingly bought into them and made them our own.

Take a minute to just sit with the idea that what you have done in the past, or continue to do now, has not worked—as evidenced by the fact that you still have whatever it is in your life you do not want. Can you see that?

Now, try something new. Be curious. Allow yourself to truly consider the possibilities available to you. They are infinite. Curiosity is magical. In becoming aware of your story, triggers, feelings, patterns and beliefs, you can recognize your part in any situation, and take action to shift the experience, for yourself and your family.

Client Triumph—It's Never Too Late

I recently had a couple come to me about their relationship with their grown son, who was currently living at home. As I typically do, I asked them to tell me about his childhood and what it was and is like to live with him. They both shared their stories about how their son's behavior and sensory challenges affected them personally and in their roles as parents. I felt such compassion for this couple. They felt truly alone and lost, judged by peers and family members. Yet, their biggest fear was that they had failed their child.

Delving into their stories, we found fear-based patterning that started in their own childhoods. Triggers, for both of them, related to how they often had not felt seen, heard or understood when they were young.

First, I shared three specific tools (Choose Empathy, Choose Forgiveness and Love, and Choose Meditation, all found in Chapter 9). Then I offered them a different way of looking at the whole picture. What would happen, I asked, if they allowed all of their emotions to come to the surface, without any filter? What if they saw the situation, their son and themselves as just there, to be loved? As you can imagine, it was an emotional session and as they left my office I sent with them a blessing of love and possibility.

At our next visit, about two weeks later, the dad seemed to almost skip into my office. When I asked him how things were going he said, "Amazing. Everything is changing!" He went on to share that he'd been practicing one of the techniques we'd discussed and that the whole situation was shifting. It was, he said, as if his son was revisiting the stages of bonding with his parents that had been absent in earlier years. Here he was, a man in his early twenties, asking to borrow clothes and requesting back rubs! This was after only one session.

These parents took charge of how they had been seeing their son and decided to love him, the situation and themselves just as they were. By addressing their feelings, they were able to empty their backpacks of substantial and long-held pain. By putting a few suggested tools in place, they cleared their underlying patterns. Their ability and willingness to open to the possibility of change produced an immediate, family-wide shift.

In the next session, we went over additional techniques for awareness and release. They now had a wealth of options in their toolbox that would allow them to keep shifting and transforming, for their son's sake and their own.

One important thing to mention is that this couple really committed to doing their work. I never met the son, nor did I feel it was necessary. They were ready to release their stories and embrace a new way of being. Each was then able to move from self-blame, guilt and shame into a place of unconditional love.

Was everything easy and stress-free from that moment on? No, but they were committed to looking at all problems and difficulties as opportunities! And, as they felt their backpacks start to fill again, they took immediate action to shed the weight.

This Shift is Available to You, Too

Is it really possible that someone could experience such a life-changing transformation in a few weeks? Is this also possible for you? Yes, and yes!!!

Everything we need in order to uncover our lifelong patterns, fears and triggers is available if we are willing to do the work. We can take our current life situation and turn it into an ongoing, live training session. And when we do that, triggering events become instant, on-the-spot opportunities for personal growth.

The first step toward this shift is to take a vacation from guilt. In **The Third Peace,** we will talk more about guilt, but I want to touch on it here.

Guilt plays such a heavy part in our programming, it almost seems impossible to avoid. I spent many years thinking that everything I experienced was my *fault*. "If I only had done things better," I thought, "none of this would be happening."

For the purposes of this book and where we are, I am asking you to suspend your automatic guilt response. Take a little vacation from blaming yourself. Trust me, it's worth it.

Four Reasons to Take a Vacation from Guilt Right Now:

1. Promoting guilt goes against everything we talked about in Chapter 4, True Self versus Ego. You are not your human faults or mistakes. You are a unique creation of Infinite Love who has temporarily forgotten this (and will over and over again).

2. Would a little girl who unknowingly kills a butterfly deserve a harsh reprimand? Certainly not. She didn't see the butterfly, nor did she intend to hurt it. If we are not aware of the potential harm in our actions, why blame ourselves? This does not mean we ignore personal responsibility for the consequences of our words and actions. Rather, we take responsibility *without* guilt or blame. (I return to this concept and scenario in Chapter 13, Response-Ability and Diligence.)

3. When we fight guilt, it digs in to fight back. We're giving it the attention it wants, so it stays for more. If we let guilt go, it dissipates.

4. I am asking nicely. If you are willing to hold off on guilt right now, we can look at the upcoming tools and illustrative stories with clear eyes and a light heart.

Feels good, right? You are now ready for the second step toward this shift—coupling theory with empowered action. If you feel guilt come up as you read the next sections, know that we will return to it and put it in its rightful place—a fire pit.

Coupling Theory with Action

You may, like me, have worked hard to gain enough knowledge to be the kind of parent you would like to be and create the life you desire. And you may, also like me, have noticed that learning does not necessarily lead to growth, especially when no action is taken.

For years, I studied spiritual theories and read many amazing books about the power of mindfulness and intentionality. As I mentioned, I am fascinated by the power we have to create our own reality. I love the science of quantum physics and epigenetics, which means "above genetics" (in other words, *beyond* what genetics has been believed to determine). I had the theories down pat, and could explain in detail how I felt when exploring and absorbing the philosophy. Meditation, when I found the time to do it, brought me to a peaceful place, where my mind was still and I experienced a strong connection to Infinite Love.

And, I was still living in chaos much of the time. My kiddos were in a constant state of conflict with each other and/or me, the house was a mess and we had little structure to our days, a fact that was a source of extreme frustration. In addition, I spent little, if any, time taking care of my own needs. In fact, I was fairly miserable, at least until I found the next great spiritual author.

Whenever I dove into a new book, I felt motivated, happy and hopeful. But inevitably, when I finished the book, I eased right back into my lifelong patterns of playing the victim or martyr and sabotaging any chances to get what I really wanted. On top of that, I believed my happiness was dependent on the happiness of others, which left me feeling helpless.

I had heard many times that we are never given more than we can handle. On a few occasions in my younger years, that thought comforted me in some way. It seemed honorable to be able to handle all that was *given* to me. But as a mother of two, desperately seeking something different from what I was experiencing, I wanted to scream at anyone who even implied the so-called wisdom of this adage. I could not and was not handling the challenges in my life. Or was I? Well, I lived to tell about it, so I guess on some level I was.

Fundamentally, I didn't believe Infinite Love was giving me this pile of junk to deal with. When I really stepped back, I knew that *I* was choosing these experiences and that it was possible to look at them as opportunities. That was quite the shift for me. Taking this level of responsibility, without blame and shame, led me from a place of victimhood to a place of empowerment. I began to see that my True Self, or some piece of me that was connected to my Divine plan, was beautifully orchestrating these intensely challenging events that almost took me over the edge. Why? Because what was offered on the other side was life-changing—in a wondrous way.

My life was shifting, though it felt slower than booting up a computer in the 80s. Little did I know that all of the theories I was immersing myself in were being absorbed deep inside, building a powerful foundation. Throughout the course of gaining this knowledge, I was gathering, and using, processes and healing techniques that would initiate and accelerate the shift I was yearning for. Combined with strategies I'd built as a therapist and parent, these became the basis for the Action Peaces you see in this book.

Here is an example of a time I coupled theory with action to create a shift.

A Personal Peace—A Conscious Shift, in the Moment

I was standing in our newly renovated kitchen, which allowed me to look straight into the living room. I no longer had to guess what the latest altercation between my children looked like. It was as if I'd switched on a really loud reality show, except there was no off button.

There before me were two beautiful cherubs, screaming at each other about the rules of a new game. In that moment, I knew their argument had little or nothing to do with what they were playing. There was more to it. I decided to really observe what was going on, without being upset or triggered, from a place of connection with Infinite Love.

What might my children teach me about my own destructive thoughts, habits and ways of looking at life? And how might these thoughts be transformed into something useful that could help us have the life I knew we deserved?

The process unfolded with little effort. I observed, I translated, I flipped what I saw (and understood) into an affirmation.

Observation:

My son wanted to make the rules and dictate how the game needed to be played. The rules could change at any time, as long as they benefitted him. He came across as loud and demanding.

Translation:

Feeling powerless is scary and can lead us to attempt to control one another. Having some control is better than having none.

Affirmation:

I don't need to be in control of anyone or anything. I am powerful and peaceful and can hand everything over to Infinite Love.

Observation:

My daughter was crying, screaming and extremely upset because my son was getting to make the rules. She shouted, "It's not fair."

Translation:

Fear and lack were plentiful. There was a theme of injustice—not having what one needed because of another. This was the victim/villain role, played out in full force.

Affirmation:

In this human experience, things do not always appear fair. I am safe, know what I desire and have no need to participate in this pattern of being an innocent victim.

As I watched the show before me, I jotted down a few more affirmations, coming up with about five in all. When I finished, I folded the paper and put it in my pocket for the day, as I often do with things that inspire me. I said NOTHING to my children.

Within seconds, the fight fizzled out and they began playing peacefully. I was stunned. All I had done was objectively observe the scenario, map out what patterns they were playing out, and write down replacement affirmations to reference throughout the day. Actions coupled with theory! And, everything had shifted. It was as if my witnessing the children from a non-triggered, connected place allowed the adverse energy to be seen and released. This was even better than having an off switch.

I didn't stop to second-guess or analyze the moment. I just said two very powerful words, "Thank you."

When to Do the Work—Now or Later?

In later chapters, we'll discuss being proactive toward upcoming events that have a history of ending in turmoil. We will also talk about doing the work to heal events from your past. For now, let's focus on situations that are occurring in the moment or are from the recent past. Here, you have two options as to when to do your "Coupling Theory with Action" work—as soon as you feel triggered or anytime thereafter. Right away is ideal. However, that is not always feasible, especially if you don't realize you are feeling triggered. Also, when first learning any approach, it is sometimes helpful to practice after the fact, when you feel calm and centered.

Doing Your Work Later

If you're not able to do your work right as you are triggered, carve out some alone time as soon after the event as possible, preferably that day or the next. As for how much time you'll need, plan on anything from five minutes to two hours to a weekend away—whatever it takes.

You may be thinking that you just don't have that kind of time. Now that you're familiar with your story and patterns, as well as the difference between your ego and your True Self, and how damaging that heavy backpack can be, you understand that you *can* find the time if you are ready and willing. You will get pretty crafty with your schedule when this work becomes a priority. I have had phone sessions with many moms who holed up in the bathroom, asking their husbands or a friend to hang out with the kids.

The benefit of setting aside time after the fact to work through what happened during the upset is that you can familiarize yourself with the tools without a sense of urgency. It's like exercising a muscle or learning a new yoga sequence; with practice and focus, it gets easier and becomes automatic. When we do this work in privacy, with minimal interruption, we're giving a gift to ourselves and our whole family. The clarity and relief that accompany letting go of our thoughts, feelings and patterns will be felt by all.

And what, you may wonder, does this work consist of? The Action Peaces at the end of this chapter are a great place to start, as are the tools you will learn coming up, in **The Second Peace**.

What This May Look Like—Reflecting on a Previous Event
Ginny had been doing her work for quite some time. She spent abundant quality time with her kids and diligently recognized and cleared her underlying patterns. She also practiced and taught meditation regularly.

One morning, she called to ask if we could schedule a last-minute phone session. She felt triggered from events that had taken place the night before and needed to talk. It seemed her sister-in-law was in town and had managed to push every one of Ginny's buttons. The worst was that she had spent the evening dealing out judgments of their mutual family members. Many of the things her brother's wife criticized were ideals that Ginny valued, such as eating healthy food and setting boundaries for her children's screen time.

Ginny tended to sink into old patterns and fears during such heated discussions. She felt defensive and knew she was acting from her ego when she attempted to combat the perceived attacks. Perhaps what bothered her most was that she was aware of this pattern and did it anyway.

That morning, Ginny awoke feeling sick and drained—heavy with sadness and anger. It was as if her sister-in-law *knew* each tender spot and jabbed at them repeatedly. Ginny was in a fearful place, filled with self-doubt and shame. What if her sister-in-law was right? What if the trials Ginny was experiencing with her kids *were* her fault? Was she too rigid? Had she passed her own struggles on to her kids and totally screwed them up? (Notice how guilt accompanies self-doubt.)

After listening to the story and Ginny's reaction, I encouraged her to sit quietly and really feel all that had come up for her. The emotions and bodily sensations that arise in times of upset are a map to our patterns and beliefs. On the surface, Ginny felt *anger,* directed at her sister-in-law. Under that was the *anxiety* that she had passed down her own challenges and, in turn, created exactly what she did not want for her children. And even deeper, under that, was a major childhood *fear* and a pattern. As Ginny said, "As a kid, I was not allowed to be who I was. I shut down, just like I did last night." There. We had gotten to it. The core fear and belief—that Ginny wasn't good enough and it was not safe to be herself.

After letting this settle, I offered Ginny a theater analogy. All of our lives are an elaborate stage production—our family and friends are the actors, and we are the writer and star. Ginny's sister-in-law played the exact role that Ginny's mother had played for her as a child and and adult. Her mother, and now her sister-in-law, provided Ginny with the opportunity to either doubt herself... or to own her True Self as a unique creation of Infinite Love.

We did a clearing meditation (see the Streamside Meditation at the end of this chapter) and, by the time we were done, Ginny was at peace. Later that day, she sent a text: "Stillness, my heart is lighter. Thank you, dear Kristen. That was a divine experience. Love and Gratitude. I am literally chuckling."

Ginny was able to see the situation for what it was—a wonderful opportunity to clear the big stuff she'd been holding onto. In the moment, she'd been triggered and immersed in the drama and pain. By choosing to do her work after the fact, Ginny was able to send her sister-in-law off in peace and love.

You may be wondering how this might help Ginny as a parent. By taking the opportunity to remove another layer of an old pattern, Ginny moved closer to living from her True Self. The more she connects into her own Divinity, the more she is able to look at her world from a place of love. And that means, when she is with her children, she is better able to see that they are also unique beings who might be playing out roles, or casting her in a role, that help their ego selves. Either way, everyone in the family benefits, even though Ginny is the only one doing the work.

Doing Your Work Now

Whether you use the tools as you are triggered or afterward, you are addressing the root causes of your conflict and showing yourself that you value sanity enough to do something about what is happening in and around you.

What I gained from my "breakfast reality show," during which I observed, translated, and made affirmations inspired by my children, was a recognition of the power of doing my work in the moment.

Prior to the realization that becoming a conscious observer can transform any situation, I took mental notes throughout the day on the "bad" thoughts, feelings and experiences I needed to meditate on and release "later," when I had a moment to sit. Perhaps before bed. Or the next morning. In other words, whenever I had extra time—if I still remembered and had the energy. Meanwhile, I continued to carry the heavy ideas and strong feelings in my invisible backpack, and they continued to weigh me down.

When these tools become second nature, you can practice them in the moment. It's not always easy, but it is simple. Once you know your options, it comes down to choice. Einstein taught that we can't solve a problem with the same consciousness that created it. Our True Self, the part of us that does this work, can empty our ego-filled backpack, leading to healing and transformation.

Action Peace—Reflecting Back

In many situations, it is helpful to spend time reflecting on and letting go of emotions that do not serve your True Self or the people around you. For this Action Peace, call to mind a recent eruption that occurred in your living room, the car or grocery store. Imagine you are there, witnessing the whole situation.

In the space provided below, write down your observation and your translation. Flip that into an affirmation (or two or ten). At random times of the day—or when you feel triggered—reference and repeat your affirmations.

OBSERVATION	TRANSLATION	AFFIRMATION

A great way to aid this process is to put your affirmation on a slip of paper, or a memo in your phone, and set a reminder to go off periodically during the day.

Action Peace—Live Time

Try this exercise in live time, like I did while observing my children in the Personal Peace above. Use your cell phone or label a number of 3 x 5 cards with "Observation," "Translation" and "Affirmation." Keep these handy and fill them in during or immediately after a conflict with your child(ren).

Action Peace—Streamside Meditation

Sit quietly and visualize yourself resting next to a gently flowing stream. Allow any feelings or concerns to arise. Sit with them for a minute or two. By going deeper into the feeling, you can pinpoint the underlying pattern or fear. When you have that awareness, imagine that your family and friends have joined you at the stream in silent support.

Look around—the ground is covered with colorful leaves and feathers. Choose one and place your fear or worry on that feather or leaf. When you are ready, place it into the stream. Watch as the water gently carries your anxieties downstream to Infinite Love.

Do this over and over until you feel peace come over your body. As you feel lighter and freer, look down. You will see a glowing white flower. Pick up this flower and hold it at the center of your chest. Breathe in feelings of gratitude for the opportunities in your life and for the shift that is occurring. Thank your friends and relatives as well.

The Second Peace

───────────❋───────────

The Power Tools

You MAY HAVE recognized some of the concepts and theories in **The First Peace**, or everything I've said might be brand new. Even if they are very familiar, you may have found it challenging to put them into practice. Sometimes we can feel overwhelmed by our parenting experience. This is common to us all and can be especially intense when our kids do and say things we don't know how to handle. We worry that their behaviors are symptoms that something's wrong and we want to help. But we feel stuck and even desperate at times, not knowing the best approach.

Trust that the "hidden peace" is not far away. In fact, it is right there with you and always has been. The deeper connection and harmony you are seeking have been hiding under layers of guilt, anger, frustration and more. These emotions overflowed from your invisible backpack into your body and covered the light within, leaving you feeling helpless, sad and distraught. Little or none of your light can be seen or felt.

The Second Peace will help you retrieve that light by providing relevant information, real life examples and specific steps to increase understanding, clarity and, of course, peace!

In the last chapter, Power Up, you learned how to create shifts as you do your work in the moment or during quiet, reflective times shortly thereafter. You know that change is possible and you're ready to move into **The Power Tools,** a four-part flow I developed as a "go to" sequence to be used in the moment, as soon as we feel triggered. These tools are so powerful—each gets its own chapter.

I call this process "The Four C's":

1. **Consciously Observe** – Step outside of yourself in order to look inward, at the one who is triggered, and really feel what has come up for you.
2. **Connect** – Actively select an affirmation, breathing pattern, movement or prayer that brings you closer to Divine Love and your True Self.
3. **Choose** – Select from a number of options designed to release baggage and put you in a place of freedom, choice and power.
4. **Create** – Powerfully intend new thoughts, new emotions and a new story.

The Four C's is not a cookie cutter solution, but one that can be tailored for each person in each situation. From a variety of options, you will find the tools that work best for you. Sometimes you may want to do all four C's sequentially, other times you may choose to do just one or two.

Along the way, you'll discover that the more you commit to doing this work for yourself and your family, the easier it will become. Know that I am with you in Spirit and sending Love!

CHAPTER 7

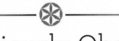

Consciously Observe
Step Out to Look In

"I can't believe I am going to tell you this: When I'm
mad at you, I try to say as much mean things as I can
that will get you mad, on purpose."
(Long pause.)
"I feel so much better."

~ ANDREW, AGE 8

THE FIRST STEP of the Four C's is **Consciously Observe.** To consciously observe means to look at yourself from a different perspective and simply be aware of what has come up in your thoughts and in your body. During or following a triggering event, imagine stepping outside of your body to clearly see your reactions, thoughts and feelings.

In moments of upheaval—upset, anger, rage, sadness, hostility, frustration, desperation—what is there to do? When your child refuses to put on his shoes after the fourth or fourteenth request, for instance, some feelings may come up. Especially if you skipped your coffee that morning or are already running late.

It is good to remember that you may not be reacting to an isolated event. When we're super annoyed and ready to boil over, it's typically due to a series of events that may or may not even be related to our children. Often, we're responding to intense feelings linked to long-held patterns and beliefs that have been reactivated by the triggering event.

The point is, the more self-aware you become—the more actively you become your own observer—the more you will see your interactions during these times as if in slow motion. As you speak words peppered with frustration and resentment, you will *hear* yourself and become totally aware that the reason you are frustrated with your child's comment, action or choice is because of something that happened earlier that you didn't address. Or perhaps a pattern that has perpetuated for years is driving you crazy. Either way, awareness and observation of your thoughts, actions, beliefs and feelings is your first step.

Client Triumph—Seeing Others Truly

In this example, the work I did to consciously observe my thoughts, take ownership of them and subsequently change them resulted in a shift for one of my clients and for his teacher.

As I entered the classroom of a kindergarten child I was working with, I saw that he was crying at his desk as he attempted to copy sentences from the board. I believed he was stressed because of a heavy demand, on his eyes and hands, to perform a task he was not developmentally ready for. The more I thought about this, the deeper I went into the story. I felt totally triggered that this child was being *forced* to do work at a level too advanced for his body and brain. Adding to the story, I began to blame the school system for what I saw as unrealistic expectations that were being placed on little ones at younger and younger ages.

From there, I moved into "rescue" mode, taking him to my office for our therapy session rather than working with him in his classroom. There, we spent our time playing games and completing tasks (to build his eye-hand coordination) that I made sure placed limited demands on him. At the end of our session, knowing I had to return him to a setting in which he was not able to do what was asked, I felt sad and helpless.

That evening, it hit me. I was perceiving this child from a place of fear and lack—delving deep into the victim/villain duality. As soon as I realized this, I knew what I had to do.

I consciously observed the beliefs that accompanied my version of this scenario and this child. One by one, I let them go. I then asked Infinite Love to show me the truth of this kiddo. In that instant, I knew in my heart, and in my gut, that he had everything he needed to accomplish all that was expected of him throughout his school day.

The next time I was scheduled to work with this student, I entered the room to find him easily and accurately copying from the board. The scene brought tears to my eyes. I was filled with gratitude.

I spoke to the teacher about how wonderfully he appeared to be doing. In reply, she said, "Yes, but now he is having trouble with…" and went on to list multiple other challenges he was experiencing. I was so bummed out. This child had made major strides in a two-week period, and she was not willing to celebrate even for a moment.

I strongly believe that, to reach their optimal potential, all children need a nurturing, supportive environment. Next to parents, a child's teacher is the person who has the most influence on him or her, both individually and as a member of the classroom community. I again felt helpless that this teacher, who spent so much time with this child, was focused only on what he couldn't do.

In a moment of grace, I realized that I was now observing the teacher from a fear-based viewpoint. I'd been so concerned about the student that I'd gone directly back to a victim/villain scenario. I shifted my attention and focused on how I was observing the teacher. I used a similar process as I had with the child, seeing that she, too, was and is a unique expression of Infinite Love. Over the course of the year, she and I became closer and closer, coming to a place of mutual respect. To this day, I think of her fondly.

I can't express how powerful it is to be mindful of your own thoughts and feelings. It's not easy to do this work. But when we commit to seeing others with eyes of love, it is difficult for them not to respond in turn.

The Window into Healing

Recalling that a large portion of our thoughts, actions and beliefs are a result of our subconscious mind, 95% as demonstrated in Figure 2.1, I am guided to share a realization I had regarding this fact. Upon learning this concept, I felt excited and could understand why I had been unable reprogram my patterns via my conscious thoughts alone. Almost immediately, a sense of defeat flooded my body. If so much of my programming was based in my subconscious, how in the world could I make any changes?

And then, it came to me:

The window into healing is through our feelings!

The emotions we experience as the result of a trigger, or those that tend to be habitually present in our resting state (stress, anxiety, annoyance, etc.), are a direct link to our subconscious. We may not be aware of the deeply held beliefs behind them, but we can certainly take note of how we are feeling at any given moment.

Let's go further into what it looks and feels like to be aware of our emotions.

Watch Your Feelings

As I've said, the first thing to do when you feel triggered is to consciously observe what comes up. Actively choose to look at the situation from a place outside of your thoughts, patterns and beliefs. It helps to name your feelings. Say to yourself, "Oh, I see that I am feeling anger as a result of...."

As you tune into that feeling, you can sit with it, stand with it, run with it, whatever. Without judging yourself, recognize it as simply what has come up. If we ignore an uncomfortable feeling or try to cover it up in any way, it can get incorporated into our body as discomfort and possibly dis-ease.

Each of our thoughts has its own neural pathway. As you saw in the story loop, these neural pathways strengthen when we have repetitive thoughts and feelings that result in deep-seated beliefs and patterns. As Dr. Joe Dispenza says, "Neurons that fire together, wire together." In automatically reacting to triggering events, we subconsciously allow our thoughts and emotions to take the upper hand. Conversely, as soon as we choose to take note of our feelings and mindfully observe ourselves—the one having the thought or experiencing the feeling—we weaken the power flowing to that automatic, neurological loop.

Watch Your Words

Once you have noticed your thoughts, notice your word choice as well, both in your self-talk and what you share aloud. Being mindful of what you say and how you say it, you can immediately shift the energy behind your words.

Word choice is crucial, especially when it comes to labeling our emotions. For instance, I do not say to myself, "I am frustrated," as that would mean I accept that feeling as a part of my being, of what and who I am. I may *feel* frustrated, but I *am* never frustrated. And neither are you. We are Divine beings of Infinite Love that, due to an emotion-based reaction to external and/or internal circumstance, have temporarily forgotten this.

Instead, we can say, "There is frustration in this situation," or "Hmmm, I notice some frustration has come up," or "There is a $#!&-load of frustration in my world right now!!!" This may sound silly and unnatural, but bringing awareness to our language helps us see our emotions for what they are. In the process, it also keeps us from over-identifying with those feelings and allows us to let them go. Our feelings are not who or what we are. Who we are is our True Self in a human body, experiencing a human emotion in the moment.

Here are some additional choices to consider:

- **Replace "but" with "and":** When we use the word "but" we negate everything that comes before it. For example, if we say, "I love you, but I can't play with you right now," our kids hear that we don't love them and we're not going to play with them. They are also likely to feel that whatever we are doing at the time is more important than they are.

  Expand the love in your message through the words you use. For instance, consider, "I love you and I hear that you want to read together. I would like that too, *and* I am doing the dishes now. When I'm done cleaning up, I'll find you and we can read." Or, simply, "I hear you want to read a book with me, *and* I want you to know I am going to finish the dishes first."

- **Say "You may…" rather than "You need to…":** I know this sounds crazy, *and* if you are willing to try it you may see a difference. No one wants to be told they *need* to do something. From partners or spouses to kids, we all want to feel as if we have a choice. Using the oh-so-common shoe example, I often say to my kids, "It is time to head out. You may put your shoes on now." It is almost a gentle invitation—a strong suggestion, if you will.

Along a similar vein, the phrase "Would you be willing to…" can also be helpful. It immediately turns a demand to a request.

To put this concept into the here and now, read the following and notice how you respond: "In order to reap the benefits of what I am sharing in this book, you need to meditate twice a day for twenty minutes in complete silence. If you don't, nothing will change."

Do you hear/sense an almost threatening undertone? How badly does that make you want to meditate?

Now, what if I state it this way: "Would you be willing to set aside twenty minutes of quiet time to meditate and reflect on your day?"

How do you feel when this is offered as a suggestion? Of course, this is not the best language to use in every case. If your child is running toward the street, you aren't going to say, "You may stop running," or "Would you be willing to turn around and run toward me?" You get to decide when and how you might incorporate this type of terminology. My main point is to observe yourself and how your word selection can influence the tone of the moment.

- **The dreaded "S" word—*Should*:** This is very relevant in self-talk as well as in our communication with others. When we use the words "should" or "shouldn't," we instantly imply fault or blame, which can quickly lead to shame and, of course, guilt.

  Think about this sentence: "I should have remembered my grocery bag—it was right there by the door." Versus, "Well, it looks like I left that grocery bag behind." The first is charged with blame, while the second is more objective, free of any guilt.

  With regard to our kids, tune into the difference in the following examples. When we say, "You should have listened when I told you to tie your shoes the first time," they hear, "I did something wrong and I'm a bad person." Instead, try, "I see you tripped on your laces. It's important to me to know you are safe. Do you want some help tying your shoes?"

A Real World Example of How This Can Work

Let's tie observing our thoughts, feelings and word choices together in a totally hypothetical situation. (Really, this has never happened! Wink, wink.)

It's almost time for breakfast and I realize I forgot to send an important email the previous night. I say to myself, "You should have done it right away instead of waiting like you always do." In response, underlying feelings of regret and self-blame start to bubble. If I don't consciously observe these feelings and release them, I will subconsciously move through the rest of the morning already on edge.

Next, I decide to quickly send the email, which puts the kiddos and me behind schedule. Now, I've added angst and tension to regret and self-blame. Increasing the load in my backpack like this leaves me wide open to upset. When my son chooses this day to organize an elaborate obstacle course that *must* be completed before getting in the car for school, a significant amount of annoyance is triggered.

Now I feel a myriad of unpleasant emotions. If these go unchecked, the rest of the day will most likely follow suit. Without even knowing it, I will magnetize even more challenges to confirm, and continue, my initial emotions. In this triggered state, I will be on the defensive and potentially move toward being short with my kids or reacting negatively to any other disturbances.

However, just because the day started out in a challenging fashion doesn't mean it has to continue that way. During any one of these triggers, I can observe my feelings and implement tools from Chapter 9 in order to move through the experience with grace and ease.

This works the other way around as well. Say it is a morning when we are way ahead of schedule. I'm well rested and just found a $20 bill in my coat pocket. In this scenario, I find my son's obstacle course innovative and confirm his above average intelligence before getting in line to go next.

When I regularly remind myself to be aware of my feelings and do the work needed to release what I no longer want, I spend more and more time in a state of gratitude. And, as a result, I continue to magnetize more and more to be grateful for.

Look Back—at You

Whatever feelings come up, the act of consciously observing takes you one step closer to your True Self. This is almost as if you *choose* to step out of your physical being for a time. You shift a portion of your awareness away from the situation to look at what you, the *feeler*, are experiencing. Eckhart Tolle expounds on this principle in his book *The Power of Now*:

> Whenever you are able to observe your mind, you are no longer trapped in it. Another factor has come in, something that is not of the mind: the witnessing presence.
>
> Be present as the watcher of your mind—of your thoughts and emotions as well as your reactions in various situations. Be at least as interested in your reactions as in the situation or person that causes you to react. Notice also how often your attention is in the past or future. Don't judge or analyze what you observe. Watch the thought, feel the emotion, observe the reaction. Don't make a personal problem out of them. You will then feel something more powerful than any of those things that you observe: the still, observing presence itself behind the content of your mind, the silent watcher.

So beautiful. If you've never considered this, give it a try.

Commit to the Process

Once you decide you're going to take responsibility for how you perceive your life and how you react to your children (and others, too), you will likely see and feel a shift. Just like with your awareness of your story, being keenly conscious of your feelings during or soon after a trigger allows you to observe and shift from the inside out.

This work is simple, yet not easy. It takes commitment, diligence and perseverance. Be gentle with yourself. Days may go by in which you fall back into old patterns. Dust yourself off and reset, consciously observing your feelings. Pay attention to your surroundings, your thoughts and your words.

To aid in this practice, try one of the Action Peaces below, and then move on to the next chapter—Connecting.

Action Peace—What Am I Observing?

Bring to mind a person with whom you've experienced a triggering situation. This could be your child, a friend, a partner, etc. See if you can identify the feelings that come up for you. Take note of how you are observing that person, their choices, the way they communicate with you—whatever comes to mind. Ask yourself, is there a victim/villain scenario being played out? Is there another pattern? Step outside of yourself and just notice what it feels like in your mind and in your body. If it's helpful, use the Story Loop diagram below.

Story Loop

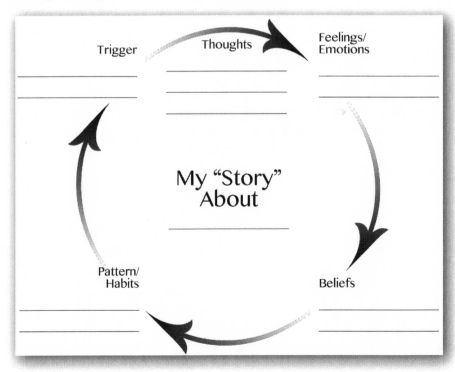

Action Peace—Observation Checklist

Put a check next to each applicable relationship or area of life where you might benefit from consciously observing your reactions, feelings and emotions. This exercise will heighten your intentionality in doing this work.

Relationships:

- Child(ren)
- Spouse
- Parents
- In-laws
- Extended Family
- Friends
- Acquaintances
- Co-workers
- Neighbors
- Staff from child's school
- Coaches
- Child's peers
- Parents of child's peers
- Medical professionals

Areas of Life:

- Emotional Health
- Physical well-being
- Body image
- Finances
- Household order (or lack thereof)
- Neighborhood
- Work/career

- Recreational activities
- Civic organizations
- Charitable organizations
- Politics
- School policies and procedures

CHAPTER 8

Connect
Join with Infinite Love

"I have a fortress in my mind and I have pictures of
God in there.
God always comes to visit because we are neighbors."

~ TESSA, AGE 6½

ONCE YOU HAVE **Consciously Observed** yourself and your feelings, you can
move to step two of the Four C's: **Connect.**

Connecting is an important component of this work, yet you may wonder—to whom or what are you connecting? You are connecting to your True
Self, Infinite Love and the True Self of your child (or any other person you're
with when triggered). The act of connecting to Infinite Love builds intentionality for more purposeful action. You are not just going through the motions
here, you are moving toward a joining with Infinite Love *in* you and Infinite
Love *as* you.

There are a multitude of ways to connect. Ultimately, this step is about
taking the time to focus on a new way of experiencing yourself and your child.
Once we set the intention to join with Infinite Love, we start to create fresh
neural pathways that will support us in new ways of viewing our world.

Client Triumph—Reaching Kids through Our Work
When I asked attendees at a half-day workshop on parenting with
peace to introduce themselves and share what drew them to the class,
Molly was the first to step forward. Her eight-year-old son had a sei-
zure disorder and she had heard about the class from his neurologist,
who she greatly respected. She said she was hoping to learn some tools

to help her son in a variety of areas—physical health, school performance and behavioral challenges.

Once she found out that one of the focal points of the class was the role parents play in family dynamics, she admitted she was skeptical. She wondered how in the world working on her "stuff" would help her kids. I am sure she was not alone in this thought. Many parents, myself included, stumble upon the necessity of doing this deeper inner work when looking for a way to help, or "fix," their children.

In introducing the Power Tools to the class, I discussed the work of social physiologist and associate Harvard professor Amy Cuddy. In her popular TED talk, "Your Body Language Shapes Who You Are," Amy teaches that standing or sitting in certain positions, what she calls *power poses,* helps decrease levels of cortisol, our stress hormone, and increase testosterone, which, among other things, boosts confidence. As Amy so eloquently says, "Our bodies change our minds and our minds can change our behavior and our behavior can change outcomes."

During a movement break, I had the class practice the power poses. As they experimented, I explained that I often do these poses following a triggering interaction with my children.

Something about the entire parenting with peace approach clicked with Molly. Absorbing this information along with what we talked about in the fields of epigenetics, quantum physics and neuroscience, she decided to run with it. Over the next few days, she immersed herself in TED talks, YouTube videos, audio recordings and more. She incorporated action steps from the workshop into her everyday life and immediately began to see and feel changes within herself, and in her children and husband.

Molly also liked doing the power poses with her children before taking them to school. All three added affirmations like, "I love going to school. I can do the work and have fun." At one point, when she was running late and feeling stressed, her son Brandon said, "Mom, just do a power pose." On another occasion, when her six- and eight-year-old boys were playing with their train set, she heard one son tell the other, "Just keep saying, 'the bridge will be fine, the bridge will be fine.'"

The following is an email from Molly:

This morning, my son screamed, "I don't want to get up! I won't put these clothes on!" I spoke nicely, telling him that he could take a few minutes to think positive thoughts and then get dressed. He said, "NO!" I calmly replied that it was necessary to get up and dress for school. He hid under his bed. I went into the bathroom and breathed in and out, and sent him loving, peaceful thoughts. I did the color [visualization], then told him I was going to take the dogs out. When I came back, he was dressed and happy!!!! Yay!!!

You, too, can realize this kind of shift for yourself and your family. As discussed, the level of change we experience is directly related to what we believe is possible. Like so many parents I have worked with, Molly is open to seeing a different way.

Let's explore a number of techniques to help you strengthen your connections and infuse your life with Divine Love.

Options for Connecting

Connecting to the Divine is a very personal process, and our needs change at different times of our lives. You may already have such practices in place. If so, you can use what already works or try something new. The connection activities below only take a few seconds. Several are described in detail in the Action Peaces that follow.

- **Breathe**. According to www.etymonline.com, the word "inspire" comes from the Latin *inspirare*, "to breathe." Thus, breathing, or *in*spiring, is an act of bringing in Spirit. Typically, we only use about 10% of our lung capacity during regular, everyday activities. Taking a few deep breaths expands the muscles between our ribs and lifts our diaphragm, thereby delivering more oxygen to our cells. Another benefit is that we break the pattern of shallow breathing that we step into when a triggering event occurs. There are myriad specialized techniques that you can incorporate into your practice of connecting. You may be familiar with *pranayama*, or box breathing, used in yoga. See the Action Peace—Simple Breathing Exercise below for details on another technique.

- **Repeat a Mantra or Prayer.** My go-to mantra is "I consciously choose my thoughts." This brings awareness that whatever I am thinking in the moment is a choice. Regardless of what thoughts got me into a given situation, I can choose something else. Or, if I feel rushed or am running late, I slowly say to myself, "I have all the time I need." Some people like to use one or more lines from a familiar prayer. Find or create phrases that are meaningful to you. If you have used a particular mantra in the past and have seen no difference, take a break from it. We are looking to grow new neural pathways, not reinforce an action or behavior that is not effective.
- **Call On Infinite Love.** Say the word(s) "Spirit" or "Divine Love be with me" aloud or in your mind. On two separate occasions, I was in a near accident while driving. I shouted God's name and, both times, literally experienced time and space slowing. No accidents took place.
- **Visualize an Image**. We all have images that evoke feelings of peace, love, and well-being. Picturing the True Self images (either from the figures in Chapter 4 or of your own creation) may work for you. Or, you could try visualizing the vastness of the Milky Way, imagining yourself on a beach or bringing to mind a picture of your child as a newborn. I like to incorporate a visualization from an ancient Hawaiian healing technique in which I imagine a series of colors washing over my body. (More on this later.)
- **Place Your Hand on Your Heart.** There is a reason why so many traditions use the image of the heart as their central motif. It is the focal point of our feeling selves. Placing a hand to our heart is a physical way to intend a stronger emotional and spiritual connection to our True Self.

- **Practice a Power Pose**. Place legs apart with your hands on your hips (Wonder Woman/Superman pose), or with your arms above your head, as if you just won a race. Hold for two minutes to decrease stress and increase confidence. You can also check out Amy Cuddy's TED talk for more details or to see her demonstrate the poses.

No matter what practice(s) you adopt, know that our way of connecting can be fluid and change from situation to situation. You may find your groove in one particular option, or you may float around from a mantra to a visualization to a power pose. Regardless, taking the time to connect will bring you closer and closer to your True Self.

A Personal Peace—Breathe in Peace and Focus

When my husband and I decided to renovate the kitchen of our 1950's ranch home, we had no clue what we were in for. One of the many opportunities for inner growth that presented itself concerned the final balance. Though my husband and I were fully prepared to pay the balance upon completion of the project, there were, along the way, several discrepancies between how we viewed the job and how the contractors viewed it.

After many delays, and several requests for more money, I had pages of documentation detailing project delays and errors caused by their choices and actions. In preparation for our final meeting, I felt extremely anxious over how everything would go down. Even now, writing this, I recall my dread. The night before the meeting, I called a good friend who used to be in construction and also studied mindfulness. He reminded me that the most important thing I could do was breathe. Recognizing the power of his suggestion, I knew this would make a difference to how I felt and responding during the meeting. Regardless of how ridiculous I might appear, I decided to make my breath a priority.

Multiple times during this meeting, I stopped mid-sentence to take a deep breath. The two men and my husband looked on in uncomfortable silence. I didn't care, as it helped me stay focused on my intention for peace.

After we each stated our piece, no one spoke for several minutes. I again focused on breathing deep and waited. Finally, the main contractor suggested we just pay the initially agreed upon balance. I wrote the check with gratitude and will forever remember the power of taking full, cleansing breaths during intense experiences.

In the process, I was also able to shift an old pattern. Because I had a tendency to take care of others' needs over my own, I'd been tempted to offer the contractor more money. By focusing on my breath, I was able to remain solid in the knowledge that what my husband and I had offered was fair and just. I started a new neural pathway in those last few minutes. I was beginning to know what it felt like to connect to my True Self—that part of me that can state my needs and take appropriate actions.

When to Connect

Connecting is an important part of the Four C's and of the process of bringing peace and love into your family. The above techniques can be used at any point—before, during or after consciously observing and naming your emotions, when you're triggered and when you're not—to bring you one step closer to perceiving and experiencing the infinite possibilities life has to offer.

Jon Kabat Zinn, professor emeritus of the University of Massachusetts Medical School and founder of the Stress Reduction Clinic, defines mindfulness as the act of "paying attention in a particular way; on purpose, in the present moment and non-judgmentally." Being mindful in the ordinary moments of our daily lives, when nothing feels stressful or challenging, helps us exercise relaxation. It's a way to train our brain and body to know what it feels like to be calm, peaceful and centered. And, as discussed, this is extremely helpful in programming our neurochemistry in order to shorten the duration and intensity of our feelings when we're triggered.

Each of the following Action Peaces offer an excellent opportunity to practice mindfulness.

Action Peace—Simple Breathing Exercise

Figure 8.1 is a visual model of a simple breathing technique. By practicing during quiet, downtime, your body will more readily assume a relaxation response in the moments that you simply breathe deeply, without a particular pattern.

First, close your eyes. Take a deep breath in for a count of six. Hold for a count of four. Breathe out for a count of six and, again, hold for a count of four. Repeat this cycle seven to ten times.

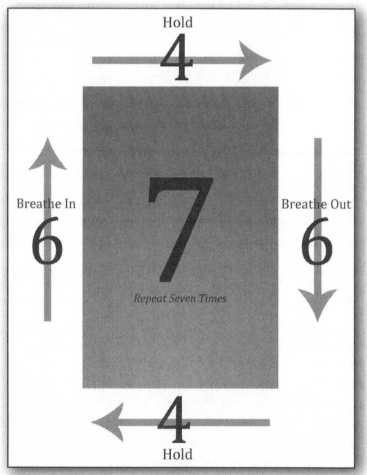

Figure 8.1 Simple 6/4 Breathing Technique

Action Peace—Choose a Meaningful Mantra

I've listed a number of my favorites below. Choose one that is meaningful to you, or create your own.

- I have all the time I need.
- My family is peaceful and well.
- I see all challenges as opportunities.
- I welcome with grace and ease a solution that is highest and best for all.
- I am the change I want to see.
- I am Love.
- Repeat *Our Father, Om Shanti,* or another name for the Divine that speaks to you.

Repeating a mantra/prayer regularly will make it easily accessible during times of stress. Write yours on a sticky note or decorative slip of paper and place on your bathroom mirror.

Action Peace—Select a Peaceful Image

Sit quietly and review relaxing scenes from your past. Do you love to watch the ocean or sit near a bonfire, mesmerized by the flames? What visualization represents Infinite Love to you? Write the details below:

As with your mantra, keep this present in your mind call on when a little "connecting" is needed.

CHAPTER 9

Choose
Select a Way to Let Go

"Mommy, I have something for you to remember.
If you want to be happy or sad, you can decide."

~ ANDREW, 6 DAYS BEFORE HIS 4TH BIRTHDAY

AFTER YOU CONSCIOUSLY **Observe** and **Connect**, you are ready for the meat
(or kale, for vegans) of doing your work to live as your True Self. Number
three in the Four C's is **Choose**. Although this sounds so simple, know that
the act of deliberately choosing a method to release your story and embrace
your True Self is extremely powerful. When you make a mindful decision to
do your work, there is no way to play the victim or martyr or to delve into
guilt. You are now ready to let go of your limiting thoughts, patterns and
beliefs, by standing in your power and actively making a choice to do things
differently.

Life brings us opportunities to use these practices over and over again and
having a variety of options can make a huge difference in how we respond.
Sometimes we are up for a complete shift in consciousness. At other times,
we need the path of least resistance—the easiest, gentlest approach to ease the
situation at hand.

By choosing to acknowledge our feelings and limiting beliefs and alter our
thoughts and our story, we change the environment within and around us.
This choice affects the ones we love on a quantum level (see "mirror neurons"
in Chapter 4). Our children move into a new way of being simply by sensing
this new environment. At the very least, we are no longer triggered by what
they say and do. We can be present for them, choosing compassion and understanding. When they are ready, we can support them in another way of being.

Client Triumph—Choose New Tools to Shift Perspective

Dianne came to me at her wits' end. She spent the first twenty minutes of our session relating a laundry list of professionals she and her daughter had been to—from psychologists to counselors to MDs and several other specialists in between. My initial impression was that she was trying to scare me off. I know now that she simply wanted me to know they had tried *everything,* and nothing seemed to offer what it was she really wanted… a peaceful and harmonious home, family connection and effective and loving communication.

Dianne had visited my website and watched my free videos, so she had a bit of background on what we would address. I started with the concept of her story and we discussed triggers, patterns and beliefs. She immediately softened, perhaps sensing that my primary intention was to connect with and genuinely hear her.

Dianne's daughter Madison had severe ADHD. She tended to keep it together at school, with friends and around town, and then let loose on her family at home. This looked like making rude and hurtful comments, complaining about meals, putting her feet up on the dinner table, screaming at her parents, etc.

As you know by now, when we perceive our children from the eyes of the one wearing the backpack, we see the same behaviors over and over. As our session came to a close, I selected a technique (a guided meditation) to help Dianne release the feelings, patterns and beliefs she was carrying in her backpack. I then suggested action steps she could take at home, including practices from our session and a meditation found on my website (www.kristenoliver.com). I also directed her to the work of Dr. Joe Dispenza. With that, she was on her way with a new set of tools.

To my delight, Dianne soon reported that things with Madison were beginning to shift. Dianne took responsibility for working through her own feelings, patterns and beliefs and started actively choosing specific tools to address her needs and feelings during quiet times as well as when she was triggered. As she did, she felt less and less upset by Madison's words and actions. Though Madison still exhibited some of the same behaviors, Dianne did not feel angry like she had in the past. For her part, Madison went from complaining about meals and throwing long and loud tantrums to eating respectfully and joking and laughing with her mom. She even told her mom that she was her best friend.

Over the course of our work together, Dianne shared one story after another of growth for herself and her family. They enjoyed the best holiday season they'd ever had, for instance, despite having visited family members who were steeped in their own patterns of trauma and drama. Knowing that her sister and sister's partner tended to look for the negative side of situations, focusing intently on perceived problems and challenges, Dianne set an intention to have fun regardless of the energy in their home. When we spoke, she was beside herself with gratitude for how easily she and her husband and three kids were able to laugh and create adventures, while her extended family members argued and gossiped.

Dianne went on to use the same techniques to shift her perceptions about certain foods she was sensitive to. Following a trip to Europe with her husband, she told me that all of her sensitivities had faded away and she could, and did, eat anything she wanted. This included French bread and exotic cheeses that had previously caused considerable intestinal discomfort. I asked her what the biggest influence had been in this process and she said, "You told me I could heal my sensitivities, and I believed you."

Dianne's commitment reminded me that, when implemented wholeheartedly, this work can help families make tremendous shifts in a relatively short period of time.

Okay, What Are My Choices Here?

Once you've allowed yourself to feel what comes up for a chosen length of time, there are myriad options to formally and powerfully release and reprogram your mind and body to bring forth a new story. For now, let's focus on those I've found most helpful in my practice and with my own children.

As an observant, connected parent, you can choose:

- Acceptance
- Empathy
- Leaning in
- Releasing baggage
- Meditation
- Forgiveness and Love

Let's take an in depth look at these options, following a natural progression from simplest to most complex.

1. Choose Acceptance

What? Acceptance? Is this crazy? Not at all.

When you choose to just *be* with what is, without judgment and without trying to change anyone or anything, you surrender to the situation. Because this is a choice, there is strength in such surrender that seems quite the opposite from what we can mistake for acceptance—passivity and victimhood.

A Personal Peace—A Gift for Us All

Following a guided meditation in which I reflected on what I had needed as a child, I realized that in moments of intense emotion— such as the episodes of uncontrollable crying—what I had needed most was to be accepted no matter what. I'd needed to know that I was allowed to feel whatever it was that came up. I didn't want to be told, "It's okay, stop crying." I wanted *permission* to cry, even if I had no logical reason to do so.

The morning after this meditation, I was given an amazing opportunity when my kiddos began to argue. As things became heated between them, I caught myself falling into an old pattern and realized I really did not know what to do. I did know that whatever each felt was real to them and any use of reason would be be futile.

I chose to go to my son first because his anger and frustration appeared more intense than what my daughter had expressed. Though I still didn't know what to do, I knew I did not want my reaction to be automatic. I sat with him for a bit in silence, and then it came to me. First, I let go of my agenda to be on time for school, having peace and calm the entire way. Then, I stepped into a place of acceptance. All of what he was doing and saying—I would allow all of it and just *be* with him.

I sat next to him and rubbed his back, imagining he was me as a child. In that state of absolute presence, I was able to give him exactly what I'd wanted—complete acceptance. The experience was truly profound. I was overcome with feelings of unconditional love, for my son and for myself. I don't keep data on duration and intensity of such conflicts, but I can say that the whole episode, from start to finish, felt significantly shorter than when I tried to reason with him or tell him what he'd done to instigate the argument in the first place.

I then went to my daughter, who is two years younger than Andrew, and repeated the same process. I sat with her from a place of abundance and just accepted all of what she expressed. Again, the negative feelings seemed to dissipate easily, and I felt full of love.

To my surprise and complete delight, we were not only on time that morning, we were early. The three of us sat in the parking lot of their school, enjoying each other's company before it was time to go in. The particulars of the argument were so far in the past, it seemed like it had happened weeks ago. I found myself feeling grateful for the argument, knowing that, from it, we had all received a gift.

Remember, choosing acceptance doesn't necessarily mean you don't take action. Sometimes, as in the story above, you'll be guided to sit with and comfort your child. In other situations, choosing acceptance will mean that you simply let your child's tantrum fully play out, without resistance.

This choice is at the top of the list because it takes the least amount of effort. You simply allow yourself to go into surrender mode, accepting what is in the moment. Maybe next time you will choose something further down on the list. For now, this is what you can handle.

2. Choose Empathy

So often our kids just want to know that they are *seen* and *heard*. Who am I kidding? Adults want the same thing!

I am inspired by communication theories and strategies based in compassion and empathy. Many people in this field mediate between individuals or groups in conflict, allowing all parties to be heard and feel witnessed from a place of mutual respect. With compassion, the participating parties are then able to move toward reasonable solutions.

It's not always easy to choose empathy when you are triggered by something your child has done or said. However, once you do some work on your stuff, genuine empathy can be a powerful tool.

Client Triumph—Hair Brushing Analysis

After we reviewed the concept of empathy and compassionate communication, the parents of Emily, a beautiful eight-year-old, returned to a follow-up session with a life-changing story. Emily had some sensory challenges and one of her issues was brushing her hair. The whole process felt like torture to her.

One Saturday, her dad got out a white board and markers, sat on her bed, and listened to what she had to say. As she detailed the discomfort of getting her hair brushed, he made a series of charts that visually exhibited what she was saying to him. They did this and other empathy-based activities that he came up with for an hour and a half! The next day, they did a variation of the same activities for a similar amount of time. On the third day, Emily came to her parents with a hairbrush and *asked* them to brush her hair.

Thanks to her father's choices, Emily felt seen, heard and loved to the point that she willingly shifted the challenge of brushing her hair into an opportunity to bond with her parents.

Honing your empathy skills for others helps them feel seen, heard, and loved. What more could a child want?

What about Me?

I would also like to emphasize *self*-empathy. In our society, children aren't taught to empathize with themselves. Can you imagine hearing an elementary school teacher say, "Just be gentle with yourself when you make mistakes" or "It is helpful to love yourself, no matter what"?

Sometimes our power comes in providing ourselves with what is most needed. For example, in a private session with the parents of five children, they related how the whole family had gotten together to make gingerbread houses. What started as a fun holiday activity quickly turned into a vortex of chaos and arguing. The mom, who had just wanted to build strong family memories, experienced frustration that the kids couldn't pull it together. And so much anger came up for the dad, he walked out. In the end, the clients laughed as the mom told me she took a picture of the gingerbread house instead of one of the family as they made it. We joked that in the future they could show this to their kids as proof that they did, in fact, enjoy some fun family activities together.

When conflicts like this arise, it can be so powerful to take the time to empathize with yourself as well as with others involved. This could be as easy as saying, "Wow, I can't believe this. I just wanted to enjoy a fun family project and now everyone is arguing, including my husband and me. This stinks and I don't like it."

Again, there is power in choice. The kind of energy we're talking about is that of a loving grandmother coming over to put her hand on your back. It's hard to subconsciously play the victim at the same time that you are comforting and loving yourself.

3. Choose Leaning In

As I've explained, once challenging emotions have been triggered, the key is to allow yourself to feel what comes up. You can do this for thirty seconds, five minutes, an hour or several days. Realizing that this, too, is a choice will empower you.

How is leaning in to our experience different from being stuck in our story? If our intention is to stay locked in our story, it's difficult to feel our emotions. Being stuck is more about "this happened" or "that happened." Leaning in is about being fully conscious of your emotions. Let the anger, frustration, sadness, etc. have their time in the limelight. Many of us are taught not to express ourselves as children. As a defense mechanism, we learn to stifle our emotions effectively in order to "survive" in our family, school, or social circle.

When a triggering event or circumstance arises and the situation appears to be unresolvable in the immediate future, really allow yourself to sit with everything that comes up. Old patterns and roles may surface. Recognize them. Greet them. Just *be* with it all. Go deeper into the feeling, exploring its potential origins. When you get there, you will know it.

From a place of fully feeling all that arises, you can then choose to release the emotions. As time progresses and you start to reprogram your subconscious patterns, you may be a bit firmer with yourself when you witness an old belief resurfacing. For example, when I have done extensive work on a particular belief and feel it shift and release, temptation to reignite the old habit can sneak back in. When I recognize this, I revaluate. Do I need to fully feel or have I exhausted this and want to move on? When I feel empowered to move on, I say "cancel" to the belief and immediately move toward something new.

Getting Hit with Old Emotions

Let's say you've made progress in increasing communication with your child, fully loving and accepting him, and, seemingly out of nowhere, he lashes out or hits you when something doesn't go his way. You are flooded with a ton of emotions, judgments, beliefs, etc. What can you do?

In the moment your anger is directed at your child, ask yourself:

What is under that?

Maybe you thought you were past all this. And:

What is under that?

A need for mutual respect, ease, flow with life. And:

What is under that?

A fear that your life is not what you thought it would be. And:

What is under that?

The fear that you are not loved or that you are not "good" enough to have what you want. And:

Under that?

Feeling unloved and unsupported as a child or having had the experience that, in your family, love and support were conditional. If you didn't do something in the exact right way, you didn't feel loved.

This is intense stuff. At least it looks and feels that way.

Now, go back the triggering event—in this case, the son who lashed out. What was *he* feeling? His upset arose from *his* fear of not doing something exactly right or a situation that did not go the way he thought it should. In his way, he is providing an opportunity for you to feel this and let it go. Is it also possible that your reaction is a result of things not going just the way you want them to go? This is yet another example of how we can own that we are always "observing" our lives, as was detailed in Chapter 2, Patterns and Beliefs. You can also return to the Action Peace—Reflecting on Your Child at the end of Chapter 4 to gain more insight on situations like this.

Avoiding the Trap—"That *made* me feel..."

In the above scenario, you may be tempted to believe and even say to your son, "When you hit me, that makes me feel sad." As you may recall, I shared this same concept in Chapter 3, and I feel it is worth repeating.

When you tell another "You made me feel..." or "That made me feel...," you completely hand your power over to them. No one can *make* you feel any certain way. You are always in control of your reaction to whatever arises. Whether conscious or subconscious, your response and the accompanying feelings are always a choice. And remember, when you really feel your connection to all things, you actually magnetize the exact right scenario to provide an opportunity for healing.

A Personal Peace—Triggers, Tears and Healing

A couple of years ago, my mom and I were having a somewhat heated discussion. As some old triggers resurfaced and my emotions started to brew, I found myself trying to rein in tears. Finally, Mom said something that allowed it all to flow.

This was a response I chose, whether consciously or subconsciously. So, when she immediately said, "Don't cry," I firmly responded, for the first time in my life, "I want to cry and I'm going to cry. I am going to feel what has come up because I choose to. I don't want to keep it in."

She was surprised at my reaction and told me she hadn't wanted to upset me or make me cry. I told her that anything she says to me only has the power *I* give it. I could tell by her expression that she did not quite understand, that she still believed her words could *make* me feel upset. I was inspired to share my analogy from Chapter 4, about how I imagine Mother Theresa was so in tune with her True Self, I was sure she wouldn't let another's fears stop her from moving forward with her life's purpose.

I'm not sure my mom agreed. I do know that the example gave us an opportunity to connect over the idea of what Mother Theresa was all about—pure, unconditional Love.

Following this visit, I did my work to release the old pattern of holding back my emotions. I truly felt wonderful, *knowing* that I could choose to feel what came up for me and be empowered in letting go. I didn't ask my mom to change in any way. Rather, I took responsibility for my reactions and for drawing this opportunity into my life. And, I loved it all—my mom, the experience and, most of all, myself.

About a month later, my parents came to visit. My mom had brought a few magazine articles she'd copied for me. (She often passes on reading material she finds meaningful.) As she handed them to me, she said, "Now, I don't want this to make you upset…"

I smiled. Here was a chance to lovingly assert myself from a place of peace and clarity. I calmly told her that no article has that kind of power over me. I repeated that no one and no thing can *make* me feel any particular way. I am in charge of my feelings, always. We laughed and I graciously accepted the articles, knowing my mom loves me and that this is one of the many ways she expresses that love.

As I am writing this, I am filled with love and gratitude for my mother and for the precious opportunities our relationship provides.

Fully feeling can be intense. If you have covered up your emotions for years, it can be *really* intense. Be gentle with yourself. Ultimately, your intention in this process will determine the outcome. If you lean into your experience as a form of self-punishment, you will bring forth more of the same. If you feel all that arises with the goal of honoring your experience and then letting it go, you will find yourself gaining courage and confidence.

4. Choose Release

Real change can occur when we actively let go of lifelong patterning or everyday stressors. By recognizing the trigger, connecting to Infinite Love, and consciously choosing to free that pattern from your experience, you can and will rewire your brain to create a new story—one that encompasses all that you truly desire and deserve.

In other words, we must change our thoughts (our mind) and change our feelings (our body) in order to begin a new story. When we get stuck in the same loops of thinking and feeling, we continue to get more of the story that supports those patterns and beliefs.

What this May Look Like—Empowered by Positivity

As often happens with boys of late elementary school age, when I asked Jason what he wanted help with, he replied, "Nothing." As we proceeded to get to know each other and build trust, we completed a number of activities that demonstrated how our thoughts affect outcomes and how our bodies respond to positive versus negative thinking.

At our third session, Jason shared that he was having trouble with math. He really hated it. We talked about how fighting against something seems to make it push back even harder. Following this discussion, Jason said he would try to welcome math concepts like an old friend.

In saying yes to math instead of resisting it, Jason found the work became easier and even a bit fun. Was it his favorite subject? Absolutely not. This kiddo would rather be out in the woods building forts and climbing trees. But as math was a part of his school's academic expectations, he opened up to the power of choosing to look at perceived challenges in a completely different way.

Jason's mom also reported a significant shift in his attitude and performance in this area. In fact, she said his confidence in *all* areas had increased because he was empowered to identify blocks and welcome all that came with them.

A Powerful Way to LET GO

As we move through our days, we typically resist what we do not want, either consciously or subconsciously. The problem with this is, as Carl Jung so insightfully stated, that "What you resist, persists." Or as James Redfield, author of *The Celestine Prophesy*, puts it, "Where attention goes, energy flows."

As is true with most of the concepts I share in this book, you must be open to at least the *possibility* of letting go in order for this process to be effective.

When we reject or say "no" to a physical ailment, for instance, or an overwhelming emotion or challenging relationship, we send energy to, and thus perpetuate, that condition in our lives. It's like building a dam to hold back the rushing waters of a flood: As we push against what we don't want, it pushes right back and stays right there with us.

If saying "no" hasn't worked, what would happen if we said "yes"?

Identify the trigger in an undesirable situation in your life. Now, try saying "yes" to it in your mind. Say "yes" to your feelings, the people involved, pretty much everything. Repeat this process over and over until you feel a shift. If something comes up as you are saying "yes," move through the new trigger and feelings in the same way. This is a form of surrender, if you will—recognizing what *is,* allowing it to simply be, and moving toward something different.

The first few times I tried this, the image of a Ferris wheel came to mind. The gondolas represented triggers or feelings; each time one passed by, I practiced saying "yes" to it. Eventually, the Ferris wheel unscrewed from its base and just rolled away.

Keep in mind that this process also works in reverse. That is, when we give attention to what we *don't* have in our lives, we block ourselves from receiving something new. For example, if I focus on how little support I have and how much I *really* want it, I unintentionally confirm its deficiency.

Clients often ask, "Should I surrender to what is going on with my kids or should I try to intend something new?" The answer is yes, to both. You can allow what is occurring without resistance *and* focus on your desires moving forward. Striking a balance takes practice. Remember to be gentle with yourself.

After you practice saying "yes," you can then focus on the feelings that go with having what you most deeply desire. (This idea is expanded upon in Chapter 10, Create.)

5. Choose Meditation

Meditation techniques range from sitting quietly for a period of time and focusing on your breath, to lengthy guided meditations, to elaborate practices formulated by spiritual masters. I enjoy a variety of meditation approaches and feel that clearing my mind is integral to connecting with Infinite Love and living from the perspective of my True Self.

So many times, clients request specific details about my meditation practice. I recall feeling the same way when I first started. My biggest thoughts and questions were linked to my biggest fears:

- I've never meditated before.
- I don't know how to meditate.
- What if I can't do it correctly?
- Where do I even start?

I started small, with daily silent meditations, focusing on the space between my eyes or the breath going in and out of my nose. Eventually, I was meditating for twenty minutes daily, without exception. I felt more grounded and connected, which allowed me to be much more aware of what appeared to "disconnect" me. Then I got pregnant with my first child. During my first trimester, whenever I closed my eyes I felt nauseated. As I didn't have the awareness that I could release the nausea, my meditation practice was placed on hold. (That was part of an old story for me! I experienced a beautiful healing in that area with my second pregnancy—see the Personal Peace below.)

Once the nausea subsided, I began practicing prenatal yoga and meditation, including guided meditations that led me through various visualization and fear-release processes. Although the birth was intense (to put it lightly), I meditated through 17 hours of labor and delivered Andrew without pain meds, which was my goal. The nurses in the birthing center kept peeking in to watch me lying with my eyes shut, relaxing as much as possible while experiencing the biggest of contractions. I rather felt like a zoo animal, but I didn't let that affect my focus.

Interestingly, there were two fears I had difficulty fully releasing. By the time I had Tessa, I was pretty clear of even those. She was born quickly and easily after a short, though still intense, three-hour labor.

With two little ones, I didn't find much time to meditate. After things settled a bit and I chose to make more time for myself, I returned to exploring different methods of getting quiet and centering. Because it was such a priority, this was a regular topic of conversation in our home, which is evident in the story below.

What this May Look Like—Halfway Healed

As a weekly volunteer at my children's alternative, outdoor school, I spent the morning doing a quantum physics experiment with an engaged group of kids. We selected the number three to focus on as we rolled a six-sided die 36 times. Our goal was to see if three would appear significantly more than the other numbers. To our delight, we rolled the number three twice as often as the average rolls of the others. (This really only works when I am not invested in the outcome!)

After lunch, the group was stampeding toward a blanket that was the meeting area for our next class—drama. A larger child tripped and fell, taking my daughter down with him. I was sure she had broken a bone. As I scooped up my screaming four-year-old, I felt extraordinarily calm. This I can only attribute to grace.

We moved away from the group and started praying and visualizing. I, of course, wanted a miraculous instant healing, but when I asked Infinite Love if it was highest and best to go to the hospital, I clearly got a "yes." As we packed up, I asked all of the children to make a picture in their mind of my daughter perfectly healthy and whole, just as she was created. Just as we had done by focusing on rolling a three, I asked this group of powerful children to focus on Tessa's healing.

As we drove to the nearest hospital, I went through all of the healing techniques I had absorbed throughout the years. I was blessing, cleaning, seeing Truly, you name it. At a stoplight, I turned to see my daughter in the backseat with her eyes closed. Knowing it's not recommended to sleep immediately following an injury, I nudged her knee and asked her to wake up. She opened her eyes and said, "I am not sleeping. I'm meditating."

Hmmm... was this the case, or did she really want to sleep and knew I would let it slide if I thought she was meditating? I tapped her knee again and requested that she stay awake. More firmly now, she said, "I am meditating, Mom! It's already halfway healed."

During an extraordinary experience, the ER staff brought us snacks and frequently inquired whether we needed anything. After a minimal wait, we were informed that my daughter's collar bone was broken—halfway through.

Over the next few days, she and I spoke of the experience regularly, allowing her to release any trauma. A friend of mine led a healing ceremony for Tessa and we also reached out to others who would visualize her perfect health and wellness.

My daughter wore the prescribed sling on and off for about five days. She moved her arm more and more each hour, it seemed. In the waiting room at our follow-up visit, I begged her to put the sling on. Knowing she didn't need it, my daughter boldly refused, which brought some attention our way. All the while, my ego was bellowing, "Bad mom over here, call social services. Her daughter broke a bone thirteen days ago and isn't following sling protocol."

When the physician's assistant and doctor entered the room, they asked my daughter what had happened. She detailed the fall and, like a little actress, proceeded to lift her hand and rest her forearm on her head. Both practitioners gazed in amazement. After the initial surprise subsided, the orthopedist said my daughter was much further along in her healing than they would have expected. She no longer needed the sling, and no additional visits were necessary.

More recently, my dad also broke his collarbone. Our relationship and connection has progressed and I felt guided to share the details of Tessa's healing. It was a magical exchange. I was able to be compassionate, while also sharing what is truly possible for our minds, bodies and spirits. He embraced the information and started to investigate the power of meditation for himself.

Before moving on, I will add that I currently either meditate or sit quietly multiple times a day, typically upon waking, before going to bed, before each client and during or after any triggering events. I use a variety of mindfulness strategies and meditation approaches. Some take a few minutes, others take up to an hour or more. I have learned many of these approaches from others, and some have been revealed to me directly by Infinite Love.

6. Choose Forgiveness and Love

I saved this choice for last because it can be difficult to believe we can heal everything simply by loving and forgiving others and, ultimately, ourselves.

I've also found that, in order to truly love and forgive, it can be beneficial to first release old patterns via one of the methods listed above.

Remember when I mentioned that each thought has its own neural pathway? We can completely blast apart old thought patterns and create new ones through one simple act—offering ourselves unconditional love. Take note, I said *simple*, not easy. It is, in my opinion, virtually impossible to have harsh feelings toward another when we truly love ourselves no matter what.

A Personal Peace—From Forgiveness to Healing

As I mentioned, I experienced varying degrees of nausea and vomiting in both of my pregnancies. In my first, I often felt extremely ill in the morning and evening but was able to make it through my workday without vomiting. In my second pregnancy, both the nausea and vomiting, which occurred up to seven or eight times a day, increased significantly. I recall numerous occasions of having Andrew crying and pulling on my pant leg as I threw up in the kitchen sink after breakfast. (Sorry for the graphic image, but I want you to understand how monumental this healing was.)

Funny side note, being sick did serve me in one instance. I was summoned for jury duty on a murder trial—not ideal for an emotional, pregnant momma, right? After telling the attorneys, judge and fellow potential jurors that I'd thrown up three times that morning and had a bag in my purse in case it happened again, they immediately agreed I was not the best candidate to sit on this trial.

Aside from being released from jury duty, the intensity of my symptoms and emotions were almost unbearable. As grace would have it, prior to learning I was pregnant, I had planned a trip to Michelle Longo O'Donnell's annual "Living beyond Disease" retreat in Texas. Michelle is an RN who felt moved to leave Western medicine and open a holistic healing clinic for people from around the world. I was drawn to study with her after reading she had healed her daughter, who had been born prematurely and suffered severe physical and intellectual deficiencies as a result. (Her daughter is now an attorney, married with children!) As much as I dreaded the cross-country travel, I knew this was a great opportunity.

During the first day of the retreat, Michelle referenced an ancient Hawaiian healing technique that emphasizes taking responsibility for all you experience and "cleaning out" memories that simply replay over and over. This was the third time that I had heard of this technique, called Ho'oponopono (discussed in more detail in Chapter 13), in a short period of time so it caught my attention. Infinite Love often speaks to us this way, through what some consider "coincidence" but I call synchronicity or Divine intervention.

As the presenter explained the steps in this technique, I gleaned a basic understanding of what it would entail. In my case, I could intend to access the memories on automatic replay in my life—those of fear (and searing pain) left over from my first pregnancy, those involving my extended family or even the collective memories of our culture. Once I identified those memories, I could release and clear them from my backpack.

This would be an act of radical forgiveness. And, I finally felt ready and willing to do the work it would require.

During our next break, I sat quietly with a pen and paper and closed my eyes, intending to bring up memories to clear. In other words, I entered a relaxed and reflective place and asked that those memories be revealed. One by one, various thoughts and beliefs I had been carrying for years emerged from the backpack. I found myself crying, as I realized how much fear I had been carrying. Writing down each belief—mine, those of my family, and collective past and present cultural and societal beliefs—I filled six pages. And then I chose to love and forgive all of it. I remained in this place of meditation, emotional release and forgiveness as long as I felt necessary.

I felt drained yet lighter as I headed in to dinner. The conference was on a beautiful ranch with all meals served cafeteria style. The food was above average for a cafeteria and, to my surprise, I felt

hungry and requested a full plate of food, then went back for seconds. I felt nourished for the first time in weeks. Joy filled my body.
Exposing, releasing and forgiving all of the baggage that was weighing me down led to a full healing—I felt healthy, vibrant and alive.
Best of all, I never threw up again!

I didn't announce what had happened to everyone, or anyone for that matter. I have read, and I believe, that the energy of
such experiences can dissipate when we share them with others.
And the experience was so sacred, I didn't want anyone else's story
to filter in. I also didn't want any sort of credit or a pat on the
back. I just wanted to enjoy the gratitude and magnificence of the
moment. To this day, I am very intentional about only sharing
when I feel my experience might help others understand a concept
or know what is possible for them. It is never to say "Lucky me,
I've had a healing."

There were many others in the audience who underwent such
transformations. One man shared that his son was no longer autistic
since he began doing this work. Inspired by the lecturer, I made a
point to talk with her about a child I worked with. I wanted to buy
her book and give it to this child's mom. She looked into my eyes and
firmly yet lovingly said, "No, you do the work." I understood: I could
take responsibility for how I was experiencing this child, and love and
forgive it all.

This child was far on the autism spectrum, had difficulty communicating, and demonstrated a great deal of developmental delays. I
almost dreaded working with him. I felt guilty for these thoughts, and
viewed his mom with compassion, knowing she never got a break. She
even had to follow us from room to room during each session because
he didn't want her to leave his side. I'm being brutally honest here,
again so you can understand the magnitude of what occurred.

While still at the retreat, I again employed the Ho'oponopono
technique—forgiving my thoughts, beliefs and perceptions surrounding both the child and autism in general. I then forgave

anyone anywhere who might have similar perceptions. This process was again very emotional. When I was done, I felt free and filled with love.

Upon returning from the conference, I entered the therapy clinic with growing delight and curiosity. I felt no hesitation or dread, and I made sure I had no expectations.

When the child walked in, he immediately proceeded to the therapy gym—without his mom. I motioned for her to have a seat in the waiting area, hoping she would enjoy her time with a magazine, book or just silence. It's difficult to describe what happened next. This child and I connected in a way that goes beyond words. He completed all therapy activities calmly and with more accuracy than ever before. It felt as if we were communicating from our hearts rather than through words or even thoughts. At the end of the session, he gave me a long hug. We had barely touched in the past, let alone hugged. I was speechless and forever changed.

Did his autism go away? No, but his experience had certainly changed. As additional confirmation, the owner of the clinic asked me what I was doing differently and what I had learned at the conference, because she saw a new child. To this day, I am grateful to this little guy for the gift he gave me. I learned the power of taking responsibility for how I perceive others, and the power of true forgiveness.

Radical forgiveness is a big concept. It all goes back to what we talked about in Chapter 4, True Self versus Ego. Once you observe your story and the contents of your backpack, you have the opportunity to recognize the influence your memories and experiences have on how you judge yourself and others. Look again at Figure 4.6 (below). Remember, when we see with the eyes of the one wearing our backpack, we see our children through the lens of events that took place in the past. Forgiveness is releasing the contents of the backpack and opening up to seeing our children from the perspective of our True Self.

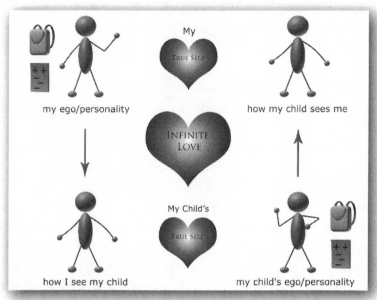

Figure 4.6 How You Perceive Your Child

The act of radically forgiving your child's behaviors, difficulties, tantrums, etc. as well as forgiving yourself for seeing him or her this way, leads to building a relationship based in limitless love. When you awaken your True Self and witness your child's True Self, genuine healing can occur.

Figure 4.7 Two True Selves Really *Seeing* One Another

7. Choose What Works for You

There are plenty of totally amazing techniques available that not only allow us to let go but change our neurochemistry and patterning. Addressing this root causes of all dis-ease—the patterning you've adhered to since childhood—is what will really shift your experience. When you release the thoughts and feelings that come along with a trigger and let go of the experience, you actually change *who* you observe from. And, as well-known spiritual author and speaker Wayne Dyer says, "When you change the way you look at things, what you look at changes."

What works for me may not resonate with you. Take what I've shared here, modify as necessary and commit to exploring which approaches are highest and best for the unique being that you are! By making this choice and placing this as one of your top priorities, you will meaningfully and effectively release and reprogram your subconscious mind.

I regularly use the concepts and techniques I share here, along with many other methods I've learned or developed, to release my own physical ailments, intense emotions and limiting beliefs. As a result, I have experienced miraculous shifts and enjoyed creating new stories filled with abundance, joy, peace and love.

Here a few additional techniques to choose from:

- Emotional Freedom Technique, know as EMT or Tapping (Check out the work of Nick Ortner)
- Eye Movement Desensitization and Reprocessing (EMDR)
- The Silva Method
- Nia

More Than a Quick Fix—A Change in Lifestyle

We are often moved to make a shift as a result of a major challenge or difficulty that has become unbearable. Maybe our child's tantrums are out of control or we argue with a spouse or ex over contradictory parenting views. Regardless of what triggers us, our first inclination is often to find a quick fix.

Practical strategies taught in many parenting approaches can work wonders to address surface symptoms. Some of the techniques in this book can even be used as a quick fix when we're in need of immediate relief. However, the bigger challenge is *doing the work* to create lasting change. This means committing to live from a different level of understanding and to take the necessary steps to create a new lifestyle—one based in being present, intentional and conscious.

Clients and friends often ask "exactly" what I "do" to make the changes I talk about. My most profound life shifts have come as a result of committing to live from the perspective of my True Self to the very best of my ability. I made this work and my relationship with Infinite Love and infinite possibility my number one priority. Rather than viewing this as selfish, I saw that everyone I knew and all I came in contact with benefitted from my commitment. Why? Because I was able to step out of my story and awaken more and more to my True Self and to living my life's purpose. Those around me feel seen and heard in a way that was impossible when I was stuck in my own story. Remember, only the ego gives us points for being a martyr. Only our stories lead to the belief that we must make a sacrifice in order to give or receive love.

Action Peace—Exploring Your Choices

List three different "Choose" tools you'd like to try from above. After trying each, come back and fill in the details:

1. Name of tool and relevant details:

   Describe the situation:

   How did you feel before, during and after using this tool?

   What were the outcomes or results?

2. Name of tool and relevant details:

    Describe the situation:

    How did you feel before, during and after using this tool?

    What were the outcomes or results?

3. Name of tool and relevant details:

    Describe the situation:

    How did you feel before, during and after using this tool?

    What were the outcomes or results?

CHAPTER 10

Create
Powerfully Intend a New Path

"The sun came up and came over to me and went
in my heart,
and I got brighter and brighter.
That was my dream."

~ TESSA, AGE 3½

NOW THAT YOU have **Consciously Observed** your thoughts, feelings, beliefs and patterns, **Connected** to your True Self and Infinite Love and **Chosen** a method to let go, you are ready to **Create** your new story—well, really, Co-create, with Infinite Love. This will enable you to live your highest and best life with grace and ease.

Once we release any vestige of the victim role and claim our worth, we can use our connection with Infinite Love, the greatest power available to us, to bring forth more and more of what we most deeply desire—a life of joy, peace, and love for ourselves and our families.

Calling our imagination into play in a new and highly purposeful manner helps us tap into the field of infinite possibility. It seems incredible, and even unbelievable, that our brains don't know the difference between what we imagine and what we experience in life. Yet, experiment after experiment in the field of neuroscience confirms this mind-boggling concept. Test subjects include pianists who practice only in their minds and go on to play flawless orchestral concerts and athletes who display remarkable performance gains after a simple meditation. There are so many breakthrough examples, we now have indisputable scientific evidence of the abundance of beautiful opportunities that await when we tap into our True Self through imagination, visualization and reprogramming techniques.

I have mentioned the word "intention" throughout this book. Beyond its original definition—a purposeful objective—*crafting* an intention can set the underlying tone for your morning, day, even your life. The work you do with the Four C's will free you from your old story so that you can re-pattern your thoughts and consciously create the peaceful, fulfilled life you imagine.

A New Story

Let's revisit your Story Loop. In previous chapters, you observed the loop and brought awareness to each component. You felt what came up, connected to Infinite Love, and made a conscious choice to address your needs to the best of your ability.

How, then, do you create something new? How do you move into a new story, one that serves and supports you and your family?

We start by reprogramming our subconscious and building new neural pathways based in love, joy, peace and ease. In order to do this, we need new thoughts (the mind component of the loop) and new feelings (the body component).

Remember, we are always experiencing our lives through the lens of the one wearing the backpack. Our story is on automatic replay, and we receive predictable outcomes because the familiar feels good, even when the feelings themselves are unpleasant. Our brains want to be right, so we subconsciously look for that which confirms the old, habitual story.

By releasing the components of our lives that no longer serve us and by making our True Self our top priority, we magnetize new experiences into our lives. In Figure 10.1, we see how a new story fits itself into the loop we are familiar with. Once new thoughts and feelings become more dominant than former patterns and beliefs, a new story can begin. The old trauma and drama become distant memories.

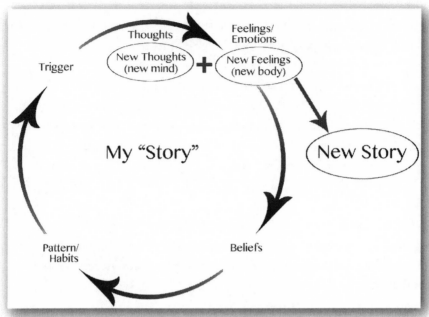

Figure 10.1 Creating a New Story

I know I've really shifted one of my own stories when it becomes difficult to recall the details. I can hardly remember my son's night terrors, for instance, or tension between my parents and me, because I have a completely new story around those situations—one of abundant health, joy and gratitude. In this way, I attract more and more experiences to be joyous and grateful for.

Powerfully Create

It's easiest to incorporate the fourth "C," **Create**, into your life right after practicing your preferred Choose method. While in meditation or following a release or forgiveness ritual, we're in a relaxed state and free of the heavy emotions that weigh down our backpack. The subconscious mind is open and primed for re-programming.

Here is a simple description of how to **Create:**

- Remain in the relaxed state you brought forth via the process you chose for your third "C."

- Understand that a new story is possible and you absolutely deserve your deepest, heartfelt desire.
- Consider what you'd like your new story to include. If your child is struggling with a learning difference and you feel sad and anxious, you might envision a new story where your child feels happy, confident and successful, and you feel relieved and at ease.
- Establish new thoughts—one or more powerful intentions that go with the new story. For instance, "My son has all he needs to meet the demands placed on him at school. I have all I need to support him."
- Identify and name the feelings that accompany the new story. These could be relief, ease, clarity, etc.
- Embody those feelings as if your new story is already a reality. Imagine filling your body, mind and spirit with these new feelings. Enjoy the sensations as they course through your being.
- Focus on a sense of gratitude, again as if the new story is already present in your life. Really *feel* the gratitude in your body. If it helps, call to mind a time when you experienced a great deal of gratitude. Tap into that energy and merge it with your current intention(s).
- If you have determined that the new story "must" include specific components, consider that you may be creating from old memories and the old story. Remember, you are not responsible for what that story looks like, only what it *feels* like. A key component here is that you and Infinite Love are co-creating something new—what comes about may not be familiar.

Know that you can create in the moment or over time, concentrating on acute issues or those that have been with you for years. The client triumph below will help you see how this might play out even during a somewhat urgent situation.

Client Triumph—Only Responsible for the Feeling

Maura sought my assistance following a personal crisis. She and her husband had a happy, healthy young son, and had hoped to expand their family. In recent weeks, they had suffered a miscarriage. Maura's wounds went deep, as you can imagine. Upon reflection, Maura realized one of the most difficult challenges of this experience was that she had not, and did not, feel heard or supported by her mother.

We did some in-depth work (both group and individual) to release the related patterns and beliefs stored deep in her backpack. Finally free of her sadness, Maura went on to do the work of powerfully intending a new story. About a year and a half later, Maura became pregnant again. She glowed with a vibrant beauty that words can't describe. As she shared her plans for the birth, I was moved by her peace and clarity. As Maura valued a gentle and non-invasive approach, she and her husband decided on a natural birth, with a midwife, at a birthing center.

One day, I was working on an upcoming presentation. I had set a strict boundary that I wouldn't answer any calls until I got a certain number of tasks accomplished, one of which was to identify the client triumph I would share. When my phone rang and I saw Maura's name, everything in my being told me to let go of that plan and answer the phone.

As I said hello, I could hear Maura crying. The midwife had found something troubling during an ultrasound and was sending her immediately to a specialist. I told her I would do anything she needed. With about twenty minutes to spare before her appointment, she asked if we could have a phone session while she waited in her car.

My intuition told me all was fine with both Maura and the baby. But I knew telling her that would not be enough. It was clear to me that Maura was at a crossroads. She had a beautiful opportunity: She could revert to her old story of fear and a lack of support or she could proceed down the intentional path she and her husband had committed to for this pregnancy.

Maura detailed (Consciously Observe) all of the emotions that were rising within her—fear about the baby's health, anxiety over being in a cold, sterile hospital environment with judgmental medical staff, etc. We then did a quick breathing exercise (Connect with Infinite Love) and a guided meditation (Choose), releasing each fear and apprehension that arose. At the end of the process, we focused on the feelings that would accompany her desired outcome—perfect health for momma and baby (Create). She imagined drawing in feelings of relief, relaxation, support, joy, confidence, grace, ease and, most of all, gratitude.

After we had moved through the Four C's, I reminded Maura that she was not responsible for how the new story played out, only the feelings that went with it. In other words, if she tried to predict the details of the new story, she would be using old thoughts and old feelings to create, which would yield a different version of the old story. By committing only to the feelings that went with the new story, Maura chose to trust Infinite Love and possibility to handle the details.

Following our conversation, I spent a moment imagining the feelings *I* would have upon receiving the news that all was well with Maura and the baby. I felt joy, awe and gratitude coursing through my being. A couple of hours later, I received a text:

Girl, we, who are one with all, just created total magic. Big expert doc, who was a super nice guy, sent us home with no additional instructions. He said he saw (nothing amiss). He said he didn't understand it, but he felt totally good sending us home with no interference.

I responded:

Of course! That's what I saw (in meditation). This little one is a reminder that anything is possible. We released all judgment and fear, anything other than the truth, which leaves only the truth to be seen and experienced—perfect Love!

Later that evening, I had the opportunity to get the full story. Maura told me the hospital had hardwood floors, dim lighting and warm colors—the opposite of what she had feared and resisted. She had a 3D ultrasound, during which the tech repeated phrases like, "Well, that looks perfect" and "This is exactly what we hope to see." When feelings of irritation and judgment arose during a conversation with a doctor, she noticed and released them, focusing instead on the feelings that went with what she wanted. "I knew that was all I was responsible for," she said.

Maura and her husband experienced a beautiful, full term pregnancy and a wondrous birth, and now have a beautiful baby girl.

Maura's experience is a great reminder that miracles are possible. In a short period of time, she transitioned from a place of darkness and fear to gratitude and relief. My job was simply to encourage and support her, remaining committed to seeing and knowing the truth—that Maura and the baby were Divine creations of love and light and infinite potential. I knew with certainty that all was well.

And, anytime I feel otherwise, I have an opportunity to release my own story and allow myself to resonate with the feelings of a new story.

You may wonder—What if, after Consciously Observing, Connecting, Choosing and Creating, the outcome is not at all what you intended? I don't want to gloss over the fact that tragedies do occur in our lives. The loss of a child at any point in life is devastating. During times of such intensity, I recommend clients honor their feelings and do their best to connect to Infinite Love—our deepest source of support and grace.

One gift that often comes with such grace, even in the face of circumstances that we didn't choose and don't want, is gratitude. Have you ever had an experience of feeling gratitude while in the midst of an enormous challenge? Let's look further into the magnetism and healing strength of this emotion.

Expanding on Gratitude

We are extremely powerful beings. Day after day and year after year we unintentionally create a succession of similarly themed stories, often based in fear and lack. Though the outcomes are not what we've wanted, we continue to powerfully devise more of the same. When we settle for mediocrity, the Universe takes note and offers us even more mediocrity.

When we are committed to clearing our old patterns and bringing forth the feelings that accompany a new story filled with abundance, ease and grace,

Infinite Love responds. The energy of unconditional love is there, just waiting for us to place our order.

As we incorporate the Four C's into everyday life, beautiful changes occur—our confirmation that this work really does make a difference. Kiddos start to communicate more effectively, spouses offer to help out with the bedtime routine, an unexpected financial gift arrives in the mail. Recently, a couple I worked with received a surprise gift of $10,000 from a relative. This happened just hours after we'd released their story of debt, connected with Infinite Love and possibility and co-created a new story of abundance. The woman texted: "The Universe has our attention!"

Once such things happen, we have the opportunity to acknowledge them with gratitude. Infinite Love sees and feels that gratitude and, subsequently, sends us more to be thankful for. Like begets like.

Feeling Your Desired Emotions

When defeat, guilt or anger have been our dominant emotions for a long period of time, we may not be familiar with what it "feels" like to experience joy or abundance. I am often asked, "How do I bring in the feeling of joy (or ease or relaxation) if I've never experienced it before?" Or, "How do I know what feelings should go with my new story?"

The simple answer is, choose what feels right to you in that specific situation.

Here are a few other suggestions:

- Recall a time when you felt something similar to what you now desire. You may have felt exhilaration when playing in the woods with friends as a child, or maybe you felt joy at the birth of your child. Your feeling is in there somewhere. You may just have to dig a bit.
- Move up the "emotion chain" a few rungs at a time. If you feel desperate and depressed, joy may seem too big of a leap. Instead, work to release the old emotions and focus on what seems manageable or possible at the time. Try bringing in the feelings of relief or curiosity.

A move from despair to relief will make it easier to move from relief to contentment and from contentment to joy.

- Ask Infinite Love to send an experience that will bring about the feelings you're looking for. If homework battles with your child are the norm, ask for an experience that shows you what peace feels like. You never know how this will be revealed. Maybe your sister will offer to take your child to a movie, giving you an afternoon to yourself to read on the couch. If that brings you peace, merge that feeling with your intention to have homework time flow more smoothly.

- Play the "What If" game. If you had a magic wand and could make the triggering situation just disappear, how would you feel? Focus on that feeling when co-creating your new story.

- Get clear on what it is you really want. Recently, I had an opportunity to make a choice on whether or not to attend a destination wedding. I really was not sure what I wanted to do. Rather than imaging myself feeling fabulous in Spain or feeling productive at home, I brought forth the sense of relief I would have when the highest and best option was revealed. A day and a half later, a series of events made it clear that going on this trip would offer a wonderful experience. I felt the relief and, from there, went on to the feelings that accompanied the story of having a spectacular time!

When we know how something works, we're more likely to believe that true change is possible. Let's take this time to explore how and why creating a new story is possible.

A Brief Look at Brain Waves

So, how does such reprogramming occur? In order to understand this, a brief description of brain waves will be helpful. Just a reminder, I am not a neuroscientist. What I share here is very basic, yet I believe it to be helpful to this process.

Figure 10.2 displays the four main types of brain waves. When we are "in" our conscious mind, we can be in either a beta or alpha state. Most of our awake time, for instance, is spent in high, mid or low beta. High beta is typically a place of intensity and stress. Mid beta is when we are alert and able to learn most efficiently. Low beta is a relaxed, attentive state of awareness, like when we are reading.

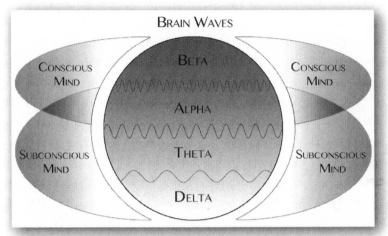

Figure 10.2 Four Types of Brain Waves

When we are in an alpha state, yet still in our conscious mind, we can be awake, yet preoccupied, perhaps even daydreaming. A good example of alpha consciousness is when you pull into your driveway or another familiar location and are not sure how you got there. You were driving safely, yet minimally in tune with the outer world. Provided nothing out of the ordinary happens, you can easily slip in, and stay in, a relaxed, more imaginative state of mind.

The alpha state can also be reached while in our subconscious mind, as in meditation, where we tune in less and less to our outer environment in order to access our inner world.

Theta brain waves are present when we are in an even deeper state of subconscious. In his book, *You Are the Placebo,* Dr. Joe Dispenza describes theta as:

A kind of twilight state where we're half-awake and half-asleep (often described as 'mind awake, body asleep'). This is the state we're shooting for in meditation, because it's the brain-wave pattern where we're the most suggestible. In theta, we can access the subconscious, because the analytical mind isn't operating—we're mostly in our inner world.

Theta is where we do the reprogramming necessary to release old patterns and beliefs that no longer serve us and allow us to bring in the feelings that go with the new story. What does this mean? In this state of deep relaxation, we can empty the backpack and release ourselves from the patterns that dictate our life experience. While in this highly suggestible state, we can reprogram our brains at the most profound level to bring forth the life we most deeply desire. New emotions are planted in our subconscious, replacing the old. Then, our lives reflect the new story that goes along with those emotions.

Delta is a state of deep sleep or dreaming. When we fall asleep with pleasant thoughts and a list of what we are grateful for, our subconscious marinates in this state of love and possibility throughout the night. We awake refreshed and curious about the wonderful things that will occur in the coming day, weeks and months.

Gamma brain waves aren't included in the figure above but are worth a brief mention. Accessing gamma brain waves allows us enter a sort of super-consciousness, and can be associated with bursts of insight and accelerated information processing.

Two Great Times to Incorporate the Fourth "C"

Alpha and theta waves are not only accessed in meditation; we also experience these states at least two other times of the day. Each evening as we fall asleep, we pass through alpha and theta states to get to delta (or sleep/dreaming). And in the morning, we pass back through theta and alpha to get into beta.

How can we use this knowledge to our advantage?

Well, each evening, whether triggered or not, you can take the opportunity to clear any distress from the day. You can Choose a release method to free negative bits and pieces from your subconscious and go right into Create mode, breathing in the feelings that go with your new story. The new story can involve an immediate situation—how smoothly the next day will go—or more of a long term story—how amazing you'll feel as you pay off your credit card, decide what school is highest and best for your child, or resolve a disagreement with your spouse or best friend.

Regardless of what area of life you focus on, when you bring in the desirable feelings *prior* to a night's rest, you give your subconscious the opportunity to work on this new story through the night. With your first awareness of the new day, immediately return to those desirable feelings. Intentionally bring them into your body as you dance between sleep and waking. This theta state is a magical time. The more you practice dwelling there, the easier it will become to access.

Sometimes we skip the in-between brain wave states (theta and alpha) and hit the day running in beta consciousness. That's okay. You'll have another chance, either in meditation or in the evening, to work on creating. Just remember, the more you commit to incorporating these concepts day to day, the more they become a lifestyle rather than just a "technique."

What This May Look Like—Four C's for Peaceful Mornings

School mornings were a regular source of stress and frustration for my kiddos and me. Even though every morning came with the same expectations—get dressed, eat breakfast, brush teeth, make your bed, etc.—it seemed as if each day brought a new battle.

I'd identified practical strategies to ease morning stress, such as packing lunches the night before and providing my kids with a checklist of what to do each day. But, as I've said, practical strategies only really work when our old underlying patterns are cleared.

As peace was still hit or miss in this area, I knew there was more work to be done. I committed to doing the Four C's to address our morning chaos.

I was easily able to Consciously Observe how I felt—rushed, frustrated, annoyed and even angry—and as various challenges arose, I would stop and take a few moments to work on my triggers. To Connect back to my True Self and Infinite Love, I would select a breathing technique or mantra and then Choose a meditation or other technique to release. I ended with Create, breathing in the feelings that went along with having a morning of ease and flow, filled with effective and loving communication. I did this over and over.

Because life events offer the best curriculum for shifting our stories, I committed to doing the work in the moment. Upon waking each day, I immediately imagined what it would feel like to be laughing in the kitchen with my kids. It felt wonderful and joyous. I stayed with that feeling as long as I could while snoozing between my morning alarms. Each evening, as I drifted off to dreamland, I again brought the emotions of a peaceful and harmonious morning into my body.

Soon enough, my kids and I started experiencing more joy and ease in our routine. Did we laugh and skip around like fairies and elves every morning? Nope. But, in general, there was a massive shift in how I experienced this formerly daunting part of our day.

My son and daughter even started doing things without being asked, not to get "credit" or points on their scorecard—they were simply in the flow, just like me.

To this day, when we have a rough morning, I still do my work to ensure we don't fall back into old patterns. Now, when difficulties arise, there is typically a reason—a poor night's rest or a challenging situation with a friend. Rarely is it the norm that we struggle and argue before leaving for school.

Remember, we can't expect our kiddos to meet our needs. It's our responsibility to make clearing our stuff our first priority, so we can help address *their* needs.

Proactively Create

We don't always have to be facing a challenging event to practice this last "C." When things are going fine and we want to bring forth more of the same, we can choose to proactively create just for fun.

This might look like having the family imagine a super fun vacation. What might it feel like to get the fast passes at a theme park? It would be great to skip those long lines and enjoy more rides and attractions. My family chose this one! We decided not to invest in fast passes and instead imaged short lines and tons of fun. Seemingly out of nowhere, a family walked up to us and gave us their passes! The next year, we imagined the same scenario. Though we didn't receive any fast passes, we were unknowingly funneled into the fast pass lane of one of the most popular rides at the park.

We employ these same principles in other areas of life as well. For example, when hearing a friend is sick, I might say to the kids, "Luke's Mom said he's not feeling well, can we imagine him healthy and well? What will it feel like to play with him tomorrow at school and see him laughing and running?" We then release this to Infinite Love, knowing that whatever is highest and best will come forth.

These co-creating concepts can be incorporated into relationships, careers, vacations, finances, health, and on and on. There is no limit to Infinite Love.

A Personal Peace—Getting the Goat

Three years ago, my kids and I made cutout Christmas cookies, the kind you ice and decorate. They wanted to sell them at the end of our driveway like a lemonade stand. It seemed funny to make money for ourselves at that time of year, so we decided to ask for donations only. Our goal was to get $20 so we could purchase a group of chicks for a family in a third world country through the Heifer Foundation. We decorated a table, got out some musical instruments and made a huge sign that read "Donation Only." We also laid out the Heifer catalog to show customers why we were jumping up and down at the end of our driveway on a gray and chilly day.

In less than an hour, we raised $26 dollars! Some people took a few cookies, others took none, donating anywhere from fifty cents to five dollars. Two teenage boys actually circled back later in the day to give more money and see if we had met our goal.

The following November, my kids and I looked through the Heifer catalog to choose a new goal. Our decision was unanimous— if we could raise $120, we could purchase a goat. I cut out the page and taped it to a wall in the kitchen. We visualized getting the money, no problem. We brought in the feelings of giving this potentially life-changing gift to another family, who could have milk to drink and maybe even enough left over to sell. (Kids are naturally open-hearted and can easily do this kind of thing with a little practice.)

As the date got closer, I reminded my daughter and son to keep the good feelings alive and allow the vision be for Infinite Love to bring forth the highest and best for all. This allowed us to release our "agenda" and be curious as to how everything would play out.

When I told my friend Cindy what we were planning, she said she and her two nephews would love to join in. We set a date and invited additional friends to come by. Two days before the sale, Cindy called, mentioning that the forecast was calling for rain. I rarely look at the weather report, preferring to go day by day. "Well," I said, "let's join together in imagining a clear day. And, if we have to stand outside with umbrellas, that will show our determination to get this goat!" (Notice I didn't say we'd visualize "no rain." When we focus on "no" and "rain," we call in exactly what we don't want!)

Our set-up consisted of a child-sized card table covered with a holiday table cloth, a few chairs, more musical instruments, signs, the picture of the goat from the Heifer catalog and eight kids, ages five to sixty. With four dozen cookies to sell, we started at 11:00 a.m., planning to go until about 2:00. A few kids even put in some of their own money to get things started. Whenever we heard or saw cars round the corner, we yelled, "Cookies for goats," "Donations only" and whatever else came to mind. Many people smiled or waved, others continued on. A good number of people stopped to see what we were up to and we started off strong, making $50 in the first hour. The experience was exhilarating. We were almost halfway there!

After that, there were a few lulls in traffic and the giving slowed as a result. We adjusted our marketing plan, sent out some texts to friends and neighbors, and decided to move an easel slightly down the road to get additional attention. Equally important, we joined again in visioning our goal of $120 and imagined helping to change a family's life with the gift of a goat.

By about 1:30, there'd been another surge in traffic, and we were getting closer and closer to our goal. When our neighbor Steve came home, my daughter and I went over to tell him what we were doing. He was so moved, he pulled out a $20 bill and handed it to Tessa. Her face lit up as if she had just received the only Christmas gift she'd asked for. I started jumping up and down, and told him that we had only $7 to go before reaching our goal. Steve instantly opened his wallet and pulled out two fives, saying that we had made his day.

We were all so excited. We had met our goal with time to spare! Rather than stopping there, we decided to keep up the momentum. With thirty minutes to go, we envisioned raising another $40 for an additional two sets of chicks.

When all was said and done, we raised $194 dollars that day. After putting in $6 to make it an even $200, we were able to buy a goat and *four* sets of chicks. Not only did we get to help five families, each person involved in the adventure experienced the power of releasing our agenda and joining together in a greater vision for what was highest and best for all!

The following year was equally magical. We upped the ante and went for a water buffalo at $250. We invited the same friends, plus more. Though a few doubts came up, we were each able to feel how wonderful it would be to meet our goal in one afternoon. We were a battalion, screaming at the end of the driveway.

This past year, we were met with a slight challenge. The donations really didn't flow as quickly as in years past. The first guy that stopped was a young fellow, driving an old, red Honda Civic. English was his second language but he appeared to get what we were doing. He said he was going to work and that he'd be back later. Before long, as many people went by and a few more donations came in, I forgot about the encounter.

After a couple of hours, the momentum slowed and a large group of kiddos navigated inside to play. Though I wasn't ready to give up, I understood it had been a long day. With roughly $70 to go, I asked them if they would be willing to come back out for just twenty minutes more. When they agreed, I asked that they pull all their energy together and imagine the feeling of celebrating our ability to purchase a water buffalo. We focused on the family, likely from Vietnam, who would use the gift to plow fields. This would be a game changer—with that type of animal they could go from a small family garden to a farm.

Not long after, the old red Honda rounded the corner. It was the young man who had been our first "customer." In broken English he told me about work and handed me a stack of money bound with a rubber band. As I looked at what he was wearing and pieced together that he must have been kitchen staff at a local restaurant, I hesitated. This was a lot of money. Sensing my reluctance, he held up his hand, refusing to take anything back. I felt the smile on his face in my soul, touched that he was giving from a place of such heart-based generosity.

We had reached our goal. For the next 24 hours my family could talk of nothing else. Imagining the Vietnamese family, now able to make a living with their farm, we were filled with thanksgiving.

Who knows what we'll aim for this year? Maybe a heifer? As long as we believe it's possible, it'll happen.

Action Peace—Gratitude Journal

Find a new or unfilled notebook and convert it to a gratitude journal. Prior to heading off to bed each evening, list three to five things you are grateful for. It's amazing what this simple step can do to change your perspective. Just like focusing on the good feelings that go with a new story, writing what you are thankful for shifts the mind to pleasurable thoughts and feelings. As you relax and enjoy reliving those moments, you set the stage to receive more of the same the next day.

Action Peace—Proactively Create

In the book *E2*, Pam Grout suggests focusing on a butterfly and seeing how it will come into your day. I did this on a chilly November morning, after butterflies had pretty much vanished for the year. Letting go of how I would see butterflies in November, I embraced the fun of witnessing the creative power of intention and focus.

Within three hours, I received three butterfly experiences: Tessa found an old picture of Andrew with a butterfly on his head; the kids and I came across the song "Mariposa" (Spanish for butterfly) while searching the internet for something else entirely; and, as I got into my car after dropping the kids off at school, another song with "butterfly" in the chorus came on. I was exhilarated.

Take a moment to think of an experience that would simply be fun. This is your opportunity to play with Infinite Love.

1. What will you proactively create?

2. What will it feel like to have that experience?

Image those feelings as they fill your body. Now, release any attachment to what the outcome needs to look like. Move through your day with curiosity and wonderment—Infinite Love will likely surprise you in ways you'd least expect.

Action Peace—Revisit the Harmony Rating Scale

In the last four chapters, you have had a chance to practice the Four C's. You've thought about, worked with and, in many cases, shifted your old patterns and beliefs.

Before proceeding to **The Third Peace, *Moving Forward,*** take this opportunity to fill in your Harmony Rating Scale one more time. Once completed, revisit your responses in the scale from Chapter 1.

Reflect on what has shifted for you and your family since you started this process.

Today's Date: _____

Scale:

1 = Almost No Harmony
2 = Very Little Harmony
3 = Some Harmony
4 = Frequent Harmony
5 = Almost Total Harmony

AREA OF CONCERN	RATE 1-5	CURRENT OBSERVATIONS
Your Child's Areas of Concern		
Academic Performance		
Attention to Tasks		
Following Instructions		
Problem Solving		
Ability to Plan/Organize		
Impulsivity		
Ability to Complete Familiar Routing		
Motivation		
Behaviors at Home		

AREA OF CONCERN	RATE 1-5	CURRENT OBSERVATIONS
Your Child's Areas of Concern		
Behaviors at School		
Frustration/Tolerance		
Tantrums/Meltdowns (+Duration/Frequency)		
Handling Transitions		
Adapting to Change		
Anxiety		
Self-esteem		
Mood		
Social Skills		
Interactions with Parent(s)		
Interactions with Sibling(s)		
Interactions with Peers		
Appropriate Play		
Sensory Challenges		
Self-care		
Physical Strength		
Motor Skills		
Coordination		

AREA OF CONCERN	RATE 1-5	CURRENT OBSERVATIONS
Your Areas of Concern		
Anxiety		
Stress		
Family Dynamics in General		
Relationship with Spouse		
Relationship with Child(ren)		
Self-care		
Other (Note Area)		
Other (Note Area)		

Action Peace—Create What You Most Deeply Desire

Select three areas from the Harmony Rating Scale above on which to focus your Four C's efforts. Try one minor area, one of medium difficulty and one that is really challenging. List them below, along with what it might look and feel like to move into a new story in each area. Remember, when choosing your new feelings, do so as if what you desire is already a reality.

1. Area 1: _____
   What your new story might look like:

   The feelings that accompany your new story:

2. Area 2: _____
   What your new story might look like:

   The feelings that accompany your new story:

3. Area 3: _____
   What your new story might look like:

   The feelings that accompany your new story:

The Third Peace

✷

Moving Forward

IN THE **FIRST Peace—Getting Clear**, you became aware of your story, revealed your hidden patterns and beliefs and exposed the contents of your backpack. You also acknowledged your triggers and have started to experience who you really are—your True Self.

In the **Second Peace—The Power Tools**, you were presented with a go-to sequence, the Four C's, to guide you toward shifting into the life you most deeply desire—a life of family cooperation, loving communication and a genuine connection with yourself, your loved ones and Divine Love.

I'm sure it's clear by now that *The Connected Parent* approach doesn't just address surface symptoms—we're going pretty deep here. As you continue to shift from old patterns to a beautiful new story, your kids will feel that shift and respond in kind.

What's fascinating is that, at some point, you'll witness a former triggering event (i.e. a child's tantrum or an argument between siblings) and observe yourself remaining calm and peaceful throughout. You'll almost be beside yourself at the level of peace and ease you experience. I've found that this is a key step in this process. Once your needs are met, you can remain unaffected by what goes on around you and you'll be willing and able to address the needs of your kiddos. Before you know it, some of those triggers will melt away—they just won't appear to occur anymore. And, some will stick around. The difference is that you now know there are tools to get you through. You'll always have the Four C's to turn to at any given moment.

In the **Third Peace—Moving Forward**, we will expand on key concepts that will inspire you to stay on the path of abundant peace and joy, and to remember that when you get lost or fall from the path, it's okay. It really is. Such times offer another opportunity to love yourself, reconnect to Infinite Love and feel empowered all over again.

CHAPTER 11

Judgment versus Discernment
Know Your Peace

"Daddy, it's not that you're a bad cook, it's that
the food you make tastes bad."

~ Tessa, age 5

JUDGMENT IS AN automatic response that occurs without thought. Something comes up and, before we know it, we are long gone in another world—one in which we "know" what is right and wrong, or how our children, friends or family members "should" think, act, speak and feel. Judgment is fuel for the ego. Becoming aware of this is, of course, the first step. From there, though, what can we do?

Moving into a place of discernment is a powerful next action. To discern is to recognize, spot, or perceive, without judgment. In this context, discernment is being able to think and/or say, "This (situation, person, action) is just not for me. There's need to label it good or bad, it's just not something I am choosing." Or, alternately, "This (situation, person, action) is what I choose for me." We always have a choice—whether conscious, meaning we are aware of the choice, or subconscious, meaning it is part of an automatic pattern.

Once you shift and begin parenting from a clearer, more connected perspective, many opportunities will arise to help you discern what you desire and intend for yourself and your family. As they do, you may begin to notice the way others talk to or act in the presence of their children. Or you may observe characteristics in others that run counter to the path you've chosen for your family. After feeling whatever emotions come up for you and choosing a technique to let them go, remember that you can easily shift from any tendency toward judgment to a place of compassion and discernment, knowing others are free to make their choices, just as you are free to decide what is and is not for you. Discernment also helps us know when to take mindful, productive action. We do not need to tolerate abusive or inappropriate behavior.

In addition to a heightened awareness of your judgment of others, an inclination toward self-judgment may also intensify. Guilt, blame and shame may be lingering in the shadows, ready to reactivate old patterns and wounds whenever we judge, or feel judged by, others.

Client Triumph—Freed from the Binds of Judgment

I shared the concept of judgment versus discernment in a class I taught several years ago, explaining how clarity in this area can truly shift interpersonal dynamics *without* the verbal exchange we so often feel is necessary.

At the second class, one attendee, I'll call her Mandy, shared how she had put what we'd learned into action. Driving to a family reunion, with her husband and children asleep in the car, Mandy found herself ruminating over past incidents and unresolved conflicts. As myriad issues arose for each extended family member, Mandy was able to look within and compassionately observe the one who was feeling triggered by these events—herself.

In doing so, Mandy recognized that her relatives weren't good or bad, they simply made choices or set priorities that were meaningful to them. She could even consider that these were neither good nor bad. She witnessed herself judging their actions, loving and forgiving them and herself, and then moved into discernment—asking what it was she wanted for herself and her family.

Mandy had a spectacular week at the reunion—the best she could recall. As a result, she became a firm believer that doing her own work—releasing resentment, guilt, anger, shame and blame—was enough to at least shift her perception of people and events from the past. Freed from the limits she placed on herself when judging others, she was empowered to take charge of what she really wanted.

What we can learn from Mandy's experience is exciting. All it took was four hours to release years' worth of judgment, which led to forgiving herself and her family members. She was ready for a shift and did the work.

Let's not get ahead of ourselves, though. To help us make the shift from judgment to discernment, we will benefit from addressing one of the biggest barriers to peace and clarity. Do you recall that, in Chapter 6, I requested you take a vacation from guilt? Well, it's finally time to address this deeply held emotion that can lead to a lifetime of inaccurate, limiting beliefs and negative patterns.

The History of Guilt in our Lives

Guilt does not need to go hand in hand with parenting. Before I convince you of how worthless it is, however, let's look at its origin in our lives.

Guilt is an invasive derivation of fear. A dominant theme in many of our childhoods, it took on many faces, often as a powerful means for manipulation and shame. It might have been used to make a point or to get us to stop, or start, doing something. Guilt had an immeasurable influence on us and could be set in motion through a single look from a parent or authority figure. It was like an invisible force that controlled our every move.

Guilt affects people differently, depending on their unique personality. For somewhat compliant children with a strong desire to please, guilt kept us in check, as the idea of pleasing others drastically outweighed the benefits of doing something that would get us in trouble. If we were a bit more adventurous, guilt acted as punishment or reprimand. And if we were flat out defiant, guilt was used to manipulate and shame us.

Many adults in our lives saw guilt as a very good thing, as it kept our willful thoughts and unspeakable desires under control. This method and its perceived benefits are often passed down from generation to generation, like a family recipe. We only needed it to be modeled a few times by one or two predominant adult figures before we incorporated it into our experience. It likely remains a part of who we think we are to this day—errant beings, trying our best to do the right thing.

As children, we learned to weigh the pros and cons of our choices in order to determine what was more valuable—the "bad," guilt-ridden action we felt driven to do or the "good," guilt-free action the adults in our lives would have us do. For many, early childhood experiences in which we did not make the preferred choice initiated a pattern of self-judgment. More importantly, we came to believe we actually *were* these choices. On some level, guilt and its counterparts—shame, blame and fear—felt like punishments we deserved. On another level, they felt totally foreign and horrible.

When faced with a choice, neither approach truly serves us, right? How in the world can something as destructive as guilt play a positive role in our lives?

What is available to us here and now is a shift in perception. We can choose to address and release guilt. We can see and embrace the truth that we are not our actions, choices, failures or mistakes. We are beings of Infinite Love who happen to have made certain choices. I will say it again in a different way:

You are a unique creation of Love, who is temporarily (and over and over again) forgetting this. Embrace this truth and see how it changes your relationship with yourself and your children.

Releasing Residual Guilt

One of the reasons guilt influences us to such an extreme degree today is because of what we carry from the past. Think about it—there's survivor's guilt, guilt over actions taken, guilt over actions not taken, guilt about choices we made in our youth, and in our relationships, careers, and finances. The list goes on and on.

We may be tempted to believe that, while we can make changes in current situations, the past is the past and we are stuck with our old choices and the corresponding consequences. Well, that may be true, if you believe that you deserve to suffer your entire life for these choices. Once you tap into the love that is available to us all, however, you will realize that it is possible to release residual guilt from the past. In fact, this holds true for any emotion we've been holding onto.

Memories are stored, energetically, in our body. When we experience a trigger that elicits feelings of guilt, we may be linking into a very old memory. Remember, as Joe Dispenza says, "Neurons that fire together, wire together."

In other words, the feelings of lack, inadequacy and guilt that come up for us today feel familiar and are therefore strangely welcome in our body and experience. To shift those old memories, we simply do our Four C's work retroactively.

Choose a memory and take yourself back to that specific time and place. Consciously Observe what happened. Feel the arising feelings for whatever period of time you select. Let yourself cry, scream and punch pillows if necessary. Re-Connect to Infinite Love. Choose a method to shift the feelings and corresponding beliefs, and Co-Create a new story in which you are totally free from these limitations. Bring in the feelings of freedom, ease, relaxation and gratitude.

If something surfaces that needs further action, you'll know. Trust yourself. You will be able to move forward with an apology if that is what feels right. If the person you feel you wronged has passed away or you don't know how to reach them, have a meditation conversation with their True Self (more on this in the next chapter). If you feel someone else owes you something, go back in and do more releasing. Peel off yet another layer.

If, once you've taken these steps, you still feel attached to the guilt, blame or shame, or if you think you deserve punishment, let me share one last thought: Are you really serving yourself and your family by holding on to this belief? What would happen for your children if you let go of past decisions, choosing to no longer let them define you? I'll tell you: They, like you, will come into a knowing of who *they* really are—a Divine being in a physical body who makes certain choices.

"Well, then, you might ask, "if our choices don't define us, what does?"

Infinite Love.

Stay with me, and let's keep going with this.

Stepping into Discernment

Again, judgment is a way of viewing someone or something as being one of two polar opposites—right/wrong, good/bad, blessing/curse, etc.

What if we don't categorize our choices as "good" or "bad"? What if they just *are*? Well, if our choices just are, we have the opportunity to discern how we feel about them. If we like how we feel and our choices are in alignment with what we most desire for ourselves and our families, we can keep making similar choices. If we don't like how we feel, we can make different choices. It is that simple.

When we make our choices from the perspective of our True Self, we experience our life and decisions from a place of love and discernment. From this place, we experience the freedom and true power to consciously choose our path. If that choice doesn't work out, it doesn't change who we are—we simply have the opportunity to choose again.

The following story is a perfect illustration of how this might look. Sometimes I still can't believe what I chose!

A Personal Peace—No Need for Sacrifice

A couple of years ago, I was out to dinner with two very good friends. One shared how much she loved spending time at the barn with her horse. I could feel her passion and the enjoyment she received in pursuing an interest she had dreamed about for years. The other friend told us about a recent tennis tournament and what she'd learned in observing the dynamics between teammates. It felt great to be in the presence of two peers who knew their worth and found time to engage so fully in their personal interests.

As I was listening, I suddenly realized I didn't have a hobby. How had that happened? In the past, I had done yoga, painted, traveled, danced, and more. I had also played tennis and even worked with horses. Without even being aware of it, I had given up all of my interests. Instead, I was always either working or with my family, two things that are certainly very important to me.

Now, from an ego perspective, this fact could go on my scorecard as a point to the positive—my being "good"— and lead to feelings of resentment and a pattern of martyrdom. Or I could discern it like this: I like how it feels to work and give time and attention to my family. It isn't good or bad that I don't have a hobby, and I would still like one.

In that moment, though, my experience was that I felt like I had "lost" myself. How was it that I could not think of one thing I did just for me?

When my friends were finished sharing, I opened up to them. I admitted I was feeling a bit distraught over the realization that I didn't appear to have any hobbies.

After a moment of loving empathy, they asked, "What do you like to do?" The first thing that popped out of my mouth was "travel." Of all of my past interests, that was the one that seemed the most unrealistic. I wasn't talking about visiting relatives or taking family trips to the beach or mountains, which I also love. I was talking about *adventure,* traveling to Europe or on a cross country road trip—the kind of journey where you have a rough plan to visit an unfamiliar place and surprises lurk around every corner. At one time, this type of travel had fed my soul.

We finished dinner and I put the conversation aside. I kept an awareness that I wanted to start doing more for myself, but I didn't feel like making any plans just yet. I remained busy with kiddos, family and work activities.

Two weeks later, I received a call from my best friend from college. She had earned an all-expenses paid trip to Quebec and was inviting me as her guest. "Wow!" I thought, "That was fast!" With my husband in full support of my going, there was only one catch—the trip was scheduled for the same weekend as my daughter's very first dance recital.

How could this be? Hadn't Infinite Love placed this trip in my path because I put in an order for travel? I hadn't been attached to the outcome and, truthfully, hadn't even thought about it since that evening. Now that this offer of Quebec had arrived, however, my mind was flooded with thoughts of martyrdom and victimhood. Why did this conflict have to arise? Of course I wanted to be with my daughter, to celebrate and support her. I couldn't miss her first recital... or could I?

No.

Well... maybe.

Oh, my. I knew I would be the worst mom in the world if I chose to miss my daughter's first recital to go on vacation with a friend. What would my family think? My friends?

As you can imagine, it was quite a dilemma. At least that's how I saw it at the time. I decided I would very carefully work through the decision-making process in the two days I had until giving my friend an answer. I wouldn't talk to my momma friends or my parents, as I really felt I wouldn't get an objective perspective. And anyway, I wasn't looking for advice, just someone to bounce my thoughts off of.

I called one of my friends from dinner. She shared in my joy and listened to my concern about the conflict. Without hesitation, she said, "I sure hope you're going on the trip." Her support and enthusiasm brought a lightheartedness to the situation that I had not yet felt.

I started to play with the idea of going to Quebec. I considered my daughter in ten or even twenty years. Of course I wanted to see her perform, *and* the idea of saying no to this adventure seemed like a sacrifice of sorts. (Sacrifice is an old story of mine, and of many other moms.)

If I attended my daughter's recital out of a sense of obligation or guilt, would that really serve her? Or, would it be more of a service if I were to break the chain of martyrdom and sacrifice? What was better—having a mom who knows her own worth and so believes she deserves to take advantage of an extraordinary opportunity for a free trip with a friend? Or a mom who would give up such a trip to watch a short performance at a dance recital? This is an oversimplification but you get my point.

I'm sure you've guessed by now that I chose to go on the trip. The looks and comments I got from a few of the dance moms when they heard my decision told me I was certainly in the minority. However, I had done enough inner work to release any sense of guilt. In fact, it was more of a symbolic success for me to claim what I knew to be true: I need not sacrifice for another to gain. Everyone, including my daughter, has exactly what they need within. Nor am I responsible for another's happiness, as we are all directly linked to Infinite Love and don't *need* anything from outside ourselves in order to be happy and whole.

On a practical level, when I told Tessa of my choice to go on the trip, she *was* sad at first. Careful to first let her feel what came up, I shared my decision-making process. Though I didn't need her permission, it felt fabulous to share my passion for travel with her and to discuss that this did not lessen my love for her. Both could occur simultaneously. Just as nothing would ever compromise my love, no action based in fear or lack, like skipping the trip due to a sense of guilt, could prove my love. I ended by telling her that love is ever-present, and transcends both space and time. From her reaction, I could tell she understood this on both a surface and a soul level.

I then asked if she would like to hold a private dress rehearsal in our living room. She agreed and did wonderfully. In addition, the teacher allowed me to sit in on their last class and watch the whole group perform. I called my daughter on the morning of the recital and told her I was with her in her heart, always. My husband gave her flowers and a little note from me on her special day. No, I wasn't there physically, but we are so connected, I was definitely there in spirit. Most importantly, Tessa came away from the experience with a deeper understanding that she is always connected to Infinite Love.

Aside from the actual trip itself, this beautiful situation was a gift in a number of ways. For one, I have become more purposeful in co-creating new stories and opportunities for myself and my family; when making an intention, I always include the phrase "for the highest and best for all involved, with grace and ease." I also received a lesson about the joy found in releasing notions of guilt and sacrifice, and know now that conflict is not necessary. When an issue does come up, I know there is an opportunity for discernment.

While judgment might lead some to label a decision to go to Quebec "bad," and a decision to stay "good," discernment allowed me to step back and choose what was "for" me or "not for" me. There have been plenty of other times when I decided to postpone or cancel something I'd planned in order to meet the request or need of a family member, client or friend. The key is in embracing the opportunity to make choices from a place of clarity and peace. I refuse to do anything out of guilt or obligation.

This situation also provided my daughter with a valuable lesson. When she finds herself battling with the idea of doing something out of guilt or obligation, I remind her of this story. She totally gets it, knowing she is able to discern what choice is "for" or "not for" her. When children know that they are infinitely loved and that they do not need to allow fear and lack to guide their decisions, they are more likely to make choices that are in alignment with love and abundance.

Parenting with Discernment and Listening to One's True Self

In much of our culture, guilt, blame and shame are viewed as highly benefi-cial in deciding between "right" and "wrong." Many parenting approaches are rooted in the use of guilt and fear as a way to control children's actions. If we have not yet released our own fear and guilt based patterns and beliefs, we may have also employed such approaches, either knowingly or unknowingly.

No one is a bad parent because they've relied on guilt to try to teach their child how to act, how to treat others or to respect the environment. As we do our own work, however, we have an opportunity to discern what we really want for our family. Does it feel good to teach from guilt and fear and obligation? Do we want more of these feelings in our relationships, or less? What do *you* want?

What if we could teach and guide our children through unconditional love, as opposed to shame and guilt? I'm not suggesting that kids be allowed to do anything they want without consequences. I am saying that it is beneficial to be clear with our intentions and to live through discernment rather than judgment.

When we love ourselves unconditionally, despite all of our perceived faults and failures, and when we don't allow our faults and failures to define us, we automatically move toward discernment. And, when children live in the pres-ence of a parent or guardian practicing discernment, they learn the power of operating from one's True Self.

For instance, I can discern that it doesn't feel good to see a child destroy a piece of furniture, hit a sibling or talk harshly to a friend. Yet, I know in my heart that my child's identity is not based upon his or her actions, just as I know my actions don't define me. My choices are my choices and they cannot change the deepest truth within me—I am a unique expression of Infinite Love. The same is true for our children.

Whenever I realize I am in a state of temporarily forgetting this, I can take responsibility and clear what's in my backpack. This allows me to address what is going on with my child in the most effective, loving way possible. And, if my child is in a state of forgetting who he or she is—making choices that are not in alignment with their highest and best—I have the opportunity to direct him or her toward remembering, through whatever conversation, action or consequence is "for" me, and "for" my child.

What This May Look Like—Free the Flow of Love

As I sat considering examples to solidify this concept, my son and daughter came into the room. They were arguing. (I told you this stuff still happens from time to time. The difference is that now I know what to do.) (*And*, sometimes I still forget.)

Based on what they each shared, I made the decision that it would be best if they took a break from one another. I felt this was fair and I wanted to move on with our day. In other words, I just wanted the situation to be over. I wanted my son to see my point and not have any more needs.

Andrew made it clear this decision was not what he wanted. He wanted to play with his sister or me rather than take the break I'd suggested. He continued to press—now arguing with me—and insisted I loved his sister more than I loved him. He obviously had an unmet need, yet, because I felt triggered, I slipped into judgment, of his words, his choices and his actions. I saw him as wrong and myself as right, and neither of us was willing to back down.

Caught up in the moment, I began to judge myself as well. Wasn't there a magic phrase that would get him to see I was right? What was it? I teach this stuff! Shouldn't I know exactly what to say?

And then it struck me: I was seeing my son as separate from me and from Infinite Love, which I can only do if I, too, am in a state of feeling separate. I had unintentionally stopped the flow of love to my son and, subsequently, to myself, like a dam to a river.

The irony of this hit me as I noted what chapter I was working on—I was so obviously in a state of judgment. I know it is impossible to come to a peaceful and loving resolution when feeling separate from another. As I paused, looking within and witnessing the one doing the judging, I felt compassion for myself and my children.

I discerned that I did not want fear-based, un-conscious communication in my home. I shifted into loving and accepting myself for allowing an old pattern to resurface. This self-love helped me move more powerfully into the perspective of my True Self. From this vantage point, I could witness the truth of my son. He just wanted to know he wasn't being left out of anything. He wanted to be seen and heard and loved unconditionally. As I tuned into this and committed to seeing him as connected to me and Infinite Love, the words and actions I chose were in alignment with my new, more conscious intention.

Perhaps you're wondering exactly what I said or did next. But that is not nearly as important as what I felt—compassion, connection, peace, forgiveness and love—for myself and my kids. And my son clearly got it. In a single moment, he shifted from being tense and argumentative to loving and relaxed.

Connection is the real key. There are no magic words that work in every situation. Just connect to your True Self and know your oneness with Infinite Love and your oneness with your children. From there, whatever you say or choose will be perfect.

Compassionate communication is powerful. *And,* if we don't take care of the root cause of our upsets—the fear of feeling separate from one another and from Infinite Love—we can become masters at communicating while continuing to act from our negative patterns. That is why, as important as loving, effective interactions are, I feel it's most important to clear our stuff first. I say this over and over because I, too, benefit from regular reminders.

There are situations where taking the time to address and clear old patterns and beliefs is not possible. None of us are going to stop to meditate and release when our child is running toward the street or taking scissors to the living room curtains. Safety comes first. Such situations are yet another time to discern: "I will step in and make sure everyone is safe *and* I will address my frustration (or fear or anger) in a few minutes."

Once we are clear and living more and more from our True Self, it gets easier to guide our children. The words and actions that demonstrate the support and love they desire and deserve will appear, with grace and ease.

Action Peace—Clarity and Discernment

In the space below, list several judgments you've made in the past, good and bad. Once you've completed the list, go back through and, in each case, flip that judgment to discernment—decide what is "for" you and "not for" you.

For example:

1. **Good**   **Bad**
   Talking respectfully   Using harsh words or
   within the family.   a condescending tone.

Discernment

My kids are hungry and tired. I am going to let this one slide.

Or

I discern that it's "for" me that we all speak respectfully to one another.
I choose to say, "I hear that you are feeling sad and frustrated. And,
mutual respect is of the utmost importance.
You may not speak to me that way."

Or

"I don't like how that sounded. Would you be willing
to say that differently?"
(Also known as a "redo," see Chapter 15)

2. **Good**   **Bad**
   Making donations—   Acquiring just to have—
   Generosity   Greed

Discernment

I like this pair of shoes and I don't need them. I won't buy them.

Or

I feel good wearing these shoes. They're comfortable and
I will wear them often. I'll buy them.

Now, try this exercise yourself:

3. Good   **Bad**

             Discernment

4. Good   **Bad**

             Discernment

5. Good   **Bad**

             Discernment

Action Peace—Guilt from the Past

Take some time to clear out your backpack. Review the following bullet points with the intention of digging up old feelings, beliefs and patterns so that you can release guilt and discern what you want for yourself right now.

1. Childhood:

I see that I made these judgments:

_____

_____

_____

_____

I discern that _____ isn't good or bad.

And, I want more _____ in my life and

less _____.

2. Teen years:
I see that I made these judgments:

_____

_____

_____

_____

I discern that _____ isn't good or bad.
And, I want more _____ in my life and
less _____.

3. Young Adulthood:
I see that I made these judgments:

_____

_____

_____

_____

I discern that _____ isn't good or bad.
And, I want more _____ in my life and
less _____.

4. Past romantic relationship(s):
I see that I made these judgments:

_____

_____

_____

_____

I discern that _____ isn't good or bad.
And, I want more _____ in my life and
less _____.

5. With my parents and/or siblings:
I see that I made these judgments:

_____

_____

_____

_____

I discern that _____ isn't good or bad.
And, I want more _____ in my life and
less _____ .

6. With my spouse, partner or ex:
I see that I made these judgments:

_____

_____

_____

_____

I discern that _____ isn't good or bad.
And, I want more _____ in my life and
less _____ .

7. During my child's infancy:
I see that I made these judgments:

_____

_____

_____

_____

I discern that _____ isn't good or bad.
And, I want more _____ in my life and
less _____ .

8. In my family life:
I see that I made these judgments:

_____

_____

_____

_____

I discern that _____ isn't good or bad.

And, I want more _____ in my life and

less _____ .

CHAPTER 12

Forgiveness and Self-Love
Be Your Own Best Friend

"You know what is importantest of all?
Loving yourself."

~ ANDREW, AGE 4½

As you recall, "Choose Forgiveness and Love" is one of the third "C" options in Chapter 9. Genuine forgiveness and *self*-love are so essential in this work, I've given each it's own chapter.

So much of the time, we focus on our children without making the time or effort to attend to our own needs. Yet, as we've discussed, it's equally important to put a little emphasis on yourself—your feelings, your needs and the steps you can take to commit to loving yourself.

As parents, even conscious parents, we are going to make mistakes daily, maybe even hourly. Once we recognize we've done so, we tend to respond with feelings of guilt, blame and shame. What would happen if we changed this dynamic, objectively observing these so-called mistakes and choosing to love and forgive ourselves immediately? How would our lives and those of our children be different if we chose Infinite Love for ourselves in every moment? I'm talking about Divine Love here, not conditional love or love that is dependent on our scorecard. When we choose to love and forgive ourselves the minute we recognize our slips, we create an environment of implicit self-acceptance. This guides our children, on an unspoken level, to respond in kind, opening the gateway to positive growth and happiness.

So, what if the key to to more respect in the home, fewer tantrums, less struggle over homework, chores, bedtime, etc. is that we, the people who brought our children into the world, simply decide to love ourselves uncondi-tionally? Radical idea, huh? I can here you thinking, "How can self-love be so powerful?" When parents choose love and forgiveness, love and forgiveness are magnetized for the whole family.

That's why I believe self-love is the fastest route to reprograming our old patterns, which are typically steeped in anger, fear, and resentment. Love dilutes these feelings, robbing them of their power. And, it is very difficult to proceed down an automatic path of limiting thoughts and behaviors while loving ourselves.

How far are you willing to go with self-love?

Client Triumph—What About my Daughter?

In many of my on-going classes, I first and foremost address the roles, actions, choices and feelings of parents. Those who attend hoping for a quick fix can be thrown off when they realize we will be discussing them rather than strategizing to fix their kiddos.

After the first class of a series, one mom, Deb, emailed me about her 13-year-old daughter, who experienced intense symptoms of ADHD. Her daughter was, she said, disorganized and late to school every day; homework took up to six hours a night. In summary, she wrote:

At my daughter's request, we wake her up extra early but she doesn't get out of bed. We have tried typical "consequences," such as not allowing her to go to social events and taking away her phone, but nothing seems to be improving. Carpool to school and other func-tions is very stressful because I don't want her to inconvenience others due to her lack of time management. Will we cover anything of this nature in the class?

Reading her email, I smiled. This is a common question, a para-phrased "So, when do we talk about what to do when a kid…"

In our second class, I offered a couple of practical strategies but stuck with my main focus—reminding the mommas to be in aware-ness of their story in order to identify negative patterns and limiting beliefs. Something happened for Deb in that class... she started to *get it*. Realizing this was a huge opportunity, she opened her heart to seeing things differently. I ended class with a visualization technique, during which we released past memories, emotions, challenges, feelings and fears.

Upon returning the third week, Deb was on fire! She announced that she'd been experiencing so much love, it was unbelievable. First, she'd decided to focus less and less energy on what her daughter *wasn't* doing and more on connecting with herself and with her teenager. Though she didn't experience any monumental shifts in regard to her daughter's ability to manage time and attend to tasks, their relationship felt closer than it ever had. More than that, she'd felt something awaken within herself. By letting go of numerous burdens, Deb was able to propel her own personal growth. Not surprisingly, her daughter noticed, lightly teasing Deb about her "new ways."

Even after the class ended, Deb kept up her work, loving herself and peeling away layers of ego fear that had started in her childhood.

Deb recently contacted me to share an update. Her daughter had approached her, saying she felt depressed and wanted to talk to someone. Rather than leap to a state of anxiety as she might have done in the past, Deb stayed grounded and told her daughter they would do whatever they needed to get her help. The level of their connection and Deb's confidence that all would work out created a beautiful space for her daughter to share her feelings and begin to learn to navigate life's challenges.

By making her work a priority and choosing to love herself, Deb became truly present for her daughter, which ultimately resulted in a connection that transcended the limitations of her diagnosis. Is there more work for them to do? Sure. Is Deb ready to do that work? Yes. By loving herself, she is able to open up more completely to love and guide her daughter.

As we are redefining so many terms here, let's look at forgiveness in a new light as well.

Genuine Forgiveness

What does it really mean to forgive? When I use this term, I am not referring to the interpretation of our childhood, which often sounded like this:

Parent to you: "You stepped on your brother's foot. Say you're sorry."

Parent to your sibling: "Now, forgive her."

The essence of our True Self goes beyond words, and so it is with true forgiveness. Forgiveness is a way of being, an immeasurable gift. When you are filled with love for yourself and another, triggering events don't even seem to matter. And yet, here's the thing—as great as this sounds, sometimes it's really difficult to get past the trigger. Trust me, I've been there—repeatedly.

One thing that helps me in such situations is to have an imaginary conversation with the other person. Whether this is a parent, friend, significant other or child, I find this an effective way to release my thoughts and feelings. So, when I'm ready for a true shift in perception, I light a candle, get myself some tea and settle down for a meditative conversation.

This is the one time I consciously let my ego roar. I say whatever I want, however I want, holding back nothing. I purge everything. If past triggers resurface, I purge those as well. Sometimes, I envision myself yelling at the person, using fear-based victim phrases like, "How could you do this to me?" or "Why is this still happening?"

Typically, this process elicits a great deal of emotion, which I often release through crying. When there is nothing left in me—no more anger, resentment, sadness, etc.—I picture myself just sitting with the other person. Then, I ask to see their True Self. At that point, I can see and feel their presence through the eyes of Infinite Love. And this leads me to forgive them.

From that place of forgiveness, I can see they were simply playing a role in my story. I unintentionally cast them in that role—the very one that initially triggered me. Without exception, I conclude by turning inward, and forgiving myself.

What This May Look Like—Withholding (Self) Love

For years, I felt resentment toward a particular friend. She was older, almost a mother-figure in a way. Though we were close, I perceived that she only loved me when I acted a certain way, said certain things or made particular choices. Not surprisingly, we recently had an explosive discussion.

What exploded? Me. I had bottled up tons of feelings I thought I had worked through and one night I just vomited them all out. (Sorry for the gross metaphor but, as a parent, I know you can handle it!)

My friend was blindsided. I didn't hold back, even though I could see she didn't understand all that I was saying. I'm not even sure I was coherent. When I finished, she took her turn, spilling her emotions about me. It wasn't a pretty sight.

With plenty of tears on both sides, we did our best to mend the perceived wounds of this conversation. Needless to say, we both felt raw, vulnerable and more than a bit shaken.

After a few days of feeling "bruised" by this encounter, I was ready meditate on it. (Notice my process here: I felt my feelings for a few days, then, when I was ready, I went inward to do the work.) Arriving at the root cause of my emotions, I found myself in a state of complete peace. I had been withholding unconditional love from my friend because I felt she should offer it to me first. After all, she was older and had more life experience. I had, quite unconsciously, placed her in a mother role.

Finally, I was ready to have a conversation meditation, as described above. In it, I released the fears and sadness I had been carrying in our relationship. I chose to unconditionally love and forgive my friend, without expectation for anything in return. After offering myself this same forgiveness, I felt free, light and overwhelmed—this time with love.

I wanted my friend to know that I forgave her but saying so would imply she'd been at fault. After years of believing just the opposite, I truly felt as if there was not an ounce of blame here. I wanted her to know, on a soul level, that I loved her. I called, intending that my words, whichever words came, would reflect that love and forgiveness. Though I never actually said, "I forgive you," our conversation went beautifully.

Since then our relationship has catapulted to a new level. At a recent get-together, she offered personal reflections on a book she was reading that linked our thoughts to our physical health. I had to smile. After years trying to offer these concepts to her, once I gave up and began loving her no matter what, she found them on her own.

Recalling this, I am reminded that withholding forgiveness keeps us bound to the past and blocks us from aligning with love. It is true—we can only love others as much as we love ourselves.

To bring this back to our children, realize that as you expand on self-love and forgiveness, you will be able to love your family more than you ever imagined. Keep in mind that you can revisit a situation at any time. Meaning, if you find that you're holding residual anger or guilt about a past situation, you can hold a conversation meditation with anyone, regardless of when the triggering event occurred. Time is an illusion. There is only now—gift yourself with the joy of releasing old patterns and beliefs so that you can be free and move forward with your new story.

My Love, Your Love, Our Love

Once we forgive, there is nothing left but love.

Love is not something that can be contained. It is contagious, and expands infinitely. Where fear begets fear, love begets love. It is the most powerful force in the Universe. And it must start with us. Why? Because we have no control over others—only ourselves.

By far, the most monumental change I made last year was my commitment to love myself regardless of my thoughts, actions, words and perceived failures and faults. Every time I made a mistake—and there were many—I took the opportunity to say, "Oops, look what I did... and I love myself anyway."

At first, I didn't really feel or believe this to be true. But I stayed with it. When I walked by a mound of dishes in the sink, I said, "I love myself anyway." If I raised my voice to my kids, I said, "I love myself anyway." When I caught myself cutting off a sweet story the kids were telling because we were late, I said, "I love myself anyway."

As I warmed up to the idea, I started to embody this self-love. I found I really *did* accept myself no matter what. Eventually, I stopped doing the things I'd previously seen as mistakes. I stopped raising my voice at my kids or harshly cutting them off when we were rushed. The kitchen started looking cleaner and cleaner.

What happens with our children when we choose to love and forgive ourselves is fascinating. By living in the spirit of self-love and forgiving ourselves for unintended shortcomings, we change our neurological patterns. The old story no longer plays, as we are magnetizing more and more to love about ourselves, our life and our family.

Remember those mirror neurons? Our children spend time in the environment we create. Because we are connected on a very deep level, they absorb the energy we project. They can absorb our stress and guilt or they can absorb acceptance, forgiveness and love. Which will we choose?

A Personal Peace—And I Love Myself Anyway

One evening close to bedtime, my son, who was seven at the time, requested that we write a story together. I enthusiastically jumped at this opportunity, knowing it would be special for both of us. My job was to transcribe as he dictated.

The story started in the woods, with a three-year-old boy who was living alone because his parents had died. The thought that my son might be projecting specific issues crossed my mind, but I was able to put those aside and simply listen.

As he got into the story, however, my ego kicked in. I went from being in the present moment to having an agenda. First I thought about what an amazing, natural chance for learning this was. We could edit the story together, type it up on the computer and maybe even print copies to give to his grandparents. As my thoughts spiraled in this direction, I blurted a suggestion. "Why don't you make the child older?" I asked. "There is no way a three-year-old could live on his own in the wild."

Every time I tell this story, I feel a bit embarrassed at how easily I slipped into ego thoughts during this creative moment. My son didn't allow this pass, with good reason. What he heard was, "Your story stinks. It's unrealistic and stupid." And possibly even "You're stupid," because, as I mentioned earlier, it is sometimes difficult to separate our actions from our identity. He screamed and threw a book across the room.

I immediately knew what I had done. Guilt flooded in as I felt how I had crushed my son's idea and his spirit. I couldn't take it back. While he sulked, I said I was going to get ready for bed and would be back in to see him.

In this time alone, I had a revelation. Yes, I had made a mistake. And I chose to love and forgive myself anyway. I'd fallen into an old pattern of prioritizing an agenda rather than being present with my son, *and* I still loved myself.

I was keenly aware of what typically happened following a "Mommy mistake." Guilt would lead me to allowing my kids to manipulate the situation, i.e., moving bedtime back so we could have a sweet, tender and loooonnnnggg conversation.

Returning to my son, I lovingly and firmly said, "I apologize for correcting your story. You were being creative and I jumped in with a what seemed like an insulting comment. I understand if you don't want to write with me. And, I want you to know that if you do decide to try this another time, I will do my best not to infringe on your ideas. I love and forgive myself for making this mistake and we are not staying up any later than your regular bedtime."

He looked stunned. Mostly, I think, because he could feel that I really had forgiven myself. He went to bed peacefully and, though I didn't request or expect it, I feel he forgave me, too.

We have since worked on similar projects and had a blast. The best result of that evening is that my son gets to grow up in an environment of self-love and self-forgiveness. He gets to experience what it is like to be in the presence of love and compassion.

I also noticed a shift in him after that—he started using an eraser! In the past, he had a pattern of tearing his work to pieces when he wasn't able to produce what he'd imagined in his mind. This was big progress.

Again, loving ourselves regardless of our mistakes is, in my opinion, the fastest way to reprogram our neural pathways. The more we practice, the more we start to link love and acceptance with the thoughts, actions and feelings that previously elicited feelings of guilt. By saying to ourselves, "And I love myself anyway," we release the cycle of trigger, negative thoughts, unfavorable feelings and limiting beliefs. We can observe ourselves and immediately take the opportunity to unconditionally love and forgive.

In what areas do you withhold love from yourself?

Action Peace—Where Do I Withhold Self-Love?

1. On a separate sheet of paper, write the sentence "If only I _____, I could love myself" as many times as you feel moved to, filling in the blank with whatever comes to mind.

    Examples:

    "If only I didn't raise my voice with the kids so much, I could love myself."

    "If only I hadn't eaten half a bag of chips and totally blown my diet, I could love myself."

    "If only I could make money at my hobby, I could love myself."

2. Now, go back and rewrite each sentence to read, "Even though I _____, I love myself anyway."

    Examples:

    "Even though I raise my voice with my kiddos, I love myself anyway."

    "Even though I blew my diet, I love myself anyway."

    "Even though I don't make as much money as I'd like, I love myself anyway."

Action Peace—Meditation Conversation

For this exercise, described in the Genuine Forgiveness section above, set aside some time when you know you won't be interrupted.

Select a person or situation that has been weighing on you. For your first attempt, I suggest this be an adult rather than your child.

Sit quietly and close your eyes.

Imagine the selected person standing in front of you.

Without censoring, allow yourself complete freedom to say whatever is on your mind. Purge it all.

Feel whatever comes up. This can be a form of deep release if you permit it to be.

Ask Infinite Love to reveal the other's True Self. See what happens.

Allow yourself to forgive this person for playing out a role for you.

Forgive yourself for casting them in that role.

Experience a new level of healing and self-love.

If you feel guided, and are able to, have a face to face conversation with the person involved. Set your intention ahead of time and pay attention to your words and thoughts throughout.

Action Peace—Write a Letter

Try writing a letter to a person involved in a recent triggering event or story. This work is 100% for you. The intention is healing, release, forgiveness and love. You will not be sending your letter. It's simply an opportunity to purge all that you have been carrying in regard to the situation.

When the letter is complete, set it aside. Pick it up a few days later and see how you feel. When you read the letter, do you still feel an emotional charge? If so, try re-reading the letter, pausing every once in a while to say, "I love and forgive you."

Jot down your feelings or anything else that comes up as a result of this exercise.

Afterwards, feel free to burn the letter (in a safe way, of course) to symbolize your complete release of the situation.

CHAPTER 13

Response-Ability and Diligence

Commit to Connection

"Mommy, I used to be shy and then I just changed my mind."

~ Tessa, age 4

As I've said, being a Connected Parent is simple but it is not easy. What do I mean by this? Well, it's simple to say, "Just recognize what comes up and let it go." Yet, when it really comes down to it, the easiest way to parent is from an automatic, disengaged and fear-based place where feelings of frustration, anger and resentment can dominate. Doing this work takes "response-ability" and diligence, being committed to your True Self and choosing your thoughts and responses consciously, consistently and continuously.

I want to make it clear that in using the word responsibility I am not implying that anything we observe or experience is our "fault." If I were to do that, we would be right back at the beginning, steeped in our ego and the false beliefs of who we *think* we are. I'm talking about what it means to take responsibility for our own growth. Fault and blame are a result of judgment. We're moving into discerning what we most deeply desire, while asking Infinite Love how best to view each situation.

Taking response-ability means that, in any given moment, we always have the ability to *choose* how we want to respond. Do we want to respond from an ego perspective, with judgment and fear? No. We have discerned that we want to respond from a place of peace and clarity—from the perspective of our True Self. The window to miracles is opened when we take responsibility.

When you find yourself dabbling in former, fear-based patterns, as we all do, you may feel like you're back at square one. This is not the case! You couldn't have made it this far, doing this work, without experiencing a shift. These moments of uncertainty provide an opportunity for us to be response-able and diligent.

How important is peace and ease in your family? Are you willing to move this work and your connection with Infinite Love to the absolute top of your priority list? One could argue that other things in life are more important, but can we really afford to place anything higher than our relationship with Infinite Love and the knowledge of our True Self and the True Selves of our children?

By committing to clear out our negative patterns and limiting beliefs, we reveal the peace and love that have always been there—the hidden peace.

Client Triumph—A Quick Shift

Leslie, whose daughter Mia had been expelled from two schools due to behavior issues, contacted me to inquire about my classes. I answered her questions and she registered for a series that was starting two days later. As we were getting off the phone, she expressed concern about a conference she had at her daughter's school the following day. She felt some urgency about this meeting because she was afraid they were going to suggest finding yet another placement for Mia.

Hearing her apprehension, I offered Leslie a crash course on taking responsibility for how she was viewing the situation and the school's staff—from a place of fear and lack. I explained that it felt as if her story was on replay: She had felt unsupported by the staff at the past two schools, as if no one had her daughter's best interest at heart, and here was a third school, wanting to meet with her.

Sad and frustrated due to past occurrences, Leslie was already on the defensive. She'd hated how the previous schools had treated her daughter. They saw her as a problem child and had been unwilling to "take her on." Ultimately, she didn't like how they had perceived her child.

I explained to Leslie that if she chose to view the current situation through a lens of fear, she would be repeating the very thing she'd found unacceptable in Mia's previous teachers—putting Mia in a box and writing her off without providing the needed support. What would happen, I asked, if she chose to release the old story and observe the new school with eyes of infinite possibility? Maybe things could be different this time. It was at least worth a try.

Leslie called late the next day to say the meeting had gone wonderfully. It turned out the school was not planning to kick Mia out at all. They'd wanted to ask how they could best assist her so she would succeed in her new setting.

Leslie was filed with relief and gratitude and celebrated her new perspective on our first day of class. Over the next few weeks, she continued to experience tremendous shifts within her family, as she fully embraced taking responsibility for what she brought to the table.

Redefining Responsibility

When I recommend that you "take responsibility for" everything in your life, it may sound like I'm placing blame. Especially if you look at dictionary definitions, which all include phrases like having a "duty to" or "control over," and being "accountable for" or even "morally obligated to" something or someone.

What I am talking about is redefining what we *think* it means to take responsibility. Blame and shame are ego traps—old patterns and beliefs bubbling to the surface. Guilt is the ego's response to these false claims. To review what we learned in Chapter 11, Judgment versus Discernment: If nothing is good or bad, it just is, then life provides us with continuous opportunities to love and bless everyone we interact with and everything that occurs.

In this light, it is a *privilege* to do this work. A privilege to be committed to living from who we really are and to who our children really are. We are not bad, they are not bad, just because a mistake is made. In fact, maybe it isn't a mistake at all. Everything is an opportunity to love, to tune in to our True Self and ask Infinite Love what is really going on. What is the truth of the person or situation before me? Unconditional Love leads us to take responsibility for knowing that we are Divine beings who are fortunate enough to realize we can choose to love everyone and everything.

Just to make this super clear—we are never responsible for a negative outcome. That is a trick of the ego. In every moment, we are *response*-able for how we choose to perceive. Do we want to view life from the perspective of the one wearing the backpack or from the perspective of our True Self?

A Personal Peace—Turning the Tables

It was about a week prior to a team progress meeting for an elementary school student I was working with. Sean had been diagnosed with ADHD and was not currently on any medication. In preparation for the meeting, I talked with his teacher about his performance. The teacher confided that she really didn't know how he would ever become "a productive member of society."

Hearing this, I felt some anger come up and a great deal of frustration and sadness. This child was completely brilliant; adventurous and creative, he loved to draw and had a dynamic personality. He also had difficulty getting his work done, sitting still and focusing during group time. And here was an influential adult writing him off before any intervention to help. How dare she see him this way?

As anger built inside me, I slipped into the old victim/villain scenario: Sean was a victim of how this teacher was seeing him, and she was to blame for some of his challenges. To me, this was not fair at all.

Suddenly, I got that I was doing the same thing to this teacher that she was doing to Sean! I was seeing her in a negative, fear-based light. Right then, I was able to step aside, observe, and take responsibility for my thoughts. I could see the anger, frustration and sadness that had come up from a place outside of myself, which allowed me to step out of the drama and the story I was creating in my mind.

That evening, I choose to meditate on my reaction to this woman. I let go of all of my ego beliefs about her as an individual and as a teacher. Once I felt clear of the story, I remained in the relaxed state that came as a result of my quiet time releasing. I felt such relief. No longer concerned, I was able to be curious about how Sean's progress meeting would go. I imagined what it would feel like to be there, offering support to his parents, feeling connected to them and to the education team, and knowing that we all had Sean's best interest at heart. I imagined filling the cells of my body with gratitude, as if the meeting had already happened.

I returned to work with a renewed viewpoint, able now to remain unattached to the results. If my mind wandered to old patterns and thoughts, I diligently returned my focus to the peace I'd attained the night before.

Prior to our gathering, I ran into Sean's teacher in the hallway. She stopped me and apologized for the comment she'd made about Sean. She told me she'd been feeling stressed and had taken it out on him. I tried to hide my surprise and focused on supporting her as she shared her thoughts.

Sean's progress meeting proved to be one of the best I have ever participated in. His teacher spent a significant amount of time prior to our review focusing on his strengths and gifts. This set the tone for all of those present as we built a new plan to assist him in areas of need.

Another Face of Responsibility

When we recognize that we are locked in various versions of a story replaying over and over, it becomes clear that we are essentially drawing in present experiences to match those of our past. We then have the opportunity to take responsibility for being the one who is, consciously or subconsciously, choosing this.

Years ago, I learned about a doctor who healed an entire ward of people who'd been declared considered criminally insane. He did this by reading their charts over and over and forgiving everything about each of them. Literally, with the exception of one patient, everyone was healed. Upon hearing this, I decided I wanted to learn from this man, Dr. Ihaleakala Hew Len.

Dr. Hew Len teaches Ho'oponopono, the ancient Hawaiian healing technique I mentioned in Chapter 9. This technique is centered around the idea that everything we experience is a result of a memory (or story) replaying itself. Any disease, anxiety or challenge is simply a recollection from our past, our family's past or our collective (humankind) past. In this approach, the practitioner *cleanses* (or forgives) these experiences as often as possible throughout the day, for as many days as it takes.

I was fortunate enough to take a course on Ho'oponopono from Dr. Hew Len, and was brought to my knees by one simple phrase. A woman from the group had asked how to help a family member with a particular difficulty. She had tried everything without any positive results and clearly felt overwhelmed, frustrated and angry about all of her efforts having been "wasted." After listening to her concerns, Dr. Hew Len asked, "Have you ever realized that you are always there?"

He went on to explain that, as a witness to this situation, she could take responsibility for her part in it. Once in awareness of this, she could choose to respond with love and forgiveness. In other words, simply by observing a situation, we are, in a sense, involved. Again, not from a place of blame or fault but from a place of love. This woman could forgive herself, all others involved, and society as a whole for all misperceptions, fears and judgments. And then she could open to love.

Do you recall that I applied the Ho'oponopono technique to a situation with a child with autism? I didn't do so because I felt responsible for the diagnosis. I did so because I made a choice to take responsibility for how I'd been viewing him and his diagnosis. I forgave myself for my perceptions based on lack and I forgave humankind for general beliefs held about autism.

The value of realizing we are always present in life, witnessing, was brought home to me when a former client returned to my classes. During the course of one workshop, she experienced a breakthrough. She had been preparing to separate from her third husband, getting her finances in order and finding another place to live. During a meditation, she lightheartedly compared all three husbands. They couldn't have been more different! And yet, they all had a pattern of lying and withholding details about various matters.

In that magical moment, she saw that *she* was the common factor in all three marriages. As a result, she was able to let go of the outcome in her current marriage. In other words, she decided to release her preparations to leave and her concerns about whether they would be married ten years from now. Instead, she chose to take responsibility for her piece in what was not working between them. She started to live as if everything was healed in their relationship. And, guess what? She and her husband experienced major shifts. They began having sex again—good sex. He began cleaning the house, something he had never done before. And, where previously she'd felt annoyed when he experienced personal and professional challenges, she began feeling genuine compassion. Best of all, she started to trust him.

Still not sure on the responsibility thing? Let's look at it another way.

The Guilt Is Back

At some point, we may come to believe that most of what we are going through with our children is a result of having passed the contents of our backpack down to them. Maybe we realize they are simply responding to the fears and issues we never dealt with. And, along with that realization, it's common to experience a return of the feelings of guilt.

First of all, I want you to know that you are not alone! At one point or another, we have all felt like we totally screwed up our children. Although I feel compassion for this, I am not going to try to make you feel better about your supposed mistakes. To do so would imply that you did something "wrong" in the first place.

What if what you did was neither bad nor good? What if it just was? You did whatever you did. What happened, happened.

As soon as we release the old belief that what we've done is "wrong" or "bad," the true energy beneath any event is revealed. This in turn opens the field of infinite possibility. We move from being a loaded observer to allowing Infinite Love to take the reins.

When we commit an act, have a thought, or make a choice that brings up guilt or regret, it is often a matter of forgetting the truth of who we are and the truth of the person we are in relationship with. What I want to remind you of is that you are pure and perfect love—the kind of love that is ever-present and unchanging.

When you are tempted to go down the guilt, blame and shame rabbit hole, think of the following hypothetical situation. The story involved came to me in a client session when the topic of guilt arose. Some may consider it somewhat harsh, but it gets the point across: Let's say you are watching a three-year-old girl with curly brown hair and a sassy orange dress, riding around on her new tricycle. She is in the moment, at one with the bike and just peddling her heart out in a state of pure joy and exuberance. Suddenly, a spectacular butterfly lands on the sidewalk. You start to say something to the little girl and, just then, she runs over the butterfly with her tricycle. She has no clue what happened and continues to peddle on and on in joyous circles.

Would you stop this girl and say, "Look at what you did! You just killed that beautiful butterfly! How could you?" Of course not. When we don't know we are doing something, how can we take responsibility for it?

Let's expand this scenario: What if the little girl was angry, riding around after an upsetting incident with a friend or sibling? In the midst of her fury, she inadvertently runs over the butterfly. Does she then deserve reprimand? Of course not. Just because she was upset doesn't mean that it is her fault the butterfly is dead.

In such moments, we may discern that we want to try to unearth our child's unmet need and address why she is so angry. We can do this from a loving place, with the intention to help her understand herself and her actions. And, we may further discern that if we reprimand a child in a situation like this, we may be planting the seed that her action was "bad," running the risk that she may come to believe *she* is bad.

Now, I must be clear, this view of responsibility is not a free ticket. Once we know that our beliefs, thoughts and actions affect our experiences, and those of the people around us, we have the opportunity to choose our responses. We can get clear about our intentions, and recognize what is in our backpack that is influencing how we're acting and perceiving. This does not have to be a difficult and arduous process. It does, however, take diligence and commitment—to ourselves first, as we can't help our children before we do this work for ourselves.

Focusing on feelings of guilt keeps us in a state of punishment and blame. This influences how we observe and perceive the world. We come to view others as guilty, and inadvertently use blame and shame in our interactions. By instead feeling our guilt fully and then releasing it to forgive ourselves and others, we are able to move forward and address the current needs of our children.

So how can we teach these concepts to children? We'll go into this in detail in the final two chapters, but here's a preview.

Warming the Toast

What is the best way to teach others the principles of mindfulness, intentional living and taking responsibility for our choices in life? By example. That means, don't even try to teach these concepts to your children until you are living them.

We know the science behind the power of thought feels right, and we have the best intentions in wanting to teach this to our children. And, there is no way they can grasp it without an example. The exception here is that some children are naturals and already living intentionally. In those cases, we're best off staying out of their way or, better yet, committing to learning real life applications from them.

For all others, I liken preparing children for this process to warming toast. Everyone knows it's easier to butter warm toast as opposed to cold toast. As you start to effectively monitor your thoughts, feelings, patterns and beliefs and nourish yourself from the inside out, you are essentially warming the toast—prepping your kiddos so the information makes sense to them and is readily absorbed.

And remember, all information is best received when we don't have an agenda to "change" our kiddos. If learning isn't a playful and joyous process, what child would be interested?

Clearing Proactively

We've explored taking responsibility for how we respond in the moment, and, in Chapter 11, we discussed retroactively clearing memories and patterns from the past to release the heavy weight of guilt in our backpacks. We also have the opportunity to be proactive in this process, choosing to do the work ahead of any event that has a history of ending in turmoil (such as a family reunion) or in preparation of seeing a friend, family member or co-worker involved in past, triggering occurrences.

Start by giving yourself a few moments to contemplate the Four C's. First, **Consciously Observe** your thoughts and feelings. Revisit the Story Loop to determine if you're feeling activated by the mere thought of spending time with a particular person. Chances are, if you haven't cleared your story completely, something will come up. Take responsibility for how you feel. Do you want to witness and communicate with this person from a place of fear, lack, resentment or anger? Do you think that the interaction will go smoothly if you enter into it wearing a heavy backpack? Probably not.

Next, **Connect** to Infinite Love and **Choose** a way to release your feelings. End by **Creating** the new thoughts and feelings that go with a preferred outcome. Remember, you're not responsible for the actual outcome, only for putting out into the universe the feelings you desire from deep within your True Self.

Your ego may demand validation or revenge. Your True Self values connection, peace, ease and love. What is more important—being "right" or participating in an exchange based in love? In every moment, we can discern and move forward from a place of empowerment.

When we start to communicate and interact more and more from our True Self, the old stories dissolve. In some cases, you will not even be able to recall how or even why something triggered you in the past.

Trust me, I recognize that it takes a great deal of commitment to live this way. And I will tell you, it's worth it. When peace is your first priority, it's much easier to take response-ability and be diligent in staying on this path. Why? Because, in being empowered—knowing that you are responsible for how you perceive others and the world—you will feel so much better mentally, physically, emotionally and spiritually. And others will feel good in your presence. It's true. It feels so good to be around someone who lives with such intention.

True Diligence

What does it take to experience lasting change? Diligence—a commitment to making this work such a priority that it becomes a way of life, not just a temporary fix.

Say you are doing this work, practicing the what you've learned, digging into your backpack. You begin to see small, medium or even large shifts in your life. Layers of your story are released. You are filled with gratitude, and may tell everyone you know how great you feel. Then, before you know it, the rug is pulled out from under you... again.

This is when you have the choice to either go back to the old story or act diligently—loving yourself anyway and going back to the Four C's, again. And then again. Understand that the work you did previously helped set the stage for a shift *and* there is more to be done.

Most Commonly Held Inaccurate Beliefs

Typically, when we experience the rug being pulled out from under us, it's due to a deeply held belief that is preventing us from a complete healing. In my experience, the most common inaccurate beliefs are:

1. I am unworthy of having what I desire—my self-worth is based on fear and lack.
2. I am responsible for others' well-being—it's my job to make others happy.
3. I am my accomplishments/failures—my identity is determined by external factors.

At first, none of these statements may resonate. Typically, clients either jump at one or more of these beliefs or say none is the case for them. If you find the latter to be true, I invite you to go a bit deeper. You may find such beliefs have been filtering through your life for a number of years.

What This May Look Like—Mr. "Fix-it"

After working jointly with a husband and wife, each decided to schedule individual sessions in order to clear their own negative patterns and limiting beliefs. A couple of sessions in, I presented to the husband the idea that he had a deeply held belief, most likely from childhood, running on replay.

After a good bit of digging, he realized that he had long identified himself as someone who "fixes things." His identity—that is, who he thought he was—was wrapped up in this belief, which is a version of "I am my accomplishments."

When I asked him how this might be playing out in current situations, he quickly saw that the problems he faced now were too big to "solve" in the sense he was used to. As a result, he felt overwhelmed, lost and defeated. Once he recognized that he was magnetizing situations into his life just to have something to solve and feel worthy about, he found value in releasing this identity.

He then shifted his intention toward co-creating what it was that he most deeply desired—a fulfilling, fun family life. Remember, we are very powerfully creating in every moment. We can create from past fears, or we can clear out our patterns and create with abundance in the now.

Many beautiful events occurred for this dad, one of which was that he was inspired to install a home-wide sound system that allowed him and his family to have access to all types of music in any given location in the house. The joy he expressed over this was tangible. This may seem so simple, yet, if music is something that feeds your True Self, you can see how big this would be.

Most Common Patterns

Recalling our story loop, let's move past the three most common beliefs and look at our patterns—the ways in which we tend to block our own fulfillment. The three most common patterns I've noticed in my life and in the lives of my clients are:

1. Playing the role of victim: "Why does this always happen to me?" (This requires a villain, which could be a child, spouse, friend, our career, finances, life circumstance, etc.)

2. Playing the martyr: "I do everything for everyone because it's the right thing to do and I get nothing in return. But don't worry about me, I'm fine. (Sacrifice is a big theme here.)

3. Self-sabotage: "I was so close to getting the deal, but lost it right at the end because (insert excuse here)." (Lack of self-worth)

When we are honest with ourselves and have a genuine desire to change, we can almost laugh at these beliefs and patterns. As we move past the massive waste of time and effort that guilt, blame and shame offer, we have an opportunity to release all three. And yes, they will resurface again and again, and we simply do the Four C's again and again until we move into a completely new way of being. In our new story, we experience abundance and peace in all areas. If, at any given time, we are not feeling gratitude, relief, joy, ease and love, we know we have another opportunity to clear something from our backpack.

Your Life's Purpose

Another way to reveal these most deeply held beliefs and negative patterns is to approach them from the opposite perspective. This means determining your life's purpose. In other words—Who are you and how are you meant to serve in this experience we call life?

What a huge question to pose almost at the end of the book! Once you get an inkling of the answers, however, you'll begin to see how you may be blocking yourself from actualizing your aspirations. You may not have a life-changing epiphany, or maybe you will. Either way, you'll likely uncover a limiting belief you've been carrying for years.

In order to discover your purpose, ask Infinite Love and your True Self for assistance. And then, pay attention.

What This May Look Like—Living Her True Purpose

I asked Jenni, a mother of two boys who came to me seeking peace and fulfillment, the following questions: "What do you like to do?" and "What feeds your spirit?"

She responded that her favorite activity was organizing and preparing gratitude gifts for the teachers and staff at her boys' school. We all know how demanding the field of education is and as I listened

I began to see what a huge job Jenni had undertaken. There are 35 teachers and 32 staff members at this school. Sensitive to the dangers of burnout, Jenni had joined the PTA with the sole purpose of creating opportunities to thank them. To this end, she organized appreciation lunches, prepared small gifts and held collection drives to purchase gift cards.

In addition, the boys' school has about 600 students. By bringing such recognition and joy to the adults, Jenni touches roughly 667 lives. When teachers and staff feel appreciated, they are better able to love and nurture students. And, when kiddos come home feeling loved and nurtured, it takes some pressure off their parents. Can you see how expressing gratitude in this way allows her to serve a much greater collective?

So what pattern was playing out that blocked Jenni from living her purpose?

As she sees it, Jenni's true purpose is enriching the community surrounding her sons, a role that was being undermined by her tendency to self-sabotage—shouldering more commitments than she could possibly handle. Jenni had so fully taken on the role of giver, she said yes to everything.

Once she recognized this pattern, she was able to prioritize. Helping out with a local consignment sale takes a ton of time and energy and is not in alignment with her purpose. Previously, she'd said yes to such requests because that was her "role." Now, whenever she is asked to participate in a volunteer opportunity, she gets to decide whether it is something she would enjoy and respond accordingly.

Jenni also began to learn the value of self-care, understanding that she can't possibly serve her purpose of honoring and loving teachers and staff if her own needs aren't met. Recently, she sent me this amazing text:

I have to tell you, it was so peaceful with (my sons) on Friday and all weekend...since our appointment. I am loving our shift into peace and calm!! Fear certainly seems to be knocking but I keep releasing... and this weekend I rested. Barely out of my PJs either day. And do you know how the kids responded?? Easy! They both played with friends a bit but generally enjoyed the downtime... even hubby followed suit! It felt divine trusting the process and timing of the Divine.

Being in response means that, in every moment, we have the power to choose. Do we want to respond out of fear (an old belief) or do we want to respond from a place of knowing anything is possible—a place of love?

The truth is, while we get breaks now and again, the work is never really finished. And, each minute we spend diligently living an intentional life, responding to triggers by clearing our old beliefs and patterns, and creating what it is we really want, we reap the rewards.

Action Peace—Discovering Your Life's Purpose

Knowing our life's purpose helps us stay focused, take responsibility for how we may be blocking our personal growth and release the chains of the ego.

To help discover your life's purpose, take a few moments to answer the following questions:

1. What do you love to do?

2. What do your loved ones say about you?

3. What activities feed your spirit?

4. If you had no limitations, what would you be doing on a regular basis?

Now, look at your present situation. Who or what is blocking you from doing these things? Who did you unintentionally cast in the role of villain in your life, or as someone you need to help or save? Remember, no blame or shame here. We unintentionally cast people in their roles to keep our stories alive. They are familiar, and our brains want to be right, so we look for ways to to confirm them. Take a few moments to consider the following questions:

1. What belief goes along with this block?

2. How are you playing out your patterns?

Action Peace—Committing to Your New Lifestyle

While breaking old patterns and releasing limiting beliefs takes diligence, it doesn't have to be burdensome. Select a few ways you can begin incorporating a regular practice of taking response-ability for your life. Some ideas include:

- Set a reminder on your cellphone with "I love you," "You are worth it!" or another meaningful phrase.
- Start each day with the fourth C. Upon your first awareness of the day, fill your body with the feelings that go with your new story.
- Meditate.
- Do the Four C's throughout the day as you experience triggers and upsets.
- Place sticky notes on your bathroom mirror to remind you of your new lifestyle.
- Wear a piece of jewelry, like a large ring. Whenever you find yourself fidgeting with it, remember your intention to be mindful and loving.
- In his TED Talk, corporate trainer, author, and advocate for positive psychology Shawn Achor suggests writing three different things you are grateful for each day for 21 days. That's 63 entries. This will help build new neural pathways, for sure.
- Volunteer with an organization of *your* choice.
- Commit anonymous random acts of kindness.
- If you feel comfortable sharing something you want to release, choose a person who will honor your absolute truth. In other words, don't tell someone who will buy into the trauma and drama of your story and help you remain stuck.

CHAPTER 14

—— ✳ ——

Intention and Intuition
Align with Infinite Love

"Love appears in your heart and that gives the peace to you."

~ TESSA, AGE 3½

THE WORD "INTENTION" has been mentioned often throughout this book. When you think beyond the standard definition as a "purpose" you plan to "achieve," you'll discover that crafting an intention sets the underlying tone for your day, and even your life. The work you've done in previous chapters freed you so you can re-pattern your thoughts and consciously create intentions that bring forth the life you desire.

How do we create these intentions? That's where intuition comes in. We all have the ability to tap into this stream of universal guidance, and listening to the little (or big) voice within is a great place to start. Many of us see ourselves as intuitive and are likely, as far as our kids are concerned, to have "mother's intuition." As we talk about intuition in this book, however, I am referring to something larger than that—namely, our direct connection to Infinite Love.

As we grow and learn more about the dangers of the *real* world, many of us lose the ease with which our inner guidance is received. This can, however, be regained. Through Consciously Observing, Connecting, Choosing and Co-creating we increase our ability to tune in and be in alignment with the higher guidance that feeds our intuition. There is a flow of vibration at the level of Infinite Love. As we open into our True Self, we can ask for this guidance, listen and receive.

Client Triumph—Intending to Clear a Family Pattern
After three attempts to attend one of my parenting classes or workshops, Jill was ready for the work and made the time. On the first day,

216

she shared that, though she didn't have any monumental problems with her daughter, she was always interested in learning more about parenting and moving forward on her personal journey.

Throughout the course, it was clear Jill loved the new information, but she admitted having some difficulty incorporating it into her everyday life. Awareness came gradually. With it, she started to "catch" herself when framing something in a negative light, and often said things like, "I know, I know, I shouldn't say it that way. I'll draw negativity to myself."

Jill had some health and relationship issues and I often offered to work with her on these areas, either in or outside of class. She always acknowledged my offer, and appeared to put it on the back burner. I was mindful to not be overbearing. I just wanted her to know that when she was ready, I'd be glad to help.

One day, Jill opened up. She detailed a series of health issues that dated back to her early twenties: a thyroid condition, chronic back pain, a history of needing heart medication and a number of other minor ailments. I knew her as a generally happy, light-hearted person. Considering all she was experiencing, she didn't appear to make these issues her "story" and, at least in class, I regularly forgot all about them.

During one divinely inspired interaction, Jill began to talk more about her childhood. I remained present and listened wholeheartedly, from a place of genuine connection. My commitment was to hold a vision of Jill completely healed; to see her with eyes of infinite possibility. She shared that her brother had a life-threatening illness at a young age, which meant her parents had spent a great deal of time at the hospital with him.

When I asked if she felt her mother's love, she said, "Of course I know my mother loves me." My intuition told me that there was something there, even if it was not at the forefront of her mind.

Upon further reflection and discussion, Jill shared that her mother had once had throat cancer. I also knew, from previous discussions, that her daughter had recently had her tonsils and adenoids removed.

When I pointed out that all of these ailments, through three generations of women, were centered in the neck and throat area, Jill's jaw dropped. "What does that mean?" she asked, tearing up.

We delved further into her relationship with her mother. I was gentle and stayed with my knowing that Jill was healthy, well and loved. Soon, I felt something shift. I could tell she was ready to face this pattern and do the work. We spent a great deal of time discussing how her throat ailments might be related to finding her voice. I asked her a number of questions about how her brother's illness had affected her childhood and family. I reminded her that our intention was for healing, not to place blame or shame on anyone.

I allowed her to verbally purge her experiences, while continuing to see her truth—that perfect health and wellness were already within her. At the end of the session, I asked if it was okay if I included her in my evening meditation, with the same intention of healing. She enthusiastically agreed.

That night, we each had a profound experience. I did my usual meditation prep and envisioned connecting with Jill and including her in my practice, almost as if she were there with me. I stayed in meditation until I felt a shift and intuitively knew there was a healing on the horizon.

Early the next morning, Jill contacted me in tears. "You were right," she said. "My mother never touched me. She was always with my brother and I had to take care of myself and my sister. I never felt seen or heard." She went on to tell me about a dream she'd had the previous night. In this dream, I was holding and hugging her and she felt an enormous sense of unconditional love.

After this experience, Jill's back pain vanished. The ball-in-the-throat sensation she had experienced for so long was gone as well. And, test results from her next doctor's appointment confirmed a dramatic improvement in the thyroid condition.

Once she chose to share her health challenges, Jill's intention was to let them go. She didn't just want to be seen and heard with me, although that was a big piece of what I offered. She intended to let go of her stories—of pain and suffering and of not being seen and heard and loved. Through the combination of her intention and my intuition, Jill experienced a huge shift.

Learning our Lessons with Grace and Ease

Is it necessary to learn our biggest life lessons through trauma and heartache? No. We can, but we don't have to. It is possible to gain without pain.

How do I know this? Because I have done it both ways. For quite a while I believed that I had to experience struggle and pain in order to really *get* the lessons life had to offer. With this belief dominant in my conscious and subconscious patterning, I shouldn't have been surprised that life appeared to be pretty tough.

A number of years ago, a friend gave me the book *Many Lives Many Masters* by Brian L. Weiss, MD. In it, he states, "We have lessons to learn… each one of us. They must be learned one at a time… in order."

"What?" I thought. "With all this work, I'm only receiving one lesson at a time?" This concept and my reaction to it led to a sort of "bring it on" mentality—an "I can handle anything, so send my next lesson now and in a big way. I'm ready to fight." This, too, had its limitations. After much trial and error, some of which is detailed in this book, I now know I can experience powerful shifts with grace and ease, in a gentle and supported manner.

As my clients know, I always set an intention at the beginning of each class, workshop and individual session. No matter the intention, I always conclude with the same words: *We ask for all of this with grace and ease, and for the highest and best for all involved.*

In asking the Universe to present our lessons with grace and ease, we welcome gentle nudges that will lead us to do our inner work without unnecessary trauma.

I am reminded of a lesson I received this past winter. While test driving the pre-owned car my husband and I were planning to purchase, the low tire pressure indicator light came on. I mentioned it to the salesman and his response was that this was common in the winter and we should just reset the computer. My gut told me it wasn't okay to sell a car that had any sort of "check engine" light on and that I should have them look at the tire before we left. In the end, I ignored this feeling and we did as the salesmen suggested.

Less than a week later, I was coming home from a friend's house in a neighboring county. It was late at night and, as I was driving, I noticed the indicator light was on again. I *knew* I had a flat tire. A series of complications ensued. Two tow trucks and 3½ hours later, I was back home with our new car.

Though frustrated that I hadn't insisted the dealership check the tires, I was also grateful. Grateful I didn't have a blowout on the highway while traveling seventy miles per hour; grateful for a cell phone to call for help; grateful for the kind and patient tow truck drivers; and grateful for unseasonably mild winter weather.

Choosing to see all challenges as opportunities, I saw that there was much to learn in this situation. First and foremost, I was reminded to listen to my intuition and ask for what I want and need in all moments.

After that night, my husband and I decided to buy four new all-weather tires at $200 each. The dealership agreed to pay for one. When the check arrived, I was surprised to see they'd sent $800, reimbursing us for all four tires. I called to explain the situation and the manager decided to let us keep the whole amount! I gladly accepted... with grace and ease.

Oh, and I feel it is relevant to mention that the morning we received the $800 check, I had created an intention for financial abundance for our family.

Let's keep going with how intuition can help us compassionately connect with our family.

It Matters Not What We Say

Get ready for a big concept here!

Regardless of what we say to our children, or even how we say it, they are much more in tune with how we *feel* about them or the situation. This is their intuition in operation. I would even go so far as to argue that it hardly matters what we say. If we are feeling frustrated, annoyed, angry or desperate, our children are aware of this on a subconscious level, no matter our words or the manner in which we attempt to get our point across. Even when we say something in a pleasant way, if our intention is to lash out, manipulate or control, our children know it. If we are fearful of a particular outcome and will do *anything* to avoid it, they know that, too. This is one of the many reasons our children are such a gift in our lives. They keep us honest and authentic, and show us when our actions indicate we're behaving otherwise.

How is it that kiddos can be so in touch with our feelings? Remember the brainwaves we talked about in Chapter 10? Children from birth to age six are in alpha and theta states pretty much all of the time. Living from their subconscious, they absorb whatever is in their environment without defense. Because their conscious mind is not yet developed, they intuitively experience what those around them think and feel. Additionally, their mirror neurons often fire to match those firing in our brains. When we are stressed, they feel similar stress or irritation. This sometimes looks like a cough or a tummy ache. More and more, I see clients coming to me concerned that their three and four-year-olds are experiencing anxiety. My first thought in these situations is always to address family dynamics and the home environment.

To help bring clarity to this idea, I often use the example of getting ready in the morning. How many parents feel as if they have to ask their children to put on their shoes hundreds of times? (Or, for older kids, get their backpack together, do their homework or complete a chore.) For the longest time, I made this request in the patient, loving voice I had perfected. In other words, I knew it was important to remain calm, so I tried to fake them out. While I projected my best Mary Poppins voice, I was boiling with fury inside. I could not understand why, every single day, this routine struck them as a brand new, unfamiliar task. It felt as if there was some elaborate secret I needed to decode before we could even begin making it out of the door on time.

After months (okay, maybe years), I realized it didn't matter what I was saying. All that mattered was what I was thinking and feeling. The kids weren't even listening to my sing-song Poppins voice. They were picking up my thoughts, my frustration, resentment and downright self-pity. Think of the teacher in the beloved *Peanuts* comic strip. We have no idea what "Wa wa wa, wa wa wa wa" means, but we can sure tell how Charlie Brown feels when he hears it. The same goes for our children.

Once I grasped this, loud and clear, I started to consciously observe what came up for me during our morning routine. This was my "stuff," my triggers, being brought to my attention. I Consciously Observed myself and what came up, Connected (breathing deeply), and then Chose a way to release all of the feelings I was experiencing.

Only then could I Create what it was I really wanted. After letting go of my annoyance and frustration as well as the guilt I experienced for feeling this way, I visualized the kids, walking to the car with their shoes on after my first request. I brought in the feelings of calm, ease and flow. Without any need to gather formal data about the average time it took to get shoes on and the average number of requests, I could *feel* that everything went more smoothly when I imagined and consciously intended what I wanted rather than what I didn't want.

A very important part of this concept is nonattachment. In other words, not having expectations about the outcome but instead focusing on your intention. Chose a visual image and then ask Infinite Love to allow what is highest and best to shine through. This can be difficult but after a few confirming events, you will feel more comfortable turning everything over to your Highest Love.

Here's the thing—it's the process of doing the work that makes the difference. Even if my kids had instantly started putting their shoes on without hesitation, without taking the time to clear out my underlying issues, I would have found another way to manifest the same old feelings. You know by now that when our negative thoughts or limiting beliefs aren't removed, they continue to contribute to our story.

What This May Look Like—Flip the Channel

During one of my parenting classes, I shared a fascinating interaction I'd had with my son. One morning, he emerged from his room feeling moody and spoke harshly to me upon first glance. I was not triggered at all. I made a conscious choice to observe him and myself from a place of peace and love. And, I simultaneously discerned that I did not want negative energy between us as we started our day.

In my mind, I addressed him, firmly and lovingly saying, "You may not talk to me that way. Peace is most important, and we speak to each other respectfully in this house." Again, I was not triggered

Five or ten seconds later, he said, "Okay." I hadn't said a word, mind you, yet everything shifted—his attitude and his tone of voice was calm and courteous. He'd tuned into what I was thinking and feeling, without any verbal exchange.

I invited my students to give this a try, reminding them how important it is to not be triggered. If we are triggered, it's best to save this experiment for later and move into the Four C's. Otherwise, we can bring to mind our powerful connection and speak to our children from our heart to theirs—from True Self to True Self.

The next week, one attendee described a similar encounter with her teenage daughter, Anna. This mom had observed that certain, drama-filled reality shows had a negative influence on how Anna communicated with her and others. As a result, she had begun setting firm boundaries on what she would allow her to watch.

When making dinner that week, she noticed Anna flip to one of the forbidden shows. She was not triggered by this fact, yet she wanted to maintain the set boundaries. In her mind, she spoke to Anna firmly and lovingly, reminding her she was not to watch that show. To her delight, Anna changed the channel within seconds, and without her mom saying a word.

Is this the magic bullet you've been looking for? You know by now that it's not. That said, it is powerful to grasp just how strong our unspoken connection is to our children. Keeping this work of clearing your stuff as your number one priority means you will find yourself getting triggered less and less often. Your children will feel this and respond accordingly. With pure intention, you access the deepest, heart-based connection between you and your child.

Highly Sensitive Adults Often Have Highly Sensitive Kids

I'm not a fan of any sort of label, be it a diagnosis with multiple symptoms or the idea of a child being "gifted." For one thing, I believe we are all gifted, and we all have various opportunities to work through our challenges. That said, it is important to address kids who are particularly sensitive to sounds, tastes, textures, lights, etc., as they are often highly sensitive to others' emotions as well.

Such sensory processing challenges used to be rare and symptoms were often written off or reserved to describe kiddos on the autism spectrum. For various reasons, more and more people today appear to be experiencing a variety of sensitivities. (There are many books on the topic of causation, so I won't delve into that here.) Not in that they are exceptionally sympathetic or compassionate to others. Rather, the kind of sensitivity I am referring to is the ability to *feel* what another is feeling.

As a highly sensitive child moves through his or her day, they sponge up the emotions of everyone they come in contact with. This can be challenging for everyone involved, particularly as it's not always clear if such emotions are coming from an experience that child had, or if they are tuning in to and expressing the emotions of someone around them.

This concept may make perfect sense to you, or it may be altogether foreign. I'll share a personal story from my family that may shed some light on what I am describing.

A Personal Peace—A Series of Irritations

As I've mentioned, I believe physical ailments are often linked to our emotional state. A few years ago, my son experienced a series of irritations that eventually led to a pretty big insight for both of us.

It started with a cough. Despite my diligent cleaning efforts (insert a bit of sarcasm), we figured out it was possible he was sensitive to dust. My good friend and integrative pediatrician Sheila Kilbane, MD, mentioned that carpets can also be an irritant, so I removed the carpeting in his room as well. However, this only had a minimal impact on Andrew's cough, especially at night.

With no other answers in sight, we continued to explore his sensitivity to dust. One night, we had a powerful shift as we realized we had made dust the enemy, inadvertently giving it a quite a bit of power in our lives. I asked Andrew to go within and ask what the real definition of dust was. (This may sound slightly outlandish, but I've discovered this method often works for children.)

He got quiet for a while and then said, "Well, if everything is God, then dust is God, too, just small pieces of God." We talked about this and I suggested he see if he could accept this definition over the one we had previously held about dust being the bad guy. He seemed to be taking some extra time while contemplating this. Then I realized he was asleep and breathing freely. The irritation quickly melted away. Or so I thought.

Over the course of the next couple of weeks, Andrew experienced a case of ringworm, a full body rash, and a number of yellow jacket stings. Ringworm is a highly contagious fungus, which meant he couldn't go to school. We started treatment and ended up getting to spend the day together.

Intuitively, I knew I was missing an important piece to this puzzle. It hit me that we were engaged in a whole series of irritations. As soon as one seemed to be resolved, another took its place. I sat Andrew down for a heart to heart conversation and asked him what was irritating him. I listened and continued asking as many open-ended questions as possible. I wasn't triggered, just dedicated to helping him work through the root cause of his recent issues.

To my surprise, he told me about two boys at his school who were constantly arguing. I understood the arguments didn't include Andrew, but he obviously felt the anger, sadness and discord as if he were directly involved. I was a sensitive child and continue to be sensitive to others' emotions as an adult. This is one of the qualities that helps me guide clients through their challenges. Yet, it didn't occur to me until then that Andrew was equally sensitive. And, just like myself as a child, he wasn't aware that he was absorbing others' stuff, and he certainly didn't have the tools to clear the resulting emotions.

It all made sense. The timing of the discord between the boys at school coincided with his cough and the other irritations. I took him through a simplified, child's version of the Four C's. Together we created a series of visualizations and the corresponding feelings that would help him clear his emotions as well as any he might be picking up from others.

Each day, I reminded him to do this before and after school. The irritations all went away, and I witnessed my son come into a very empowered place. He still has a tendency to take on others' emotions. As long as I am not triggered, I can help to remind him and guide him to release these emotions.

This is emotional hygiene. We brush our teeth daily and wash our clothes and bodies, yet we let old emotions linger on in our environment. By bringing awareness to the impact others can have on us, we are reminded of how important it is to clean out our emotions on a regular basis and co-create, with Infinite Love, what we most deeply desire—inner peace, connection with others and love.

Expanding Intuition

The first step in expanding intuition is remembering we are all Divine expressions of Love and Light and Truth, connected to one another and to Infinite Love through an invisible field of energy. What does this mean? Think of Infinite Love as the trunk and branches of an enormous tree—we are all leaves on that tree, vital and life giving. No one is left out.

I recall feeling very resentful of a friend who often received amazing visions during meditation. This prevented me from going deeper into my own practice and receiving the same. It was not until I decided to be genuinely happy for her that I was able to make room in my heart and mind that this was possible for me, too. I cleared my fears concerning self-worth and asked Infinite Love to help me expand my intuitive gifts. Just like everything in this book, when I released all negative thoughts and inaccurate beliefs, I was able to focus on what I most deeply desired. All I had to do was ask and listen.

The changes were small at first, the lessons gentle and not so gentle. I'd get a feeling I should drive a different route to a familiar destination, and then find out there was a backup and I'd saved twenty minutes on my drive.

And when I don't listen, well...

I'll never forget the day I drove my one-month-old minivan full of kids to a gardening adventure. The night before, a little voice in my head said to replace the trash bag I normally keep in the van, as I had thrown out the old one. I somehow forgot and intended to ask my friend for one when I picked up her daughter, Sally. Things were a little chaotic at Sally's house, and I decided to forgo the request. In other words, I made a conscious decision to ignore my intuition.

Fifteen minutes into the trip, just after I'd turned onto the highway, Sally began crying. "Kristen," she blurted from the back seat, "I don't feel good." I'm sure you know what comes next. As I scrambled to empty a packed grocery bag and toss it into the back, Sally vomited. Having an empty trash bag in the van would have been pretty convenient.

When we reached our destination, I called my friend, concerned that Sally might be ill. She apologized instantly. Despite Sally's tendency to get carsick, she had gone against her better judgment and allowed her daughter to bring along a crayons and a coloring book for the ride.

We laughed and I took the situation as a gentle reminder to listen to my intuition. The more we listen and the more grateful we are for these gentle nudges, the more Infinite Love will respond by offering these opportunities. Many times, when we do listen to the gentle nudge, we never hear about the delays or near misses. When we don't listen, however, we inevitably end up seeing how beneficial it would have been to listen.

It is all about building trust and a genuine relationship with Infinite Love. As you make the care and growth of your True Self your top priority, your connection to Infinite Love becomes unquestionable.

Action Peace—Talk True Self to True Self

Begin by clearing out any emotions or limiting beliefs you have about a triggering situation with your child. Then, sit quietly and have a heart to heart conversation with him or her in your mind. You can do this exercise while they are asleep, in another room or right in front of you.

1. Set an intention, being mindful to come from a place of peace and love rather than fear, control or manipulation.

2. Jot down what happened:

3. Did you have any expectations? For instance, did you find yourself wanting your child to meet a particular need of yours? (Remember, we can't expect our kids to meet our needs.)

Try this exercise several times and see how the results change based on your intentions.

Action Peace—Enhancing Intuition

What are your beliefs about how *connected* you are to Infinite Love? Do you feel you are intuitive? Or do you feel this gift is reserved for others and not available to you?

In the spaces below, go through the Four C's to release any fears, resentment, anger, or lack of self-worth in this area.

1. Consciously Observe—Identify your trigger, thoughts, feelings, and beliefs.

2. Connect—How do you want to join with Infinite Love?

3. Choose—Select a technique or intention.

4. Create—Label and feel the feelings of the new story.

As you create, be sure to bring in the feelings that go with experiencing what it would be like to experience receiving guidance from Infinite Love. Reflect on the following:

- I feel I am intuitive in these areas:

- I would like a stronger connection with Infinite Love in these areas:

- Upon receiving this guidance, I will feel:

Practice saying, "I commit to listening to my intuition, knowing that Infinite Love will respond by giving me more intuitive experiences."

Action Peace—Setting Family Intentions

Start with something simple. For example, try setting the intention to have a peaceful movie night with the family. Ask each person what they really desire for the experience. Maybe it's to have fun. Maybe it's to laugh. Maybe it's to relax and just enjoy being with one another. If you have the opportunity, have each person say how it will feel when their intention happens. Feelings might be peace, joy, relaxation, happiness, etc.

Remember to do your work ahead of time, letting go of any expectations as to what this needs to look like. Just focus on the feelings that go with a fun-filled evening.

CHAPTER 15

The Connected Family
Share the Peace

"I liked connecting with the trees."

~ ANDREW, AGE 8

"I liked that we were all together."

~ TESSA, AGE 6

BUSY LIVES AND overloaded schedules can make it difficult to recall the power of pure, uninterrupted connection time. And yet, connection is what we are really looking for in any relationship. Children know this on a deep level and ask for our attention in a multitude of ways. Sometimes, this looks like undesirable behavior. Other times, it can look like expressions of pleasure, as illustrated by the responses my children gave above when asked what they liked most about a family trip to California.

When we do the inner work I suggest throughout *The Connected Parent*, life-changing shifts are possible. Accessing the root cause of our challenges allows us to remove any blocks we unintentionally created to a joyful family life. Then, and only then, do practical parenting strategies make a difference. Before I reached my own awareness of this process, I spent years carting my kids around to various practitioners and reading books on parenting approaches in an attempt to "fix" them. Only after I worked on my own stuff did we make lasting changes.

It would be nice to be able to say that once you've done the work described in this book your life will be filled with gumdrops, tulips and polka-dotted bows. The fact is, though many of my clients report feeling happier and healthier than ever before, there is always room for more growth and a deeper awakening. Our children mature and change. Our relationships evolve and shift. New learning opportunities are presented on a regular basis. The difference is that now you know that something else, something beyond stress and struggle, is possible for you and your family. You are aware of your stories and you have the tools—the Four C's—to identify negative thoughts, emotions, beliefs and patterns, release what is not serving you, and bring forth what you most deeply desire.

Three Important Questions

We only experience the changes we most desire when we are completely ready. And, we don't have to hit rock bottom in order for that to happen. (I have, many times. That's okay, too.)

To gauge a client's readiness to shift their experiences, I ask three very specific questions. I offer them here so you can check in with yourself:

On a scale of 1 – 10:

1. How ready are you for a new story?

2. How possible do you believe it is to receive what you most deeply desire?

3. How willing are you to do the work required?

If you remember, we typically experience a shift equal to the degree we believe one is possible. Anytime a client answers with 10s on all three questions, I know something big is about to happen. This is not necessary to start on this path, however. If you answered all three questions with an 8, 9 or 10, you are ready and have a wonderful awakening ahead of you.

If you aren't quite there yet, try to identify the limiting belief or fear that is blocking you from knowing you deserve the gifts that are available. For instance, do you find a new story scary because you don't know what to expect? Deep down, do you feel unworthy of having what you most deeply desire? Or perhaps you have tried approaches in the past that didn't make a difference, making it difficult to believe that a shift is possible now.

No matter your reasons, keep doing your work with the Four C's. Consciously Observe these thoughts and beliefs and their accompanying feelings. Let yourself really feel what comes up. Connect to Infinite Love and Choose a way to release your story. Then, imagine what is possible to Create.

And remember, this work can be applied to all areas of life—health, career, finances, relationships, even our pets. Below are some examples of shifts that happened for clients who were ready for a new story, believed it was possible to receive what they most deeply desired, and were willing to do the work.

What this May Look Like—Five Different Experiences
Lucy

After four months of feeling sick and undergoing a great deal of Western and integrative medical testing, Lucy sent the following email:

> *So I have Lyme disease. Apparently. It's connected to my other diagnoses and symptoms, i.e. parasites, clinical depression, weight gain etc... Bloodwork shows it is creating autoimmune problems.*
> *Whatever.*
> *I'm not having Lyme or anything else. I am not sick.*

Lucy then asked a number of questions about the Four C's, specifically how she might incorporate the process into her busy life, which included three children under the age of five.

At our next visit, Lucy practically ran into my office. She was empowered and on fire! Through meditation and diligent practice of the Four C's, she had healed herself of all symptoms. Follow-up testing confirmed her huge awakening—Lyme disease was negative. Of course it was.

I asked why she thought she'd been able to heal these long standing symptoms. Her answer? "Because I *believed* it was possible."

Lucy went on to heal a long-held story involving her sister, and even manifested free accommodations for her entire extended family in a seven-bedroom home on the beach. One day after meditating on how fabulous it would be to have an affordable vacation with all of her siblings and their children, she received a home swap request from a family who wanted to stay in her house for a wedding.

Janie

Not long after suffering a miscarriage and processing months of emotional trauma, Janie became pregnant and delivered a beautiful baby girl. Days later, the baby became sick and had to return to the hospital. Doctors told Janie the baby had meningitis and that they suspected it was bacterial rather than the less severe viral form.

Janie and her husband, who are also doctors, sat with this news for a brief time. And then they completely disregarded the possibility that this illness would have a lasting effect on their newborn baby. Janie knew with absolute certainty that the meningitis was viral and that her daughter would be perfectly fine. Further test results proved this was indeed the case. Her baby was—and still is—thriving.

Samantha

The wonderful thing about this process of awakening is that it can be helpful in so many situations. Following routine surgery for her beloved dog, Samantha was told he could potentially develop a severe complication common for his breed. Despite this, Samantha remained in a state of knowing all was well. She was so solid in this belief that she didn't question her pet's health for even a second. To the vet's surprise, subsequent tests came back normal. Samantha wasn't surprised at all.

Denise

Denise and her husband came to me because their daughter Andrea, who had Sensory Processing Disorder (SPD), had developed a pattern of lengthy and intense tantrums and outbursts. According to Denise, she was also moody and had what she and her husband called a "difficult personality." They had tried a variety of dietary and therapeutic approaches that were only mildly successful. Ready for something different, each was prepared to look within and clear their own stories, including the one they were telling themselves about their daughter.

Denise began incorporating the Four C's, especially meditation, into her daily routine. Here's an email I received from her shortly after the start of the school year:

In September, (John) and I had to speak at a convention. My talk was about 'thoughts have power.' Your ears were probably ringing that day because I told them that I had met an amazing woman who changed my life—that was you! I proceeded to share with them one of my more recent stories about Andrea.

For years, the start of school has been hard. The night before school, I was always up with (Andrea) until 4am with lots of tears, anxiety, worries, etc. About 2 weeks before school started this year, I made an intentional decision to meditate on what a great summer it had been. All of my thoughts were focused on gratitude... and on not allowing myself to worry about Andrea. The night before school started, I went into her room to tuck her into bed. She asked me to lay down with her. I did so, the whole time replaying the great times we'd had in my mind. I never verbalized any of this to her. As I kissed her goodnight and stood to walk out of her room, I said, 'Andrea, I love you, sleep well.'

Without any prompting from me, she said, 'Mom, it was a great summer.' With that, she turned over and went straight to sleep. I left her room in tears. In that moment, I saw that my thoughts not only affect how I feel and think but they also affect the ACTIONS of others.

Since the talk, several folks who were (at the conference) have contacted me and asked about SPD. Two of them had been at a total loss about what was going on with their child. They have since received the SPD diagnosis. What a gift to be able to help others.

Thank you for all that you do! I feel like I have learned so much from you and yet I still have so much more to learn. I truly appreciate you! PS. I am now meditating that (my husband) will start meditating. haha!
Thanks,
Denise

Andi

Andi dove into the work of identifying and releasing her story of feeling like an outsider and "not good enough" when she realized her son was playing out the same patterns. After witnessing a complete shift in his attitude, she sent this email:

Just have to share that (my son) is having the best start to his school year. I honestly believe that the layer of my story I let go of while he was at camp had a significant impact on him. I would call what I am watching a miracle.

Andi subsequently invited her two sisters to join her in a session (with me) to address concerns they were having regarding their mother.

These three sisters were all on the same page about how they were viewing their mom—she was coming across as needy, playing the victim, and appearing to manipulate others on a regular basis. All three were willing to take responsibility for how they were perceiving their mom, and for using this opportunity to clear out their backpacks. Following a big release, we exchanged the following texts:

ANDI: Our mom is the happiest and most upbeat I have seen her in a long time. This is crazy stuff.
ME: Yippee!
ANDI: I don't even understand—it is so dramatic of a change.
ME: Aw, come on! You are all powerful… keep it up!
ANDI: I mean, I'm open but seeing this is insane. I need to silence the fear that thinks it is only temporary. Maybe she fell in love or met someone. lol. I love that you are not surprised by the news.

ME: Just stay in gratitude. Being grateful brings more to be grateful for. And yes, let go of the fear. It's worthless at this point. Keep in mind that when another sees us in our truth, we cannot help but move more into it. You are seeing her more truly and she is responding.
ANDI: That is a powerful statement. Thank you.

We are all so connected to our loved ones and to all of life. When we really know and feel this, the temptation to call a synchronistic event a coincidence starts to fade. Know that the work you are doing is beneficial to your family and to everyone you know and come in contact with.

Client Triumph—Tapped into Each Other

When the following client first came to me, we dug up a great deal of old feelings, beliefs and patterns. We went through the Four C's together and, after a sizable clearing, realized there was more to go. Unable to make it to my next class, she decided to do some work on her own. First, she Consciously Observed and Connected. For her third C, Choose, she used the Emotional Freedom Technique (EFT, sometimes called "tapping"). The reverberations of the shifts she Created that night continued through the next day. She wrote:

I was hoping to catch your online talk last night, but I didn't get away until 7:30. Instead, I watched some videos about EFT. I've known about EFT for years, since 2000… but it has been a LONG time since I practiced it. Definitely since before (my daughter) was born.

I felt inspired by what they were talking about and some of it reminded me of the techniques you share. I watched a lot of different people and approaches… and even learned a new tapping spot I'd never seen before, on the inner thigh.

I spent at least two hours tapping on some of the topics you and I covered in our first session together. I did it until I couldn't keep my eyes open and then fell asleep.

This morning, Katie was asking to watch a cartoon and I was having trouble deciding how to respond. She was starting to get upset (she's been tantrumming a lot lately), but then out of nowhere she started tapping the same spot on her leg. (She) tapped repeatedly all the way up her body, stopping at the collarbone meridian. It wasn't perfect, she's two... but it was eerily close. I asked her sort of casually... "What were you doing there? Are you tapping?" She just looked at me and did it again... this time hitting the points even more accurately, going all the way up, above her collarbone onto her face and finishing on the crown of her head.

I was so shocked... it was as if she had 'tapped in' to my experience the night before and was now utilizing the coping skills I had practiced. I know the two of us are deeply connected, but this was definitely beyond anything I had witnessed before as evidence of that connection and its capacities.

Fascinating! Feel free to share if you are ever inspired to do so.

Well, I'm inspired. I love this story because it exemplifies the deep bond we have with our children. We know our children feel our anger, resentment, dismay and on and on, even when those feeling are not linked to them. This client shows the positive side of this connection. In following up, she shared that she does her best to follow through when she says a request will be met later. This builds the necessary trust between her and her daughter. This doesn't mean they don't experience challenges. This connected momma makes sure to do the Four C's—her deep inner work—so she doesn't pass her stories on to her daughter.

In this massive field of consciousness, we are all connected!

All Relationships Offer Opportunities

Because relationships are a critical aspect of every stage of our lives, opportunities to grow are available at all times. Here's an example from one of my workshops: After completing an exercise in which an attendee reflected on the relationship she'd had with her parents when she was younger, she suddenly realized that she had cast her own daughter to play out the role of her mother. She laughed as she shared with the group that her daughter constantly criticized her, just like her mother. Once she cleared all components of her story, she was able to free her daughter from this role. Once she moved into a place of getting her needs met from within, her outer world began to reflect this abundance back to her. Her daughter stopped playing the role of critic or villain and they began having more loving and peaceful interactions.

Our children are not alone in this capacity. When we have a subconscious pattern on replay, anyone (or anything) can jump in to play out the triggering role. In fact, the more we heal and shift a particular relationship, the more it seems we end up projecting our stories onto a different loved one.

I have experienced this firsthand and often observe it with my clients. Once parents start to peel away challenges with one child, difficulties somehow shift to another child, spouse, in-law, friend or co-worker. This is why it's so important to do our work. If we don't release the root, inaccurate beliefs, someone else will appear to help us keep the story alive.

I've had countless sessions with parents in which they discuss the dynamics with their significant other the entire time. We often laugh as they stop to realize the reason they'd sought my help was to address difficulties with their *children*. The truth is, children often play out similar dynamics as those we experience with a spouse or even a parent.

Remember, seeing life from the perspective of our fear-based ego leads to projecting our fears onto others. Our subconscious mind holds inaccurate beliefs and seeks out situations to confirm them. We unknowingly cast others to play out a particular role in order to remain in our story. In this way, we hand our power over to them, which allows us to play the victim, martyr or self-saboteur. By recognizing such patterns, we have the opportunity to empower ourselves, releasing the entire story.

Given that we all project onto one another, it stands to reason that our loved ones also cast us in various roles to keep their story alive. It's important to realize that we aren't responsible for maintaining these roles. For example, if your significant other has a tendency to depend on you for comfort and security in social situations, and you spend an entire evening talking with a friend at a party, he or she may become angry, accusing you of being inconsiderate and rude. This is not your stuff. This is your partner projecting their fears onto you. Always go back to your feelings. If you feel peaceful, it's not your story and the work is not yours to do.

However, if you feel triggered by such comments, this is your next opportunity. What role is your spouse playing that keeps your story alive? Do you believe you're responsible for his or her well-being? Remember, your subconscious wants to confirm its inaccurate beliefs, too. Regardless of the situation, when you do your work, you may discern that you'd like to have a conversation about what happened at the party. Be clear as to what is yours (by paying attention to your feelings) and what is theirs, and be intentional about your approach.

I often say, "Life is the curriculum that allows you to connect with your True Self." We don't need to take a three-week silent retreat on a tropical island to find ourselves, though that may sound delightful. We have everyone and everything right here in our daily experience to reveal our most deeply held negative patterns and limiting beliefs.

What if My Significant Other Isn't on Board with this Way of Parenting?

I get asked this question in every parenting class and workshop I teach. It seems impossible to experience a lasting shift in our family life if a spouse, partner or ex will not join forces in any approach. Those laid out in *The Connected Parent* are no different.

In response, I'll take this opportunity to reiterate that we do not have the power to change others. No one wants to be forced into a particular way of seeing things. The very best way for us to experience the lasting changes we desire is to live from our True Self to the best of our ability. When we are diligent and take responsibility for our piece in every situation we encounter, we set the stage for others to transform as well.

What This May Look Like—Shifting by Example

One mom who had a series of individual sessions with me attended a group class I was holding. She shared with the other moms that she never pushed her husband to explore the concepts we covered during our time together. She did her own work—releasing the emotions, patterns and beliefs from her past that were continuing to play out with her children—and watched her life shift before her eyes. In the process, she made a conscious effort to release all frustrations regarding her husband's parenting approach and how he spoke to their kids.

Over time, the shift she experienced with her children became obvious to her husband. Without prompting, he came to her one day and requested assistance in how to communicate more effectively with their son. She gently accepted his invitation and supported the two of them in their efforts at compassionate communication.

This mom's commitment to cleaning and clearing her own patterns offered an opportunity for the entire family. Her husband felt this shift and desired a similar connection with her and their children. Had she attempted to force him into this approach, he likely would have resisted.

A Quick Review of Compassionate Communication

There are many parenting approaches that suggest numerous methods for communicating with children. Personally, I am not a fan of punishment and reward systems because I don't feel they are effective.

The most important thing we can do is be mindful of our intentions for compassionate communication and remain truly *present* with our children, particularly during times of conflict. Of course, this is only possible if you aren't triggered.

With this intention firmly in your mind, do your best to discern whether your children are in a place in which they can reason. Depending on where they are developmentally, it may be best to just listen or share compassion in a non-verbal manner. If you feel they are open to some guidance or would benefit from talking things out, first remind yourself of your intention to have a conscious interaction. Choose whether you want to interact from your ego or from your True Self, and whether you want to engage with their ego or their True Self.

Remember, all trying behaviors are a result of unmet needs and subconscious patterns. When our children are arguing, hitting or doing something else we may not like, they are acting out of an unmet need—for attention, acceptance, connection, etc. Once we've cleared our own baggage, it's our job as parents to help discover what those needs are and address them, or to teach children how to express themselves and meet their needs from within, through their own connection with Infinite Love.

You already have the tools for this process. We can use a version of the Four C's to compassionately guide our children into a knowing of themselves and into discernment rather than judgment, guilt, blame and shame.

First and foremost, we all want to be seen and heard—to matter. When we reflect back to our kids what we see, we are guiding them to Consciously Observe.

For instance, say your children are having an argument. To one, you might say, "I see you hit your brother. I'm wondering if you are feeling angry because he took your toy? It's okay to feel angry, and you may not use your hands for hurting." And to the other, "It looks like you took your sister's toy. I'm guessing you want to play with it. Is that right? How might you use words to ask for it? What about…"

Continuing with the Four C's, move into a way to help your children Connect, Choose and Create. See the children's story at the end of the chapter as an example.

I absolutely love learning from my clients. Lucy, who shared her experience of physical healing earlier in this chapter, told me that she releases triggers and feelings throughout the day by writing them on a small notepad and throwing away the pieces of paper. Positive thoughts get written on sticky notes and posted around the house. She transferred this approach to address the needs of her children. When one of her three kiddos is upset, Lucy grabs a pen and paper and asks them what they would like her to write on their behalf. If they are still upset after one attempt, she writes it again. This allows the children to be seen and heard. Lucy takes the time to listen compassionately. She also partners with them in releasing their emotions. By spending time in this mom's presence, her children gain awareness of their feelings and, at a young age, learn to let them go.

Setting Boundaries Increases Peace, Love and Growth

Setting loving boundaries is one challenge many intentional parents face. It isn't always easy to find, and enforce, the right constraints to guide, support and safeguard our children without hindering their potential.

On one hand, if we don't set clear limits, our children have little or no framework on which to build. This can cause them to feel unsafe, insecure, alone and overwhelmed. Yet, when we set rigid expectations with little wiggle room, we restrict their growth and make them feel dependent on us as their guidance system—both inner and outer. Stifled, they can develop low self-worth, feeling that we don't trust they have what it takes to navigate the world.

Connected Parents can draw on the wisdom needed to determine how to set boundaries in each instance that arises. By genuinely connecting with our children, we *know* them and can determine exactly what boundaries and limitations will help them to feel safe while still allowing infinite potential for social, emotional, physical, cognitive and spiritual development.

Here's a visual of how this works:

Say we place a marble on a plate (tons of freedom) and carry the plate around, trying to move through the day without spilling the marble. This is difficult because the plate doesn't have any edges or barriers. We have to remain alert and make a great number of little adjustments moment by moment to ensure the marble doesn't fall. As keeping the plate steady in the face of all that movement creates a lot of work, stress arises. Any disruption can easily knock us off balance. And when that happens, the marble falls.

If we put the marble in a pot with a solid lid (complete restriction), we ensure that it is safe but we can't see or guide it. We can't check on the marble while it is covered and there is very limited potential for it to go anywhere other than the bottom of the pot.

By placing the marble in a bowl with easy, curved edges (infinite possibilities for upward growth), we can see and guide it while leaving it free to move about and explore. The sides of the bowl help support, but do not confine, the marble.

Tying this metaphor to our children: You, as the parent, set loving boundaries that gently "hold" your child, while leaving room for them to discover infinite possibilities. Being solid in who you are, the creator and shaper of the bowl, allows you to lovingly discern what works best for your children and your family. With compassion and clarity, you take environmental influences and the specific needs of your children into consideration, and design the kind of bowl that fosters confidence, creativity, and emotional and cognitive intelligence.

What more could we ask for?

Create Your Family Connection Plan

Staying "connected" is a choice.

And while I truly believe in doing our deep, inner work so that we, as parents, can dig up and release our underlying negative patterns and limiting beliefs, freeing ourselves to take care of our own needs and, in turn, meet the needs of our children, connection is a key component of peaceful, harmonious families.

The following are a few practical ideas that my family and clients find helpful in promoting genuine family connection—the kind that leads to forming life-long memories. Pick and choose among them, and, if you like, brainstorm with your family to create a solid, fun-filled plan to use on an ongoing basis.

1. **Have a Regular Family Fun Night (or even a whole day!)**
    Weekly, monthly or as often as you can, set aside an entire evening (or a whole day!) to devote to just *being* together.

    In this busy day and age, one of the biggest gifts we can give ourselves and our children is time together. Undivided, unplugged, undistracted time and attention to do what feels good—play. It really doesn't matter what activity you plan, only that you are together, engaged in something that brings everyone pleasure.

    The key is to commit to avoiding unnecessary interruptions. Inevitably, your phone will ring or you will get a text or two (or ten). Unless it is a true emergency, leave it until later. Beyond true emergencies, very few things need our immediate attention. Every call or text is an absence on our part and when we leave our kids during time we've set aside to be together, they get the message that they are second to our devices.

I know this from personal experience. After purchasing a new computer, I spent so much time on it, it seemed to be surgically attached to my fingers. Or at least that's what my son thought. At one point, he said he wished he could burn it in the fire pit. What he was really saying was that he felt I was choosing my computer over him. Of course, that was not the case, as work tasks, emails, etc. are a fact of life. But I did take note and made it a point to plan specific work periods rather than going back and forth from the computer all day. During family fun night, I announce that, barring emergencies, all devices are to be put away for the night. (Texting to confirm a hair appointment is not an emergency, no matter how bad my roots look!)

Choose from the following Fun Night ideas or create your own:

- Have a flashlight or glow stick night. Turn off the lights and dance in the dark. You can also take this activity outside and catch fireflies.
- Watch a movie from your childhood. One of our favorites is *Swiss Family Robinson*—a true family adventure.
- Hold a talent show or some sort of performance. For Mother's Day this year I asked my kids to put on a show. They worked together at length to create and perform a 15-minute play, complete with wardrobe changes. During and after the show, I forgot all about the incessant bickering that had taken place between them earlier. Amazing what true connection can do.
- Plan an outdoor activity—an evening hike, a camping trip or a backyard bonfire. Bringing your family back to nature can have immeasurable benefits.
- Play some good old-fashioned board games. Or better yet, a cooperative game. What? Leave out the competition?

Sure, why not? Sometimes my family will take a traditional game and change the rules to make it a race against the clock. We have to work together to try to beat our own collective time.

- Play your own version of *America's Got Talent*. When my family did this, each person got their own turn to create four characters that competed against one another. So, my daughter performed four routines, as did my son, my husband and I. We weren't competing against each other, our characters were! It was a blast, leading to a whole night of laughs.
- Young children can appreciate Family Fun Night, too. Light a candle and sing songs in the family room before bedtime. It is never too early to start a fun routine of family connection.

2. Keep a Family Gratitude Journal

What we focus our attention on grows. When we have a mental list of what hasn't gone well for the day, we often draw more of the same into our lives. By concentrating our thoughts on what we are thankful for, we get more to be grateful for. Of course, you know this by now.

My family often goes around the table at dinnertime to share what each of us is grateful for. There is significant power in then writing these down.

Involving your kids in this process, either by sharing your lists with them, helping or encouraging them to make their own lists, or making a family list together enriches the experience and gives them practice in cultivating gratitude in their own lives.

3. Ask for or Offer a "Redo"

Sometimes I hear myself talking to my kiddos in a way I have discerned I do not want to speak to them. This typically occurs when

I'm rushing or unintentionally manipulating them in some manner. As soon as I recognize this, I love myself anyway and ask my kids for a redo. It's as simple as that. I recognize my mistake, love myself and ask for an opportunity to re-live the situation, whatever it may be. Ninety-nine percent of the time, they agree.

My kids have the same opportunity. They can either initiate a redo or take me up on an offer when I suggest it. As long as I'm not triggered and my intuition tells me they may be open to the idea, I ask them if they would like a redo. If so, I carefully resist the urge to make any last comments that support an argument from even seconds prior.

It is so empowering to know that, at any given time, any one of us can simply take responsibility for our stuff and ask for a do-over. It's miraculous what happens when we give each other unconditional love and second chances.

4. Set Intentions as a Family

Before every vacation, road trip and even some day trips, we each take a turn to set our intention for the experience. Here are some examples of what might be shared:

- To have fun
- To get to our destination safely and easily
- To be the presence of Love to all we see
- To have peace
- To spend quality time with family or friends

5. Practice Visualizations

It will be no surprise that visualizations are a regular occurrence in my home. (Or at least the suggestion of them. Sometimes my kids just want to be "normal," in which case I give them a break.)

Prior to Andrew's soccer games or Tessa's dance performances, I may suggest that they take a few minutes to visualize what they want for that event or day. After a recent goal in soccer, Andrew told me, "It was just like I imagined. Someone passed the ball to me. I dribbled a bit. Then I scored."

I always remind them to bring in the feeling that goes with what they want and to let go of what this needs to look like. In other words, we don't only focus on winning, although there is nothing wrong with that. We also focus on things like having fun and being safe or injury free.

6. Create a Kanban

My children's school, Agile Learning Centers, uses Kanban boards to provide visible feedback to students, so they can track their goals and intentions throughout the school year. Kanban ("card signal" in Japanese) was developed by Toyota, in the late 1940s, to optimize inventory control to production lines by providing visible signals about what was needed. Since then, the system has been adapted to modern materials, like sticky notes on white boards, and many settings and purposes.

Tailored to your needs, Kanban is a powerful tool to narrow your focus and prioritize tasks. (If you'd like to learn more, check out the book *Personal Kanban* by Jim Benson and Tonianne DeMaria Barry, which has a separate chapter on "Kidsban" for children.)

There are many options for creating a Kanban. One of my favorites uses a simple manila folder. Divide the folder into four columns, labeling each with child-friendly headings like "On Your Mark," "Get Set," "Go," and "Finish Line." Choose a project and write each step on its own sticky note. Enjoy advancing the sticky notes across the columns until each reaches the finish line.

I have crafted multiple Kanban boards for personal and professional use. Creating one as a family is vastly rewarding as a visual representation of what the group would like to accomplish together. Kids feel seen and heard as suggestions are added, sticky notes (and tasks) are advanced, and events and activities are completed.

Kanban also aids in accountability. If we, as parents, have a tendency to say we will do something later and then never get around to it, Kanban serves as a tangible reminder. My family has boards dedicated to movies, summer activities, weekend activities and more.

For example, this is what is on our family Kanban right now:

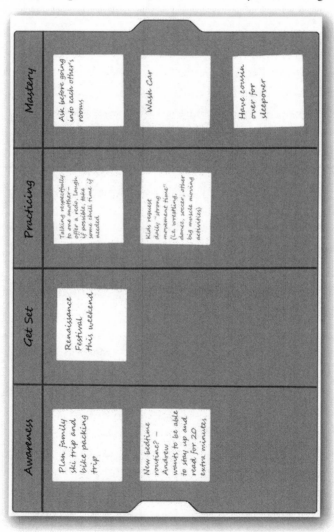

7. **Co-create a Weekly Family Meeting**

Most Family Connection Plan suggestions can be discussed at or implemented during a weekly meeting. How you structure this time is up to you and your family. Here are a few guidelines:

- Set the meeting for roughly the same day and time each week. (My family likes Sunday evenings.)
- Plan about 20 minutes, or an amount of time that is developmentally appropriate for your child(ren), for each meeting.
- Decide the structure of the meeting together. Maybe you start or end with a prayer or meditation. Maybe you each take turns selecting a snack. These details may seem inconsequential, but kids will be more invested if they have a say in how the meeting goes.
- Set clear intentions as a team. This is not just another opportunity for parents to tell kids what to do! Allow your kids to make suggestions—sometimes theirs are the most successful.
- Discuss what is going well in your home and what needs work. Be sure all family members have the opportunity to share their thoughts, feelings and ideas for potential changes.
- Decide on a plan and make sure it is clear to all.
- As challenges arise, make notes on your family meeting Kanban and discuss them at the next meeting.

To share ideas, address issues and integrate new practices during family meetings, we borrowed another idea from Agile Learning Centers, called the Community Mastery Board. Like a Kanban, the Mastery Board is divided into columns—in this case, "Awareness" (of issues or ideas noted by the group), "Implementing" (actions/tools chosen by the group), "Practicing" (to celebrate group improvement), and

"Mastery" (for practices the group becomes adept at). We sometimes include important family activities in here, too.

8. **Schedule Designated 1:1 Time**

This was suggested to me years ago by the director of my son's preschool. When I shared that his baby sister was not as popular with him as I had hoped, she suggested having special one-on-one time with Andrew while Tessa was napping. This worked fabulously. I called it "Andrew and Mommy Time" and made sure to reference it regularly. When he clearly wanted my attention but I was changing a diaper or nursing, I would remind him that we could do the activity he desired during Andrew and Mommy Time. We spent at least ten to twenty undistracted minutes together, and often much longer. To me, five minutes of genuine presence and connection is worth more than an hour of playing between distractions. Over the years, this concept has remained with us, as my husband and I try to have designated 1:1 time with each child as often as possible.

I feel it is worth mentioning that this works best when you allow your child to choose the activity. Putting dishes away during special time will likely be much less well received than playing a favorite game or reading a book they choose.

Though I can't speak to parenting a teen yet, if you have never had 1:1 time with your child, suggesting it when they are 14 may not immediately be met with enthusiasm. Even if you are getting a late start, give it a try. Set your intention and imagine having a super fun, connected experience.

While at a conference last year, I met a father of two teens who expressed regret that he didn't *know* his kids, as they were always on their phones or playing video games. Though not ideal (unplugged connection time might have been his preference), I suggested he see what would happen if he suggested playing along with them. He seemed a bit surprised, as he had never considered joining them in their preferred activity. I encouraged him, reminding him that he had nothing to lose. And, even if he was really inept at the game, they would have fun laughing and joking.

9. Use Imagination for Co-Creation

Recall that kiddos spend a significant portion of their earliest years in alpha and theta brain wave patterns—meaning, they are in an imaginative state much of the time. Their subconscious is dominant and acts like a sponge. Upon talking with Dr. Joe Dispenza about parenting, he reminded me how important it is to guide our kids in making new choices. He said he just observed his children when they were upset—letting them know they were seen and heard. When the upset was over, he never really reprimanded them. He simply asked what they would do differently the next time.

In another talk, Dr. Joe suggested telling your children an imaginary story that's really about themselves. As the parent, you can craft an ending that reflects a lesson learned or favorable outcome.

I tried this one Saturday morning when Tessa refused to go to her ice skating lesson. This wasn't like her, so I knew something was up. When I asked, she started crying and said she was being bullied by another girl in the class. This offered a wonderful opportunity, albeit not an easy one. I didn't want to make the decision as to whether I should take her to the lesson or let her bail. Intending to bring forth what was highest and best for everyone, with grace and ease, I asked Infinite Love for guidance and received a clear "Yes," to take her. Sigh. This was a tough one, but I went with my intuition.

On the way to the lesson, I told Tessa a story that began, "There once was a girl who..." I then described her situation in detail. I included what the bully had done in their last lesson. Then I went on: "The bully was scared for some reason. She didn't know who she really was and, because of this, she was harsh with the first girl (Tessa). One day, this girl realized that no one could take anything away from her. She remembered that, deep within, she had a bright light that no one could turn out unless she let them. As she realized this, the light grew and grew until it formed a blue light-bubble around her whole body. The bubble only let in love, blocking harshness and fear."

I went on to add that the bully had a pink bubble no one had ever told her about, and that all the other children in the class had colored bubbles, too. I ended, saying that once the first girl remembered her blue bubble, she felt strong and confident and was ready to enjoy her skating lesson.

As I finished, Tessa smiled but, steeped in her imagination, she wasn't absolutely certain the story was about her. "Mommy," she asked, "was that little girl's name Tessa?" I nodded and she again started to cry, this time saying, "I'm not crying because I'm sad or scared anymore. I'm crying because I'm so glad you are teaching me how to handle this."

At the rink, I decided it would be best if I spent the lesson sitting front and center, right at the edge of the ice. After all, I was the one who brought Tessa back to a place where she had been bullied. I also purposely chose not to tell the instructor about the previous week's incident.

Almost immediately, the little girl began picking on Tessa, after Tessa accidentally ran into her while skating backward. As the other girl skated by the glass, I mouthed, "It was an accident." She looked startled, like I had called her out on something. This was not my intent—my job was the same as Tessa's, to see all in and with love and to envision each in their colorful bubbles of love. After that, she magically stopped being harsh toward Tessa.

Following the lesson, when Tessa shared how she felt when she skated into the other girl, I told her what I did. She thanked me and said she hadn't been worried about it, as her bubble had kept her safe and strong. After that, Tessa finished up the package of lessons without any hesitation.

I share this situation because of its many relevant components:

- I asked for guidance and followed what I received, despite Tessa's best efforts and my own hesitation to take her back to a situation in which she was being bullied.
- With a little creative imagination, I offered Tessa a way to reprogram her story.

- I suggested the other girl also had a light bubble, helping Tessa to see the other's True Self.
- I made sure I demonstrated compassion to both girls, in the story I told Tessa and in my mind. And, I still stepped in when I felt guided to do so.
- I shared the story and what I'd witnessed with Tessa so she would know she was supported and loved.

Stories are a powerful and effective way to connect with and guide children. I wrote the story below to provide children with a simplified version of the Four C's. When shared by parents, this story can be an everyday, usable tool to empower children to release their fears and reveal their inherent worth.

Action Peace—*Will's Bubble*

Read *Will's Bubble* with your child, noting how the Four C's play into the narrative.

Points to consider:

- At the beginning of the story, Will does quite a bit of **Consciously Observing**—on his own and with the dog. He then **Connects**, in this case taking the dog up on his offer to help (just as your children connect to Infinite Love through you). The dog then **Chooses** a technique to guide Will in releasing his feelings, and shares a way he can **Create** what it is he really wants. It is not at all necessary to reference these terms with your child. They are embedded in the story.
- There are four different endings. I wrote the story this way to help kids practice understanding that we don't always get the outcome we desire, and, even when this is true, there are always opportunities available.
- When a child is feeling triggered, it is often best to Consciously Observe and simply *witness* the truth in them—their True Self. Later, when no one is triggered, consider bringing up the concepts in *Will's*

Bubble. Make it fun and playful. Tell your child the next time he or she is triggered you'll support them, just like the dog helps to support Will. You could also help them practice compassionate communication. Ask, "The next time you're feeling upset, would you be willing to try what Will does in the book?" Remember, using a phrase like "Would you be willing…?" allows your child to feel they have an option, which leads to a sense of autonomy and empowerment. When we make demands like, "You need to read this story with me and do what Will does," children feel pressured and are more likely to reject the idea.

- Once you've read the story, talk about the different endings and the power of having a way to release feelings and create a new or different outcome. It's important to make the point that we don't always get the outcome we'd hoped for. We have to deal with upsets on more than one occasion. At least now we have the tools to feel our emotions and release them, so they don't keep creating triggers that replay over and over throughout our lives.

Will's Bubble
by
Kristen Oliver

On a sunny spring day, Will was playing in Legna Park with his favorite disc. It was emerald green with a sparkly silver spiral that glowed in the sunlight. He threw the disc so high and fast, it seemed to soar through the park like a falcon. After each toss, he chased the disc through the trees and around the flowers and bushes. He liked to throw it behind his back, up to the sky and every which way. He pretended the squirrels and birds were his audience, cheering him on to throw higher and harder. One time, the disc went really far, so far Will couldn't see where it had landed. He ran in the direction he had sent the disc flying, but couldn't find it anywhere.

Where was it? He looked all over. He felt his chest getting tight as his thoughts started to race. His favorite disc was gone!

Just then, a big, fluffy dog approached him. "Hello, Will," the dog said. "What's the matter?"

"I threw my green disc super far and now I can't find it." Will said, as he started to cry. "And how do you know my name?"

"I'm what's called an angel dog. We know all kids' names, and we help them when we can. That's too bad about your disc. I see you're feeling pretty upset."

"I am, I'm feeling really, really mad! It's my favorite disc!" said Will. "It was just the right size, and it fit perfectly in my hand. And now it's gone!"

The dog looked at him with understanding eyes. "It's okay to have these feelings, Will. Feel them as long as you want and, when you're ready, I have something that can help, if you choose."

"Well, I'm still feeling mad! I can't believe my favorite disc is lost!" Will kicked a tree trunk. That didn't make him feel any better. He picked up a rock and threw it into a bush. That didn't make him feel any better, either.

Then he sat for a few minutes, clenching his fists and swiping the tears from his cheeks.

Finally, he said to the dog, "What do you have that can help me?"

"I have a container of magic bubbles around my neck. Remove the wand and dip it into the bubbles."

Will smiled a tiny bit because he absolutely loved bubbles. He took the wand and swirled it in the foamy liquid.

"When you're ready," said the dog, "put that angry feeling into your breath and slowly blow it into a bubble."

As Will did this, he felt the angry feelings leave his body. He watched the bubble as it rose up as tall as the trees, and then popped.

"Once the bubble pops, the feeling is gone. This is because you chose to let it go, Will. How're you feeling now?"

"The angry feelings are mostly gone, but I still feel really frustrated and kind of sad," said Will.

"When you're ready, you can do the same thing with those feelings; put them into your breath and release them into a bubble."

Will put his feelings of frustration into his breath and blew them into another bubble. The feelings left his body, and rose up into the sky and popped.

Will then concentrated on his feelings of sadness, and blew them into a third bubble. He watched them rise up high. When that bubble popped, too, he felt the feelings of sadness wash away.

"How do you feel now?" asked the dog.

Will drew a deep breath. His chest felt much lighter and his head felt clear. "I'm feeling so much better. I still want my disc though."

"Can you describe it to me, please?"

"It's bright green with a silver swirl on the top that sparkles."

"If you'd like to, close your eyes and imagine that you're holding your disc. Do you see a picture of it in your mind?"

Oh, yes, there it was. Will felt so happy, thinking of having it back!

"Keep that picture in your mind and breathe in the feeling of joy," said the dog. "When you choose to do so, open your eyes."

Soon, Will's eyes blinked open.

"Now, keep that happy feeling in your body, and put the picture in your breath and release it."

"But I don't want to let the picture go," said Will. "Not like the feelings of anger and sadness."

"Well, this time you're allowing the bubble to carry your wish along with the picture of what you want. What's different this time is that letting it go means you trust that the wish will be answered in the best way for everyone. And, whatever that is will be just fine. When the bubble pops, you know the answer is taken care of and everything will be alright."

Will did what the dog said, and, as he did, he felt very light and joyful.

"Wonderful, Will!" the dog said. "You've done it. The possibilities are endless! Next time you get angry, upset or sad, or if you have any other emotions you'd like to let go of, remember that, when you're ready, you can choose to put them in your breath and blow them away."

"But what will I do without the bubbles?" Will asked.

"You can choose to see the bubbles in your mind," the dog said. "They are always there for you." With that, he smiled and trotted away between the trees.

ENDING ONE:

Just then, Will looked past a large patch of yellow flowers and saw a little boy playing with the green disc. It was so big, the little boy had to pick it up with both hands. The boy looked like he had just found a treasure. He squealed with delight and threw the disc a couple of feet in front of himself.

The little boy was having so much fun with the disc, Will decided right then that he wanted him to have it. He liked the idea of this little boy sharing his love of this toy. He smiled, knowing he had other discs at home in his room. Will took a deep breath and was filled with a light, airy feeling—like he imagined the disc probably felt as it floated through the air. He turned and headed home.

ENDING TWO:

Will looked and looked for his disc. It was nowhere to be found. Just then, a large purple ball rolled right in front of him. "Hey," a girl shouted to him, "can you toss that to me, please?" As she ran in his direction, he picked up the ball and bounced it back to her. Her smile sparkled in the sun, as she said, "Thank you! I made up a new game! It's super fun, do you want to play?"

Will took a deep breath and let it go. "Sure!" he said, as he ran off with his new friend.

ENDING THREE:

Just then, a sparkle in a nearby bush caught his eye. It was the silver swirl on his disc! His special green disc had been right there the whole time. Will whispered "Thank you" under his breath and ran to pick it up.

ENDING FOUR:

Will searched for fifteen more minutes. Still no disc. He felt sad again. As he started to cry, he remembered what the big, fluffy dog had taught him. Will knew he could choose to feel, then let the feelings go. He felt the sadness and the tears. Then he took a deep breath and blew the sad feelings into an imaginary bubble. He did it again and again.

Though he never found his favorite disc, he believed what the dog had said— that his wish would be answered in the best way for everyone. He imagined how happy some other kid, who didn't have any discs at all, would feel if they found it. Or maybe a dog, whose boy would throw the disc for him. Or, what if a squirrel found it? What would a squirrel do with a disc—keep acorns in it? That thought made him smile.

Later, Will knew his wish had been answered, and in a great way, because if he hadn't lost his disc with the sparkly silver swirl, he wouldn't have met the angel dog. Now, whenever he feels upset or sad, he blows his feelings into an imaginary bubble and lets them go. It's not always easy, but Will feels happy to know he has a choice.

Action Peace—Keep Personal Connection as Your Highest Priority

Use the space below to list a few specific steps you can take right now to keep this inner work your first priority:

1.

2.

3.

Action Peace—Create a Family Connection Plan

Review the suggestions presented in this chapter and consult with friends, loved ones, or school staff who are in alignment with your values as a parent. What specific steps can you take to make heart-based connection a high priority for your whole family? The intention of the Family Connection Plan takes into account what is highest and best for everyone and focuses on grace and ease.

Choose the ideas that you plan to try this month, adding any ideas that you and your family members have:

1. Family Fun Night
2. Family Gratitude Journal
3. "Redo"
4. Family Intentions
5. Visualizations
6. Kanban
7. Family Meetings

8. Special 1:1 Time
9. Imagination Co-Creation
10. Our family ideas:

-

-

-

-

You've Uncovered the Hidden Peace

Well, here we are, at the end of the final chapter. That magic wand you were looking for? The one that would help you uncover the Hidden Peace? It's making this work your top priority. Your commitment to and diligence in practicing what you've learned will create a connected family—one filled with joy, peace and ease... and one in which the problems that arise become opportunities for each member to grow and love, more and more.

Made in the USA
Lexington, KY
21 February 2018